P9-DDF-747

Early American Beverages

JOHN HULL BROWN

Early American Beverages

BONANZA BOOKS · New York

This edition published by Bonanza Books, a division of Crown Publishers, Inc. by arrangement with the Charles E. Tuttle Co., Inc.

Library of Congress Catalog Card No. 66–17771

PRINTED IN JAPAN

Contents

Illustrations

Acknowledgments

GRATEFUL APPRECIATION is given to Dr. Louis C. Jones, Director of The New York State Historical Association, Cooperstown, New York; Miss Ruby Rounds and other staff members of that institution; Mr. Richard Carter Barret, Curator of the Bennington Museum, Old Bennington Vermont; and Mrs. Harold G. Green, staff member at that museum. Thanks are especially due Dr. Jones and Mr. Barret for permission to use the excellent photographs of items in each institution's collections.

The author is particularly grateful to Mr. Barret for permission to include valuable identification information relative to the Bennington Museum illustrations available in his book, *Bennington Pottery and Porcelain.*

To Mr. Charles V. S. Borst of Charles E. Tuttle Company, Inc., who served so ably in a consultative capacity offering multiple assistance both in organization and composition, the author is also most appreciative.

Early American Beverages

Introduction

THIS ACCOUNT of the role and importance of alcoholic and other beverages in early American life and the accompanying recipes by which they were made grew out of extensive and prolonged historical research into various aspects of history engaged in by the writer over a period of many years. Much of the relatively unknown information contained herein would not have been included without his having added constantly to his own personal library of rare printed and manuscript sources, from the seventeenth through the nineteenth centuries.

The very number of recipes here included is an indication of the widespread use of alcoholic beverages of all types in Colonial America. In fact, the use of such beverages by our Puritan ancestors antedates the consumption of tea, chocolate and coffee which were not popular until the late seventeenth century.

As for alcoholic beverages which were the most popular, there were regional differences among the New England, Middle, and Southern Colonies.

BEVERAGES OF THE NEW ENGLAND COLONIES

In New England, beer was the first luxury to be brought in. Soon the Puritan colonist learned to utilize Indian corn in the making of beer. Breweries were founded for this purpose. Laws to control the manufacture of beer and ale were enacted. The seventeenth century New England historian Josselyn refers frequently to molasses beer, for coarse sugar and molasses were often used in the brewing process.

Bark from numerous trees, such as spruce, sassafras, or birch, added to molasses and water made Birch or Spruce Beer. Even their twigs could be boiled in maple sap or in water to which were added malt, roots, and pumpkin and apple parings to make the same kind of beer. In fact, beer could be made out of a variety of ingredients, according to the theme of an early song:

Oh we can make liquor to sweeten our lips
Of pumpkins, of parsnips, of walnut-tree chips.

New England's Judge Samuel Sewall, though obviously repulsed by noisy imbibers, was not himself a teetotaler. Among the jottings in his seventeenth century diary, one finds reference to such varied beverages as ale, beer, canary, brandy, chocolate, cider, claret, mead, metheglin, punch, sack, sack-posset, sage tea, sillabub, and wine.

Among other liquor importations was an ale made of oat and wheat malts called Mumm.

Another imported beverage of seventeenth century New England was canary wine. Included among the earliest advertisements in Boston's *News Letter* was the following: "Fyall wine sold by the Pipe; Passados and Right Canary."

"Palme Wine," "Vendredi," and "Canary" are all mentioned in the Winthrop letters, the latter drink being considered by Wait Winthrop as less good than Palme Wine. "Tent Wine" was shipped to the colonists, also.

Some New Englanders were not too fond of the imported red wine, claret. As for others, Thomas Morton reports that for his imbibers at Merry Mount he "broched a hogshead, caused them to fill the Can with Lusty Liquor—Claret sparklinge neat—which was not suffered to grow pale & flat but tipled off with quick dexterity."

In early America, various strong white wines imported from southern Europe were classified as "sack", which had been popular among the English ever since the days of Shakespeare. Governor Winthrop in his writings of 1646 mentioned the arrival in port of 800 butts of sack on board four ships; this was just twelve years after the issuance of an order forbidding the sale of sack in the ordinaries.

Alice Morse Earle describes sack-posset as a "very pretty drink for weddings and feasts." It was a combination of ale and sack, thickened with cream and eggs. Sugar, mace, and nutmeg were used for seasoning. After all these ingredients were mixed together, the mixture was boiled over the fire for several hours.

Liquors continued to be imported, including aniseed cordial and gin from Holland and various wines from the Canaries, Portugal, and Spain. Earle writes that in old New England, "of these, fiery Madeiras were the favorite of all fashionable folk, and often each glass of wine was strengthened by a liberal dash of brandy."

As early as 1629, New England settlers expressed an interest in having "vine planters" sent over. Five years later, Governor Winthrop was given permission to use Governor's Island in Massachusetts Bay for a vineyard. The yearly rental fee was to be a hogshead of wine. Sometime later, two barrels of apples became the required yearly payment. In Rhode Island, vineyards were planted by French colonists.

Metheglin and mead, though mild and made from honey, yeast, and water, were intoxicating. In 1633, according to a list of various values established by the Piscataqua planters, six gallons of Metheglin were

Plate 1. *Bump Tavern, a typical upstate New York tavern of the early 19th century, was built by Jehiel Tuttle circa 1800 in Ashland near Windham for Ephraim Bump and was used as an inn for over eighty years. (Courtesy of the New York State Historical Association, Cooperstown, New York)*

equal to "2 lb. Beauer." Governor Bradford, in discussing two hogsheads of metheglin which were to be delivered at Plymouth, reports that only six gallons arrived at Plymouth, because merry-makers on board the Friendshippe decided to "drinke it up under the name leackage."

Cider was very cheap and plentiful due to the bountiful apple orchards planted so early by Blackstone, Endicott, and other settlers.

Josselyn noted, "I have had at the tap houses of Boston an ale-quart of cyder spiced and sweetened with sugar, for a groat."

The first method of making cider was pounding the apples by hand in a mortar and pestle. With the introduction of a rudimentary type of cider mill, a hollowed log together with a maul or heavy weight on a spring board were used.

Cider soon became perhaps the most popular drink for the people. It could be made locally and in great quantities. There has been recorded one orchard which produced sufficient apples to make five hundred hogsheads of cider in 1671. Fifty years later, three thousand barrels of cider were made by a village of forty families. Bennet reported in 1740: "Cider being cheap and the people used to it they do not encourage malt liquors. They pay about three shillings a barrel for cider."

From the early eighteenth century until around 1825, even the children drank cider freely at breakfast and dinner. This practice was terminated by a great sweep of temperance reform which even caused whole orchards of productive apple trees to be cut down.

From the writings of Charles Francis Adams, one learns that "to the end of John Adams's life a large tankard of hard cider was his morning draught before breakfast."

In the colleges, students were served large quantities of cider. Earle reports that it was "passed in two two-quart tankards from hand to hand down the commons table;" and "an 'Indian barrel,' whose contents were for free gift to every tramp Indian or squaw, was found in many a farmer's cellar."

Just after the Revolution a traveller in Maine described their cider as similar in taste and appearance to Madeira after it was purified by the frost and colored by the corn.

Judge Sewall's description of sillabub includes among its ingredients, cider. It was not boiled.

Fill your Sillabub Pot with Syder (for that is best for a Sillabub) and good store of Sugar and a little Nutmeg, stir it wel together, put in as much thick Cream by two or three spoonfuls at a time, as hard as you can as though you milke it in, then stir it together exceeding softly once about and let it stand two hours at least.

Cider brandy, or apple jack, resulted from the distillation of cider.

During the seventeenth century rigid laws concerning drinking were in effect in New England; however, most residents were law-abiding and temperate. By comparison, heavy drinking was the vogue among the fashionable young men of Old England.

Various mild drinks consumed by the early New Englanders included "beverige", switchel, ebulum, perry, and peachy. Some "beverige" was the West Indies variety made from sugar-cane juice with water added. The Devonshire variety was concocted from water forced through the lees of a cider mill. Other parts of Old England made "beverige" from cider, water, and spices. But in New England, beverige was a very weak drink—so much so, that it was a fore-runner of temperance drinks. In the rural areas, a summer mixture of molasses, water, and ginger was named "beverige." But an advertisement which appeared in the

August 16, 1711 edition of the *Boston News Letter* announcing the sale of the Nepture with her cargo listing "Wine, Vinegar and Beveridge" at Andrew Fanueil's warehouse must have referred to barrels of something stronger than molasses and water.

Popular in New Hampshire and central Massachusetts was a drink called switchel which was similar to "beverige". It was fortified by vinegar and rum when served to sailors. Elder and juniper berry juice with ale and spices made another mild drink, ebulum. Perry, also advertised in the *Boston News Letter,* and peachy were concocted from pears and peaches, respectively.

Stronger, so-called "aqua-vitae", drinks were also shipped into the colonies in large amounts during the 1600's.

With the importation of molasses from the West Indies by 1670, the manufacture of "rhum, a strong water drawn from the sugar cane" became profitable for New England. According to a 1651 document describing Barbadoes, one learns that, "the chief fudling they make in this island is Rumbullion alias Kill Divil—a hot hellish and terrible liquor." Various localities and people had different names for the "fudling". It was known as "ockuby" or "ahcoobee" by some Indians. Eliot and Josselyn had their own terms for this drink; the former named it "rumb", and the latter described it as "that cussed liquor, Rhum, rumbullion, or kill-devil." Earle says that "it went by the latter name and rumbooze everywhere, and was soon cheap enough."

Increase Mather in a 1686 statement deplored the availability of rum. "It is an unhappy thing that in later years a Kind of Drink called Rum has been common among us. They that are poor, and wicked too, can for a penny or two-pence make themselves drunk."

Burke was critical of both the quantity and quality of rum made in Boston. "The quantity of spirits which they distil in Boston from the molasses they import is as surprising as the cheapness at which they sell it, which is under two shillings a gallon; but they are more famous for the quantity and cheapness than for the excellency of their rum." From 1719 to around 1770, New England rum sold for three shillings a gallon, and West India rum was only two-pence more. In 1728, well over two million gallons of rum were imported and drinking was exceedingly heavy. The following lines are representative of the esteem in which alcoholic beverages were held at that time:

There's but one Reason I can Think,
Why people ever cease to drink,
Sobriety the Cause is not,
Nor Fear of being deam'd a Sot,
But if Liquor can't be got.

Rum manufacture became much more lucrative for New Englanders once it served as the means of exchange in Africa for slaves. Soon New England rum replaced the use of French brandy all along the African coast.

One gains insight into the esteem held for rum in New England through a statement made by Lazarus Redstreak in his opposition to an 1801 proposal that beer be added to or used in place of New England's usual cider or rum. Redstreak exclaimed, "Experience shows that the use of (cider) consists with sound healthy and long life. Our inhabitants are settled in favour of it. The New Englanders are of all people the longest livers. Why then try an innovation so difficult, so doubtful, to say the least, in point of health and economy, as the substibution of beer in the place of cyder?"

Alice Morse Earle claims in her *Customs and Fashions in Old New England,* (1893), "Though 'spiced punch in bowls the Indians quaffed' in 1665, I do not know of the Oriental mixed drink in New England till 1682, when John Winthrop writes of the sale of a punch-bowl."

The following poetic verse is thought to have been written by Samuel Mather in 1757, when it accompanied a gift of lemons to Sir Harry Frankland:

You know from Eastern India came
The skill of making punch as did the name.
And as the name consists of letters five,
By five ingredients is it kept alive.
To purest water sugar must be joined,
With these the grateful acid is combined.
Some any sours they get contented use,
But men of taste do that from Tagus choose.
When now these three are mixed with care
Then added be of spirit a small share.
And that you may the drink quite perfect see
Atop the musky nut must grated be.

Earle attributes the name of punch to the "Hindustani *panch,* five, referring to the five ingredients then used in the drink, namely: tea, arrack, sugar, lemons, water."

Tryer, having tasted some punch in India in 1675, described it as being an enervating liquor. But the English soon became fond of this new drink. Its name appears in many a ballad of this period.

The British soon invented a very elegant punch bowl called the Monteith. Reference is made to Monteith, a man of fashion whose mark of distinction was his scalloped coat, in the *Art of Cookery:*

New things produce new words, and so Monteith
Has by one vessel saved himself from death.

The rim of this bowl which became fashionable in the late 1690's was scalloped like Monteith's coat. Such a rim was used for hanging the ladle, wine glasses, and lemon strainer. Since the rim was separate from the bowl, it could be removed to brew the punch, and then replaced when the punch was ready.

In 1740, Bennet said of Boston society, "Madeira wine and rum punch are the liquor they drink in common."

Fashionable people always served their guests punch from the punch bowl before dinner. The bowl alone was passed and drunk from, without glasses.

In certain shops, such as J. Crosby's *Box of Lemons* in Boston, one could buy oranges, orange juice, lemons, lime juice, and shrub to add to such punches.

When Rev. Joseph McKean was ordained in 1785, at Beverly, Massachusetts, thirty bowls of punch were served eighty people before going to meeting, and out of sixty-eight diners, only six people drank tea. There were served "44 bowles of punch while at dinner; 18 bottles of wine, 8 bowles of Brandy," and a large amount of cherry rum.

In writing of New Englanders, Baron Reidesel observed, "Most of the males have a strong passion for strong drink, especially rum, and other alcoholic beverages." John

Adams stated, "if the ancients drank wine as our people drink rum and cider it is no wonder we hear of so many possessed with devils."

Bully Dawson's directions for making punch, as told in Charles Lamb's *Popular Fancies,* is no doubt identical to those of a New England host.

> The man who sees, does, or thinks of anything else while he is making Punch may as well look for the Northwest Passage on Mutton Hill. A man can never make good punch unless he is satisfied, nay positive, that no man breathing can make better. I can and do make good Punch, because I do nothing else, and this is my way of doing it. I retire to a solitary corner with my ingredients ready sorted; they are as follows, and I mix them in the order they are here written. Sugar, twelve tolerable lumps; hot water, one pint; lemons, two, the juice and peel; old Jamaica rum, two gills; brandy, one gill; porter or stout, half a gill; arrack, a slight dash. I allow myself five minutes to make a bowl in the foregoing proportions, carefully stirring the mixture as I furnish the ingredients until it actually foams; and then Kangaroos! how beautiful it is!

A drink which remained popular for at least 150 years was flip. The earliest date which the writer can find for flip's being so-called in New England is 1690. In the December, 1704 issue of the *New England Almanac,* one finds the following lines:

The days are short, the weather's cold,
By tavern fires tales are told.
Some ask for dram when first come in.
Others with flip and bounce begin.

An earthen pitcher or huge pewter mug served as a useful utensil in which to make American flip. Such a mug would be filled about two-thirds with strong beer to which would be added molasses, sugar, or dried pumpkin for sweetening, and New England rum, about a gill, for flavor. The bitter, burnt taste was gotten by plunging a red-hot loggerhead, an iron poker-shaped stirrer, into the flip making it bubble and foam.

Flip glasses, huge tumblers without handles, were the drinking vessels in which the flip was often served. Sometimes they would hold three or four quarts apiece, and, as Earle says, "speak to us distinctly of the unlimited bibulous capacities of our ancestors."

A Canton, Massachusetts tavern host made a specialty of his flip. His recipe called for a pint of cream, four eggs, four pounds of sugar. These he would mix and keep on hand. When there was a call for flip, he would fill a quart mug two-thirds full of bitter beer, add four huge spoonfuls of the above creamy mixture, a "dash", or gill, of rum, and then thrust the iron poker into it. To get the froth to gush over the top of the mug, he would add a fresh egg beaten into the mixture. Then, the drink was called "bellowstop".

Another tavern famous for its flip was Abbott's in Holden, Massachusetts. Its price during the American Revolution can be gotten from the following bill:

Jug New England Flip		9d.
Mug West India Flip		11d.
Lodging per night		3d.
Pot luck per meal		8d.
Boarding commons Men	4s.	8d.
" " Women		2s.

Earle quotes John Adams as saying, "if you spent the evening in a tavern, you found it full of people drinking drams of flip, carousing, and swearing. The old taprooms were certainly cheerful and inviting gathering-places; where mine host sat behind his cagelike counter surrounded by cans and bottles and glasses, jars of whole spices and whole loaves of sugar; where an inspiring row of barrels of New England rum, hard cider, and beer ranged in rivalry at an end of the room."

As Lowell wrote,

Where dozed a fire of beechen logs that bred
Strange fancies in its embers golden-red,
And nursed the loggerhead, whose hissing dip,
Timed by wise instinct, creamed the bowl of flip.

Cider mixed with rum became "Stonewall". Cold rum and unsweetened beer were the ingredients of "calibogus", or "bogus". Rum mixed with molasses made "black-strap". The country store would often hang a salted, dried codfish next to barrels of black-strap. One was induced to buy another draught of black-strap to quench the thirst caused by grabbing a strip of salted fish and eating it.

In Salem, the name of "whistle-belly-vengeance" was given to its drink of sour homemade beer, simmered, sweetened with molasses, filled with the crumbs of brown bread, and consumed piping hot.

Plate 2. *Saratoga Springs, New York, was famous for its many hotels and taverns as far back as around 1845 when James E. Butterworth (1817–1894) did this oil on canvas of "Main Street, Saratoga Springs." (Courtesy of the New York State Historical Association, Cooperstown, New York)*

BEVERAGES OF THE MIDDLE COLONIES

The beverages of the Middle Colonies did not differ significantly from those of New England. F. B. Lee, in *New Jersey as a Colony and as a State,* writes, "Rum, egg nog, apple and peach brandy, whisky, molasses beer, spruce beer, persimmon beer, mead, many varieties of cordials, hot rum for funerals, tiff, sillibub, Sampson, and hotch potch are a few of the drinks of the time, not to mention that famous beverage of the day, metheglin or 'perfect love'." But the favorite, and at times expensive, drinks were rum, gin, small beer, metheglin, tea, coffee, and chocolate.

As in New England, drinking was engaged in at every drawing up of a contract, the signing of a deed, the selling of a farm, the purchase of goods, and the arbitration of a suit. Every transaction and every happening in the community in public as well as in private life were accompanied by the use of liquor, which was a universal practice in those days. It is said that if either party backed out of a contract before signing, he had to furnish half a barrel of beer or a gallon of rum to relieve the pangs of disappointment. As Alice Morse Earle points out in her *Colonial Days in Old New York,* (drinking appeared at) "weddings, funerals, church-openings, deacon ordainings, and house-raisings. No farm hand in haying-field, no sailor on a vessel, no workman in in a mill, no cobbler, tailor, carpenter, mason, or tinker would work without some strong drink, some treat. The bill for liquor where many workmen were employed, as in a house-raising, was often a heavy one."

Mrs. Earle in her description of a typical day in the life of the early Dutch writes: "cans of buttermilk or good beer, brewed perhaps by the patroon, washed down this breakfast of suppawn and ryebread and grated cheese and sausage or head-cheese; beer there was in plenty, in ankers, even in tuns, in every household."

In the early days when there were no prisons, men were often imprisoned in their own houses, but subjected to prison fare, which was bread and water, or *small beer.* Francois de Bruyn was fined two hundred guilders for insulting and striking the court messenger. When he refused to pay, declaring he would rot in prison first, he was sentenced to "a respectable tavern."

Earle says, "of the drinking habits of the Dutch colonists I can say that they were those of all the colonies,—excessive. Tempered in their tastes somewhat by the universal brewing and drinking of beer, they did not use as much rum as the Puritans of New England, nor drink as deeply as the Virginia planters; but the use of liquor was universal."

In a discussion of holidays among the Dutch, Earle recalls a 1677 ordinance in Albany which stated, "Shrovetide misdemeanors were prohibited, viz.: riding at a goose, cat, hare, and ale." She explains that the fine was twenty-five guilders in seawant, "What the cat, hare, and ale part of the sport was, I do not know."

One rival to the popularity of beer was cider. It was consumed extensively in winter. In summer, other ingredients including nutmeg, sweetening, and water were added. The Swedish naturalist Kalm visited the colonies in 1749 and reported seeing horse presses used for making cider, especially in the Hudson Valley.

Apple trees had been set out early in New York. Dankers, the Labadist traveller, describes these apples as the finest in America. Ciderroyal was concocted from boiling four barrels of cider into one. "Gumption" was the name attributed by P. T. Barnum in more recent days to cider-spirits.

The February 13, 1744 issue of the *New York Gazette* carried a recipe in rhyme of one of the most popular mixed drinks, sack-posset. This was the drink of christening and wedding parties.

SACK-POSSET

From famed Barbadoes on the Western Main
Fetch sugar half a pound; fetch sack from Spain
A pint; and from the Eastern Indian Coast
Nutmeg, the glory or our Northern toast.
O'er flaming coals together let them heat
Till the all-conquering sack dissolves the sweet.
O'er such another fire set eggs, twice ten,
New born from crowing cock and speckled hen;
Stir them with steady hand, and conscience pricking
To see the untimely fate of twenty chicken.
From shining shelf take down your brazen skillet,
A quart of milk from gentle cow will fill it.
When boiled and cooked, put milk and sack to egg,
Unite them firmly like the triple League.
Then covered close, together let them dwell
Till Miss twice sings: You must not kiss and tell.
Each lad and lass snatch up their murdering spoon,
And fall on fiercely like a starved dragoon.

The drinking of sack in the colonies dates back to the first half-century of colonial existence. Though it was nearly out of vogue in New England by the late 1600's, as was pointed out earlier, its popularity in New York, in 1744, merited the above rhyme in the city's newspaper. From then on, mixed drinks made from a base of curdled hot milk, or posset, increase in variety as will be noted in the recipes that follow, and include Ale, Cold, Jelly, Lemon, Orange, Pope's, Royal, Snow, Treacle, and Wine Possets, as well as Sack Posset.

Another popular mixed drink was caudle. Upon examination of its recipe which is included later, one discovers both brandy and white wine among its ingredients. Like the various possets, caudle also has a number of variations. Raisin wine is used in Cold Caudle. Both ale and stale beer are included among many items in Oatmeal Caudle. Some of the caudles are non-alcoholic.

In those areas predominantly settled by the Scotch and Irish, rye, wheat, and later even barley, potatoes, and Indian corn were converted into whiskey.

It is thought that the first mixed drink designated as a "cocktail" was served in the year of American independence from England, for in 1776 a barmaid, Betsy Flanagan, at Halls Corners in Elmsford, New York used a cock's feathers to decorate behind the bar. When one of the imbibers asked for a glass of those "cocktails", Betsy served him a mixed drink with a feather stuck in it.

Other recipes included herein are for Whisky Toddy and Buttered Toddy. Just as with the word, "punch", the term "toddy" also has its origins in India. A 1671 description of India mentions "Toddy". But a tavern in New York in the early half of the eighteenth century, (whose vintner was Robert Todd) known by its tavern sign of the Black Horse, was famous for its Todd drinks, which were concocted principally from West India rum. According to tradition, guests at the Black Horse boasted that the American term "toddy" originated here.

Toddy, grog, and sling are three early American concoctions. Grog, as a beverage term, originated when Admiral Edward Vernon, nicknamed "Old Grog", ordered the sailors' rum to be diluted. Thereafter, any unsweetened mixture of spirit and water—in fact, any intoxicating liquor—was designated as grog. Sling was a drink made of spirits, especially gin, with water, sugar, and sometimes lemon. It was served either hot or iced. Toddy was the name given to a mixture of spirit and hot water, sweetened, as in rum toddy.

In addition to toddy, punch, posset, and caudle, one finds from the following recipes that other mixed drinks which were popular included Aleberry, Mock Arrack, Athol Brose, Bang, Bishop, Cardinal, Sherry Cobbler, Flap, Jingle, Oxford Nightcap, and others.

The Dutch were too devoted to beer drinking, and too fond of gin and schnapps, to become avid imbibers of rum very suddenly. But they resented prohibition of the sale of rum to the Indians. Their response was, "To prohibit all strong liquor to them seems very hard and very Turkish. Rum doth as little hurt as the Frenchman's Brandie, and in the whole is much more wholesome."

Dr. Eights, of Albany, in his description of the Pinkster festivities, writes that on Tuesday the "blacks" appeared and gingerbread, applejack, and cider began to be consumed. Earle concludes that in 1811 when the Common Council of Albany ordered that there were to be no more booths and prohibited all gambling, dancing, and drinking, that "when the negroes could not dance nor drink, it was but a sorry holiday, and quickly fell into desuetude."

On Long Island, however, Pinkster Day was especially celebrated. The week befores the Negroes sold swinglingtow and sassafra, in New York and Brooklyn to earn a little spending money with which to buy gingerbread and rum on Pinkster Day. Earle pictures them, "gathered around the old market in Brooklyn near the ferry, dancing for eels, blowing fish-horns, eating and drinking."

This was a festival day for the Dutch residents, as well, "going to pinkster fields for pinkster frolics," visiting, drinking schnapps, and "eating soft wafels" together.

Nor was rum left out of the punch even for the young Dutch boys and girls of Albany. In Mrs. Grant's writing of their outdoor excursions in the eighteenth century, she mentions their taking along "a basket with tea, sugar, and the other usual provisions for breakfast, with the apparatus for cooking it; a little rum and fruit for making cool weak punch, the usual beverage in the middle of the day, and now and then some cold pastry."

Little children from five to six years of age had their own parties always well supplied, writes Mrs. Grant, "with an ample provision of tea, chocolate, preserved and dried fruits, nuts and cakes of various kinds, to which was added cider or a syllabub."

In New York, in 1712, Cato's Road

House was built where the post road met the junction of 51st and 52nd streets. Cato, a slave from South Carolina who had earned sufficient funds from his cooking to buy his freedom, kept this inn for forty-eight years. Among his food specialties were terrapin, curried oysters, fried chicken and roast duck.

Cato's beverages were famous far and wide, too; for whether one drank his New York brandy-punch, South Carolina milk-punch, or his Virginia egg-nogg which he mixed in single relays by the barrelful, none ever tasted better. He seemed to know just the right number of seconds to beat the separated yolk and egg white, the precise amount of sugar, the exact number of nutmeg grains to be strewn upon the mixture, and the right amount of foamy egg white to top it all. Earle writes as follows about the charm of his establishment. "Alongside his road house he built a ballroom which would let thirty couple swing widely in energetic reels and quadrilles. When Christmas sleighing set in, the Knickerbocker braves and belles drove out there to dance; and there was *always* sleighing at Christmas in old New York—all octagenarians will tell you so."

A drink concocted from rum, loaf sugar, and perhaps a little water was called Mimbo and a favorite, especially in Pennsylvania. In 1752, York County fixed for that colony the legal "Rates in Taverns" for the purpose of "protecting (of) travellers against the extortions of tavern-keepers." The prices were given as follows:—

1 Quart Mimbo, made best W. I. Rum and Loaf: 10d.
1 Quart Mimbo, made of New England Rum and Loaf: 9d.

The word "rum" when combined with other terms, such as rumfustian and rum-barge, did not refer to the liquor by that name at all; rather, it was used as an adjective meaning powerful. Neither rumfustian nor rum-barge had any rum in them at all. Both were mixed drinks; rumfustian being made of a bottle of white wine or sherry, a quart of strong beer, half a pint of gin, the yolks of twelve eggs, nutmeg, orange peel, sugar, and spices.

Whenever the term brandy-wine was used by the Dutch, they really referred to rum. It was not long in New York before all strong waters itemized in tavern lists were New England rum, and not aqua vitae, gin, nor brandy.

A partial catalogue in one early New Jersey tavern discloses no fewer than eight wines together with cherry and currant wine of domestic manufacture.

The English chaplain Charles Wolley wrote in his journal in 1701 while visiting New York of how the English had preserved many of the old Dutch traditions in their observance of New Year's Day. "The English in New York observed one anniversary custom and that without superstition, I mean the strenarum commercium, as Suetonius calls them, a neighborly commerce of presents every New Years' Day. Some would send me a sugar-loaf, some a pair of gloves, some a bottle or two of wine."

It has been said that George Washington, unaccustomed to New Year's calling, soon adopted the custom with approval when he went to New York to live for a short time, and his receptions were most impressive.

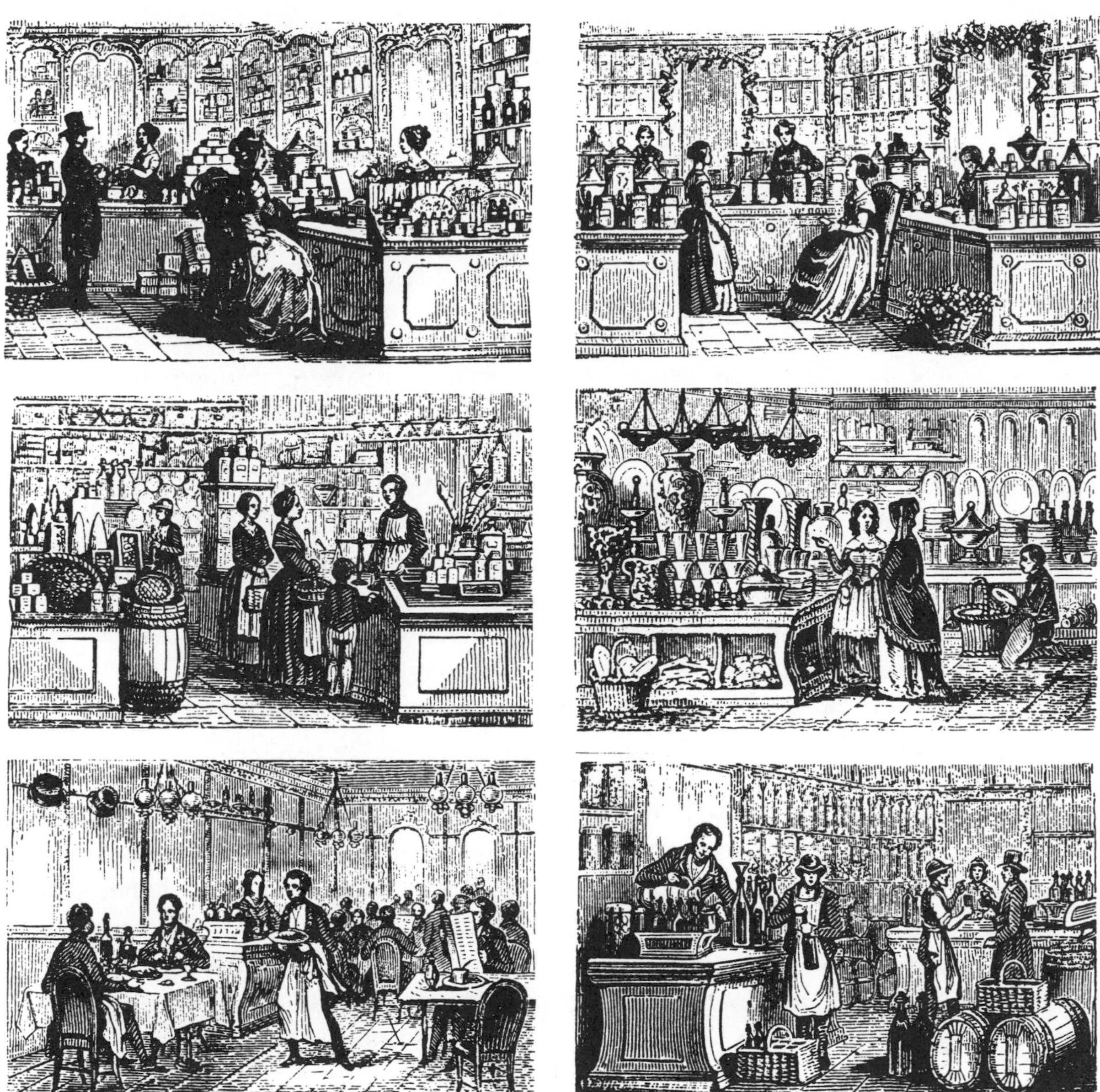

Plate 3. *Printers' standard trade cuts of a bygone day.*

Among the rhymes of the newspaper-carriers for that special days' celebration in New York, is the following verse:

The day devoted is to mirth,
And now around the social hearth
Friendship unlocks her genial springs,
And Harmony her lyre now strings.
While plenty spread her copious hoard,
And piles and crowns the festive board.

Included in the "copious hoard" piled high on "the festive board" were decanters of wine, pitchers of egg-nogg, bowls of milk punch, mounds of food, and everything the hospitable colonists could think of to make New Year's Day a festive occasion.

After Daniel Edwards, a Turkish merchant, and Pasque Rosser, his Greek servant, introduced coffee to the Londoners, there were certain Englishmen who were reluctant to accept any innovation among beverages. By them, coffee was given all sorts of abusive names, such as "syrup of soot," and "essence of old shoes." But soon after the introduction of the beverage, American coffee-houses sprang up everywhere. Such a one was the New or Royal Exchange which opened in New York as a coffee-room in 1754, some eighty-four years after Dorothy Jones was given a license to sell coffee in Boston. The New York structure was built like the English exchanges and raised on arches made of brick.

Merchant's Coffee-house stood on the southeast corner of Water and Wall streets. Every early newspaper of the area carried advertisements concerning its activities. It was a trade center where cargoes, ships, Negroes, houses, lands, and all sorts of goods were auctioned. Even an insurance office was housed here. In 1768 Alexander Macraby reported in New York: "They have a vile practice here, which is peculiar to this city; I mean that of playing backgammon (a noise I detest) which is going forward in the public coffee-houses from morning till night, frequently ten or a dozen tables at a time."

Philadelphia had its London Coffeehouse. It even had a board of trustees, according to a notice, for them to meet on the 19th at the courthouse, which was inserted in Bradford's Journal on April 15, 1754.

Bradford made application to the Governor and Council for a license, as follows:

> Having been advised to keep a Coffee-House for the benefit of merchants and traders, and as some people may be desirous at times to be furnished with other liquors besides coffee, your petitioner apprehends that it is necessary to have the government license.

William Bradford was grandson of the first printer Bradford, while his son was Washington's Attorney-General. The building in which the London Coffee-house was housed had been erected around 1702 at the corner of Front and Market streets, on Letitia Penn's land. Penn had made a gift of this land to his daughter.

By mid-eighteenth century, the Swedish visitor Kalm noted that the Dutch of New York generally had tea for breakfast. Usually it was drunk plain, without milk. Instead of adding sugar to the cup of tea, they put a small lump of it in their mouth while they drank. He adds, "Their dinner is buttermilk and bread. . . . They sometime make use of buttermilk instead of fresh milk to boil a thin kind of porridge with, which tastes very sour but not disagreeable in hot weather. . . . Their supper is generally bread and butter, or milk and bread."

One will note, upon examination of the recipes which follow, the inclusion of many medicinal beverages. A favorite among the early Dutch was one named "Vienna Drink" which was made from senna, rhubarb, and port-wine.

Among the various medicinal wine drinks which follow are Antimonial Wine; Barley Wine; Koumiss, a valuable wine of the Tartars; Scurvy-grass Wine; and Turnip Wine, as well as wines made from Ipecacuan, Iron, Rhubarb, Sacred Tincture, and Tobacco.

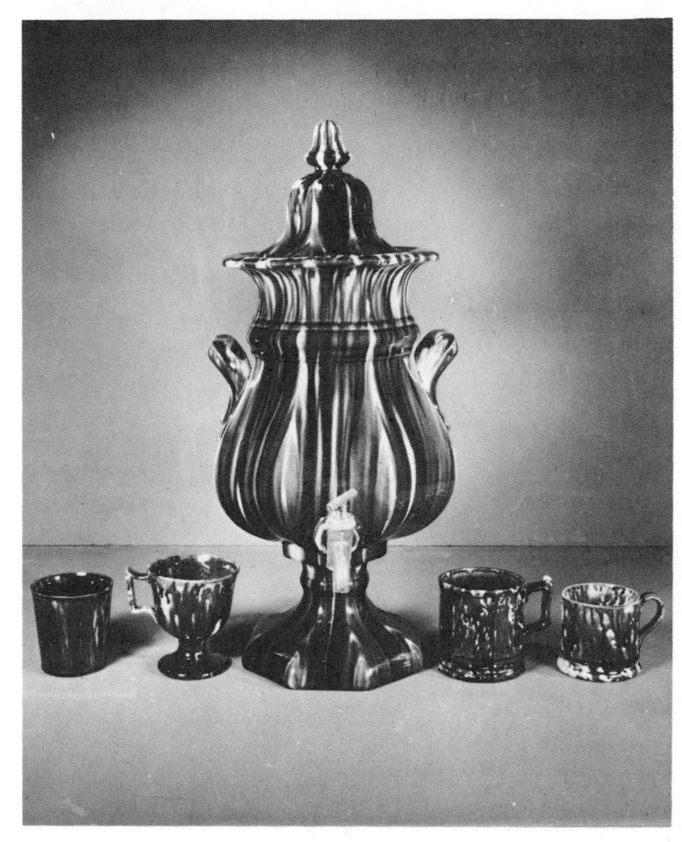

Plate 4. *This rare coffee urn, covered with flint enamel and having a pewter spigot, dates back to the period around 1849–1858. With its helmet-shaped cover it measures twenty and one-half inches tall. (Courtesy of the Bennington Museum, Bennington, Vermont)*

BEVERAGES OF THE SOUTHERN COLONIES

Popularity of various drinks abroad according to nationality was reflected within the colonies. At this time, the English were fond of ale, the Dutch beer, and the French and Spanish light wines. Thus, in the Southern Colonies where the majority of the population were British, their drinking habits were not too different from other English colonists. However, in those areas settled predominantly by the Spanish or French, light wines were by far the favorites.

Yet one did not have to be French or Spanish to enjoy wine. Among Mrs. Mary Randolph's recipes of 1828 in her book, *The Virginia Housewife: or, Methodical Cook,* can be found directions for Ginger Wine and Currant Wine.

At Chowning's Tavern in Williamsburg, wines, spiced punch, draft ale and beer were served. Raleigh Tavern, a center of Williamsburg social activity, was a place where good fellowship was "sealed by a toast of Madeira or hot rum punch, or a pint of ale drunk from a pewter tankard."

Dolly Madison's grand-niece writes of

Mrs. Madison's grief in 1804 over the parting of her favorite sister Anna from her. For the first time in their lives, they were to live apart. Her constant companion, Anna, that year married Congressman Richard Cutts from Maine—then a district of the Commonwealth of Massachusetts. Included among the wedding presents was a gift from Madame Dashcoff, wife of the Russian Minister, described by the grand-niece as being "the usual wedding present of her country—two wine-coolers, one filled with salt, the essence of life, and the other with bread, the staff of life."

In the *Memoirs and Letters of Dolly Madison,* edited by her grand-niece, mention is made of some of the gaiety at Montpelier after Mr. Madison's retirement there following his second term as President.

> One of the great occasions for bringing the neighbors together from far and near were the camp-meetings, looked forward to with great pleasure and participated in by old and young of all denominations. Barbecues, too, were at the height of their popularity. . . . Animals were roasted whole, the punch-bowl passed from lip to lip accompanied by an appetite whetted by the invigorating mountain air, "and the pleasure of clasping hands with neighbors seen only at meeting time." The Woods rang with merriment.

A. H. Wharton, in *Colonial Days an Dames,* in a discussion of wedding customs, describes one prevalent among the Scotch-Irish of Virginia "of barring the progress of the coach of the newly married pair by ropes or other obstacles, which were not removed until the groom paid toll in the form of a bottle of wine or of drinks to his persecutors."

S. G. Fisher, in his *Men, Women and Manners in Colonial Times,* writes extensively about the daily life of George Washington who, he says, "may be taken as a fair type of the usual result of Virginia life among the upper classes when it did not run to excesses." As for his drinking habits, Fisher writes, "he habitually drank from half a pint to a pint of Madeira, besides punch and beer, . . . "

The translator of Chastellux's *Travels,* in Virginia, describes an experience of his own, as follows:

> In the summer months it is very common to make a party on horseback to a limestone spring, near which there is usually some little hut with spirituous liquors, if the party are not themselves provided, where their debauch frequently terminates in a boxing match, a horse race, or perhaps both. During a day's residence at Leesburg I was myself accidentally drawn into one of these parties, where I soon experienced the strength of the liquor, which was concealed by the refreshing coolness of the water. . . .

Fisher describes the general attitudes toward drinking in his following statement: "Rude plenty combined at times with great toleration for heavy drinking was the life the people loved, and Thackeray has given a fair description of it in '*The Virginians*'." Of the less wealthy, Fisher writes, "The lower classes and poor whites were very rough and disorderly in colonial times, and spent a large part of their time drinking, gambling, and fighting at taverns and at elections."

One of the purposes for drinking was to drink healths. The October, 1737 issue of the *Virginia Gazette* in its enumeration of various social and sporting activities in Hanover County for that month, includes the following: "That after dinner the Royal Health, His Honor the Governor's, & c., are to be drunk."

Campbell says, "To eat and drink freely; to feast and dance and riot; to pamper cocks and horses; to observe the anxious, important, interesting event which of two horses can run fastest or which of two cocks can flutter and spur most dexterously; these are the grand affairs that almost engross the attention of some of our great men, and little, low-lived sinners imitate them to the utmost of their power." Today, the latter would be labeled "status seekers".

Fisher agrees with Campbell when he summarizes the social interests of the Virginians. "The Virginians loved amusements of all kinds, and there was continual visiting between plantations. Fox-hunting, cock-fighting, horse-racing, wrestling matches, and dancing parties, mingled with gambling and hard drinking, were their delight."

Estate inventories and investigations in the nineteenth century into the contents of old Virginia houses revealed all kinds of articles of comfort and pleasure. As enumerated by Fisher, some of these were: "Russia leather chairs, Turkey worked chairs, enormous quantities of damask napkins and table linen, silver and pewter-ware, . . . flagons, dram cups, beakers, tankards, . . ."

As for public facilities for drinking, by 1668 Virginia had to pass laws limiting the number of small tippling-houses and petty ordinaries within each county to only one at the court-house and possibly one at a ferry or wharf. Additional attempted restrictions were that only beer and cider could be sold at these houses. Private individuals were prohibted from selling "any sort of drink or liquor whatsoever, by retail under any color, pretence, delusion, or subtle evasion whatsoever." But stipulations such as these were of short duration. Soon, Bruce declares that "Madeira, Canary, Malaga, and Fayal wines were probably much more abundant in the Colony than in England at this time, and were drunk by classes which in the mother country were content with strong and small-beer."

As early as 1620 in Virginia, a sort of ale from maize was made. It was considered a good drink and preferable to English beer by George Thorpe. One hundred years later, Governor Berkeley wrote of Virginians: "their small-drink is either wine or water, beer, milk and water, or water alone. Their richer sort generally brew their small-beer with malt, which they have from England, though barley grows there very well; but for the want of convenience of malt-houses, the inhabitants take no care to sow it. The poorer sort brew their beer with molasses and bran; with Indian corn malted with drying in a stove; with persimmons dried in a cake and baked; with potatoes with the green stalks of Indian corn cut small and bruised, with pompions, with the Jerusalem artichoke which some people plant purposely for that use, but this is the least esteemed."

Times had changed considerably from conditions as John Hammond in his *Leah and Rachel* had described them in 1656:

Beare is indeed in some places constantly drunken, in other some nothing but Water or Milk, and Water or Beverige; and that is where the good-wives (if I may so call them) are negligent and idle; for it is not want of Corn to make Malt with, for the Country affords enough, but because they are slothful and careless; and I hope this Item will shame them out of these humours; that they will be adjudged by their drinke, what kind of Housewives they are.

Metheglin seems to have been a popular drink throughout the colonies. In Kentucky it was a favorite well into the nineteenth century. Whole plantations were planted with honey locust to supply Virginia well with metheglin, which was made here by grinding the long locust beans and mixing with them honey, herbs and water, and then fermenting.

A 1649 Virginia letter spoke of "an ancient planter of twenty-five years standing," having an excellent store of bees and "made excellent Matheglin, a pleasant and strong drink."

In Oldmixon's *History of Carolina* (1708) one learns that "the bees swarm there six or seven times a year, and the metheglin made there is as good as Malaga sack."

The latter mentioned beverage, sack, was often imported to Virginia. It was drunk generally in the American colonies during the first half-century of colonization.

Cider, another universally accepted drink, never exceeded two and one-half shillings in Virginia during the 1600's. Probably every Maryland and Virginia homestead had a supply of cider. When court was in session, it was in ample supply. Many households used huge quantities of it instead of beer or metheglin. Barrels of it were in storage for daily consumption.

Further examination of Mrs. Randolph's 1828 beverage recipes reveals that additional drinks included Orgeat, a "Necessary Refreshment at all Parties"; Cherry Shrub; Cherry Brandy; Rose Brandy; Peach Cordial; Raspberry Cordial; Mint Cordial; "A Substitute for Arrack (by dissolving two scruples flowers of Benzoin, in one quart of good rum)"; Lemon Cordial; numerous beers—Ginger, Spruce, and Molasses.

Knowing from the research of the Southern historian Philip Bruce that Madeira, Canary, Malaga, and Fayal wines were abundant in Virginia, as stated heretofore, one concluded that this may be due in part to the introduction of varieties of grapes into southern United States. One learns this fact from an interesting comment by Sir Edward Barry, Fellow of the Royal College of Physicians and of the Royal Society, in his *Observations Historical, Critical, and Medical, on the Wines of the Ancients,* published in London in 1775.

Sir Barry refers to his "ingenious friend, the honorable Charles Hamilton who has been long distinquished for his peculiar elegant taste." Hamilton is quoted then as follows:

Captain St. Pierre, who has established a great colony of vignerons in *South Carolina,* and carried there three years ago above three hundred vignerons from different parts of *Europe,* was with me several days before his departure, was charmed with my vineyard; and he had cultivated vineyards many years in *France.* He was very happy at my giving him all the cuttings of my vineyard, as he found it very difficult to get the right sort; and though his plantations are about the latitude of 33, he has not the least doubt of having excellent wine there, Which if he has, must be of infinite service to this country.

There was much tea drinking in Virginia, as elsewhere. John Ferdinand Smyth wrote as follows concerning the daily life of a rich southern planter around mid-eighteenth century:

The gentleman of fortune rises about nine o'clock; he may perhaps make an excursion to walk as far as his stable to see his horses, which is seldom more than fifty yards from his house; he returns to breakfast between nine and ten, which is generally *tea* or coffee, bread and butter, and very thin slices of venison, ham, or hung beef.

As evidence of the fact that tea is not his only daily beverage, Smyth adds:

Between twelve and one he takes a draught of bombo, or toddy, a liquor composed of water, sugar, rum, and nutmeg, which is made weak and kept cool; he dines between two and three, and at every table, whatever else there may be, a ham and greens, or cabbage, is always a standing dish. At dinner he drinks cider, toddy, punch, port, claret, and madeira, which is generally excellent here.

Smyth adds in his *Tour in the United States,* published in London, (1784), "This is his general way of living in his family, when he has no company. No doubt many differ from it, some in one respect, some in another; but more follow it than do not."

Anne Wharton in her *Colonial Days and Dames* mentions the "country visits, tea-drinkings, and all the pleasant sociability that belonged to life in the Old Dominion."

Plate 5. *Despite their warmth and coziness, typical parlors of the late 18th and early 19th centuries such as this at the Lippitt house were littled used except on state occasions. Here the minister was entertained on his semi-annual visit, which provided the occasion for serving tea. If a military officer were among the guests, he would enjoy the corner chair next to the fireplace, which was well adapted for those wearing swords. (Courtesy of the New York State Historical Association, Cooperstown, New York)*

In order to understand why our ancestors were heavy drinkers, we must remember the severity of Colonial life which certainly was mitigated by the use of alcoholic beverages.

The writer in his perusal of early American history has found many an instance when probably the availability of a rum punch or some similar refreshment may have for the moment blotted out enough of stark reality to have made victory in battle possible. After all, the early settlers of this country were not ones to enjoy killing. The warmth and cheer to be found around their own firesides were much more appealing. Farming was their prime concern. Maybe it took a bit of mug-passing to muster up the courage to kill a man in battle!

When Lemuel Cook, the last surviving Revolutionary War pensioner, was interviewed by E. B. Hillard as to his experiences in the Revolution, Cook at age 105 years gave the following account:

> It was reported Washington was going to storm New York. We had made a by-law in our regiment that every man should stick to his horse: if his horse went, he should go with him. I was waiter for the quartermaster; (Cook had enlisted at Cheshire, Connecticut when only sixteen years old.) and so had a chance to keep my horse in good condition. Baron Steuben was mustermaster. . . . Next morning I was second on parade. We marched off towards White Plains. Then 'left wheel', and struck right north. Got to King's Ferry, below Tarrytown. There were boats, scows, & c. We went right across into the Jerseys. That night I stood with my back to a tree. Then we went on to the head of Elk. There the French were. It was dusty; 'peared to me I should have choked to death. One of 'em handed me his canteen; 'Lem,' said he, 'Take a good horn—we're going to march all night. I didn't know what it was, so I took a full drink. It liked to have strangled me.

Nor did the men have the advantage of the modern electric blanket, or even a sleeping bag. Exposed to the rigors of freezing and sub-zero temperatures, at times barefoot, a bit of rum or wine no doubt provided a warming stimulant and may have prevented pneumonia. The cold is always more penetrating when one is hungry. A portion of General Washington's letter dated January 5, 1778, Valley-Forge, serves well to describe his soldier' plight in this regard: "I am now under the necessity of keeping several parties from the army threshing grain, that our supplies may not fail:—but this will not do.—As to meat, our stock is trifling, not being sufficient for more than two days, if so long, with the most sparing economy."

It was not easy to tramp or ride the wilderness trails in the early years before the establishment of a network of adequate roads. Such travel, especially during the winter season, was often arduous and fatiguing. To make the trip from Philadel-

Plate 6, next page. *An 1841 broadside announcing the reduction in stage coach fares due to competition from the railroads. Note that the stage coach agents in Albany and Schenectady promise to convey passengers from the boats "to Schenectady ir season for the Northern or Western train of Cars and that those by the Cars from the West, &c, shall arrive in Albany in season for the New York Boats." (Courtesy of the New York State Historical Association, Cooperstown, New York)*

FARE REDUCED! NO MONOPOLY!!

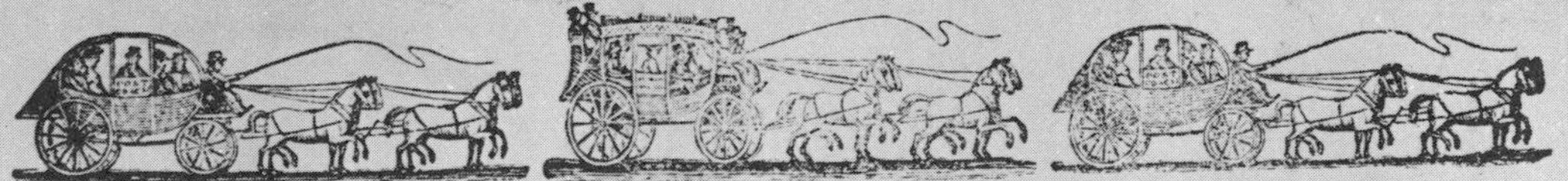

THRO' IN ONE HOUR & 45 MINUTES!

FOUR DAILY LINES OF

STAGES!

TO AND FROM SCHENECTADY.

The citizens (Albany, an ' the travelling public are respectfully informed that on and after Monday, Sept. 20, FOUR DAILY LINES of first class Stages will commence running between the cities of Albany and Schenectady, to intersect the several Rail Roads from the west and north.

The Stages will leave Albany from Thorp & Sprague's old Stage Office, corner of State-st. and Broadway, at half past 7 and 9 A. M., and half past 2 and 6 P. M., and Schenectady from Rail Road Depot, at half past 4 and 9 A. M., and half past 2 and 5 P. M., each day.

By this conveyance, passengers to and from the west will avoid the danger and inconvenience of the **TWO INCLINED PLANES,** which are unavoidably encountered by those passing over upon the Mohawk and Hudson Rail Road.

Passengers will be taken to and from the several hotels in this city and Schenectady, without extra charge. Citizens will be called for at their respective places of residence, and also taken thereto on their return, free of expense.

The proprietors pledge themselves that passengers from the boats, &c. shall be conveyed to Schenectady in season for the Northern o. Western train of Cars, and that those by the Cars from the West, &c., shall arrive i. Albany in season for the New-York Boats.

The Fare to or from Schenectady by this route will be only

FIFTY CENTS!

And No Charge for Baggage.

Either on the route, or for taking it to the boats.

ngers by this route will be free from the danger necessarily pon the Rail Road, as well as from the gross imposition often there upon them, and also to be conveyed for one half the expense, the proprie- e inouced confidently to anticipate a liberal patronage. They assure the travelli no pains shall be spared to make this conveyance every way acceptable

H. W. DANIELS, Agent, *Albany.*
J. COURTER, Agent, *Schenectady.*

Albany, Sept. 18, 1841.

phia to Baltimore by public transportation in 1783, it took Jefferson five days. Thirteen years later, nerve-jangled travelers along the same route complained of 6–10 feet deep chasms. They were in constant fear of their conveyances overturning. It still took most stagecoaches five days to make the trip.

In 1784 Josiah Quincy went to New York in a stage coach. He writes of that experience, as follows: "The journey to New York took up a week. The carriages were old and shackling and much of the harness was made of ropes. One pair of horses carried the stage eighteen miles." Quincy adds that they usually traveled until ten o'clock in the evening. After a frugal supper they retired "with a notice that we should be called at three the next morning, which generally proved to be half past two." Regardless of weather, "the traveller must rise and make ready by the help of a horn-lantern and a farthing candle, and proceed on his way over bad roads, sometimes with a driver showing no doubtful symptoms of drunkenness, which good-hearted passengers never fail to improve at every stopping place by urging upon him another toddy."

Road conditions literally drove the stage coach driver to drink. "Mud season" was another one of his problems. The story is told of one instance when the mudhole was so deep that the horses could not drag the coach through. But the passengers, when asked by the driver to get out, refused to do so. Then the driver sat down by the roadside and proceeded to light his pipe. Upon inquiry from the passengers as to why he did this, his reply is said to have been, "Since them hosses can't pull that kerrige out o' thet mudhole, an' ye wo'nt help, I'm a-goin' to wait till th' mudhole dries up." At this point, the passengers were willing to alight and help.

But the drivers never seemed to "dry up". Stephen Jenkins tells us that on the Boston Post Road, he (the driver) was expected to make ten miles an hour. "Of the two unforgivable crimes for which he might be discharged—being behind time, and drunkenness—he was more liable to be discharged for the latter than for the former. The ancient coachman was always drunk, the driver of the Concord coach never, while on duty."

But just as the terrifying experiences of road travel drove many a passenger as well as driver to drink, the arrival of rail travel did not allay the fears of all. As one veteran traveller expressed it, "You got upset in a coach—and there you were! You get upset in a rail-car—and, damme, where are you?" One wonders how courageous an astronaut this traveller would make!

Today, in certain types of heart ailments or faulty circulation, a doctor will recommend an alcoholic stimulant. No doubt, many of the medicinal beverages included among the recipes which follow, served a similar purpose.

Our forefathers seem to have had an excellent sense of taste. Many of their beverages appear to be healthful and others positively unique and delicious. One should bear in mind that scientific knowledge was limited in early America, and so the medicinal recipes contained herein should be considered from an historical rather than practical viewpoint.

However, in numerous ways one can regard our forefathers as being excellent connoisseurs; they had more time for experimentation and they were face to face with the dire necessity of concocting some medicinal beverage to aid an ailing wife or child.

Let us not forget, either, those wintry sleigh rides that ended ultimately at the great hearth where a specially brewed cup of coffee or a hot rum toddy came in mighty handy to ward off a chill.

Another reason for the popularity of alcoholic beverages was of course the lack of proper drinking water at least in the city. Besides, the English had arrived a beer-drinking and ale-drinking people—in the words of Shakespeare, they were "potent in potting." To be deprived of their favorite malt liquors in the first years of their new life in America was a bitter experience for many of the first colonists. The minister Higginson of Salem said in 1629, "Whereas my stomach could only digest and did require such drink as was both strong and stale, I can and ofttimes do drink New England water very well." Since Higginson died a short time thereafter, not all were too impressed with the virtues of water-drinking as he professed them to be. Roger Clap, an early recorder, declared, "(it was) not accounted a strange thing in those days to drink water."

Governor Winthrop in his *History of New England from 1630 to 1649* makes frequent reference to various sorts of alcoholic beverages and drinking. One such reference appears in 1642: "There arrived at Boston a small ship from the Madeiras with wine and sugar, & c. which were presently sold for pipe staves, and other commodities of the country, which were returned to the Madeiras: but the merchant himself, one Mr. Parish, staid divers months after." Again, in 1643 in his account of the "hot wars" between the Dutch and the Indians, Winthrop writes, "The occasion was this. An Indian, being drunk, had slain an old Dutchman. . . . "

Yet, according to Clap's writings as interpreted by Alice Morse Earle, "it was stated that Winthrop drank it (water) ordinarily."

William Wood writes in his *New England Prospects,* (1634) that he dares not prefer water "before good Beere as some have done, but any man would choose it before Bad Beere, Wheay or Buttermilk." In comparison with England's water, it was considered "not so sharp, but of a fatter substance, and of a more jettie colour; it is thought there can be no better water in the world." The Albany water of 1750 is described by Peter Kalm as follows:

> The water of several of the wells was very cool about this time, but had a kind of acid taste which was not very agreeable. I think this water is not very wholesome for people who are not used to it. Nearly every house in Albany has its well, the water of which is applied to common use; but for tea, brewing, and washing they commonly take the water of the river.

The water was also distasteful in New York City. If one wished very good drinking water, he had to buy it from the Tea-water Pump which supplied barrels of water to the more discriminating members of the city. A description of this landmark in the late nineteenth century is given by Charles Hemstreet in his *When Old New York Was Young*. In this account, the author designates Baxter Street as being "the limit of the city boundary shortly before the Revolution." He adds, "A little brook crossed the road right here, spanned by the earliest Kissing Bridge, where the townsfolk met friends and parted from travellers, with certain interesting ceremonies. Over there, at the southwest corner, that dilapidated peaked roof building with the number 166 above the door, stands just where the Tea-Water Pump was—a wonderful pump, the chief water-works of the city during most of the eighteenth century, that gave pure water which was supposed to contain qualities that made it especially valuable in the making of good tea."

Indeed it was not until the close of the eighteenth century that any attempt was made to provide "city water", beyond the facilities of a pump. Philadelphia was the first to attempt such a service, when in 1797 it built three underground tunnels to distribute Schuylkill River water around the city.

For these reasons we can begin to understand the resistance to the passing of excise taxes on whiskey and liquor in the post-revolutionary era.

At a town meeting held in Worcester, Massachusetts in 1782 it was declared with much vehemence that liquor was absolutely essential to farm workers' morale, and therefore those assembled were violently opposed to a state liquor excise. It was considered "contrary to the genius of a free people."

This was followed by trouble in Pennsylvania over the putting of an excise tax on whiskey in 1791. Three years later, on August 7, President Washington issued a proclamation calling out the militia to put down that state's Whisky Rebellion.

Heavy drinking of course early led to excess and as early as 1637 there were complaints among the Puritans that "much drunkenness, waste of the good creatures of God, mispense of time, and other disorders" were some of the evils at the ordinaries. Eight years later, landlords were prohibited from suffering "anyone to be drunk or drink excessively, or continue tippling above the space of half an hour in any of their said houses under penalty of 5s. for every such offence suffered; and every person found drunk in the said houses or elsewhere shall forfeit 10s.; and for every excessive drinking he shall forfeit 3s. 4d.; for sitting idle and continuing drinking above half an hour, 2s. 6d.; and it is declared to be excessive drinking of wine when above half a pint of wine is allowed at one time to one person to drink: provided that it shall be lawful for any strangers, or lodgers, or any person or persons, in an orderly way to continue in such houses of common entertainment during meal times or upon lawful business, what time their occasions shall require."

In Puritan New England, punishments were severe for drunkenness. Sometimes, they were thrust into the bilboes, which were long bars or bolts of iron with sliding shackles. Or, they were set in the stocks, and whipped. According to a 1632 order, "James Woodward shalbe sett in the bil-

Plate 7. *An old printer's cut.*

bowes for being drunke at New-Towne." The following year, on September 3, "Robert Coles was fyned ten shillings and enjoynd to stand with a white sheet of paper on his back, whereon Drunkard shalbe written in great lyres, and to stand therewith soe long as the Court find meet, for abusing himself shamefully with drinke."

Hardly a vocation was without its excessive drinkers. In seventeenth century New Amsterdam, schoolmasters drunk with rum were numerous. In the words of Goldsmith,

Let schoolmasters puzzle their brains
With grammar and nonsense and learning;
Good liquor I stoutly maintain
Gives genius a better discerning.

Jan Cornelissen, a carpenter who turned to the teaching of school, is described by Mrs. Earle as "lying drunk for a month at a time, and was incorrigibly lazy." In the Virginia colony, this sort of behavior would have resulted in his being a convicted and banished felon.

In 1668, such colonies as New Jersey attempted to correct drunkenness by either imposing a fine or by corporal punishment. As elsewhere, the offender was often placed in the stocks until he was sober. He was at least detained until morning for examination. If he was unable to give a good account of himself, he was detained until the next court.

Among the Dutch, a common punishment for soldiers who rioted or overdrank was riding the wooden horse. Earle writes, "One culprit rode with an empty scabbard in one hand and a pitcher in the other to show his inordinate love for John Barleycorn." The wooden horse in New Amsterdam was twelve feet high and stood between "Paerel" Street and the Fort.

After 1700, there appears to have been a great increase in heavy drinking in eastern Massachusetts; this extended to the western counties and Connecticut after 1725. H. B. Parkes in his "Morals and Law Enforcement in Colonial New England," in the *New England Quarterly,* (July, 1932), states that between 1700 and 1730 the number of tavern licenses in many New England towns doubled or trebled; they increased six or eight times between 1700 and 1770.

There were those who became habitual drunkards, alcoholics. An issue of the *Litchfield* (Conn.) *Monitor,* December 23, 1795, carried the following public notice dated Nassau, June 21, 1795:

Whereas the subscriber, through a pernicious habit of drinking for many years, has greatly hurt himself in purse and person, and rendered himself odious to all his acquaintances; finding there is no possibility of breaking off from the said practice, but through impossibility to find the liquor, he therefore earnestly begs and prays, that in future no person will sell him either for money or on trust, any sort of spirituous liquors, as he will not in future pay it, but will prosecute any one for action of damage against the temporal and external interest of the public's humble, serious, sober servant.

William Andrews witnessed the signature of James Chalmers to the above statement.

Such heavy drinking soon became a matter of national concern and was of course responsible for the genesis of the temperance groups which later evolved into the prohibition movement. This important social reform is discussed more in detail in the historical introduction to the section on Temperance Drinks.

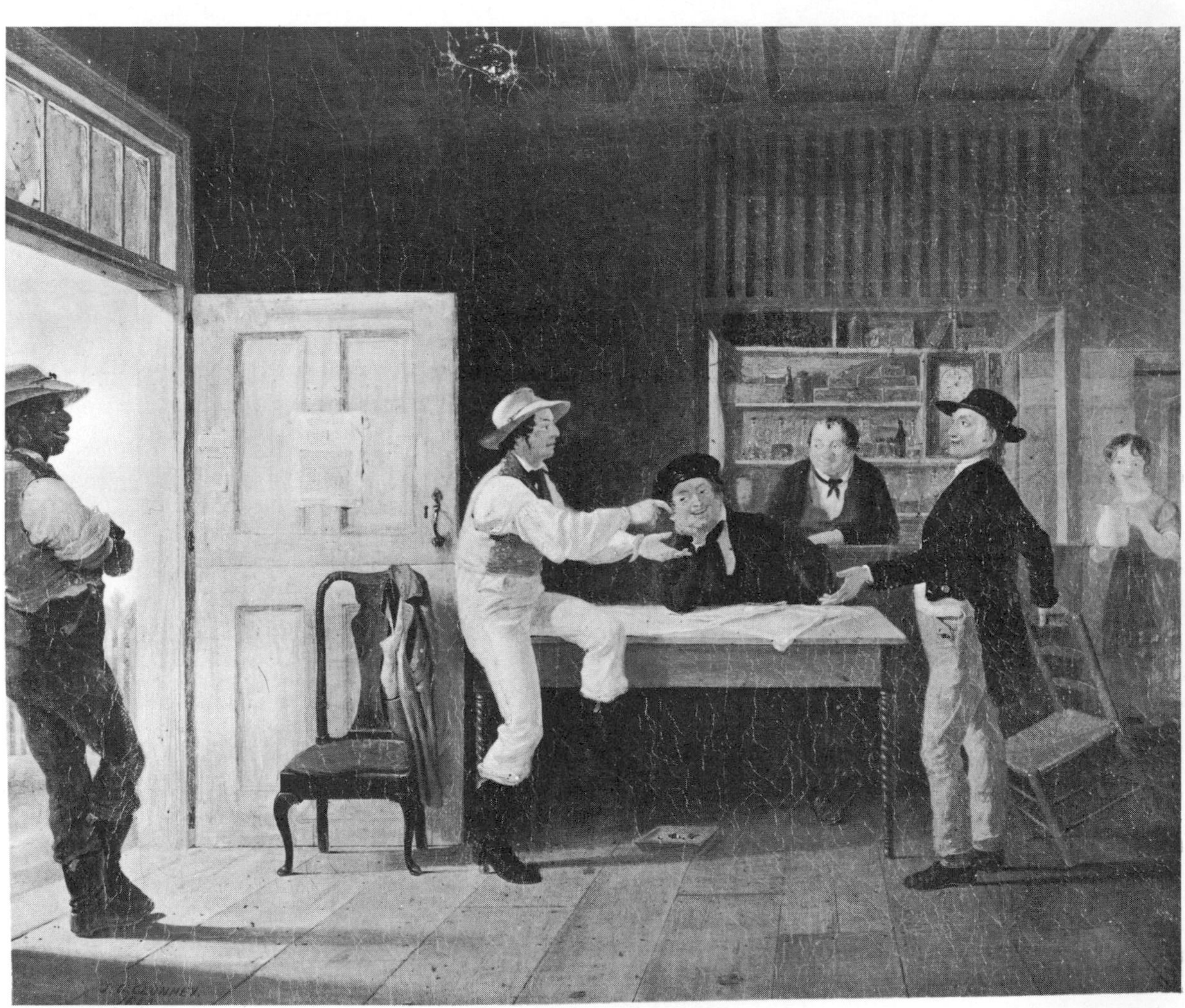

Plate 8. *"Politicians in a Country Bar" is the title of this oil painting of James G. Clonney (1812–1867), which he did in 1844.*

CHAPTER ONE

Ale and Beer

Rove not from sign to sign, but stop in here,
Where naught exceeds the prospect but the beer.
Yellow Cottage sign-board, Philadelphia

ALE, HOME-BREWED—HOW IT IS MADE: The following formula for the manufacture of a famous home-brewed ale of the English yeomanry, will convey a very clear idea of the components and mixture of ordinary ales. The middle classes of the English people usually make their ale in quantities of two barrels, that is, seventy-two gallons.

For this purpose a quarter of malt, (8 bus.) is obtained at the malt-house—or, if wished to be extra strong, nine bushels of malt—are taken, with hops, 12 lbs.; yeast, 5 qts.

The malt, being crushed or ground, is mixed with 72 gals. of water at the temperature of 160 degrees, and covered up for 3 hours, when 40 gallons are drawn off, into which the hops are put, and left to infuse. Sixty gallons of water at a temperature of 170 degrees are then added to the malt in the mash-tub, and well mixed, and after standing 2 hours, sixty gallons are drawn off. The wort from these two mashes is boiled with the hops for 2 hours, and after being cooled down to 65 degrees, is strained through a flannel bag into a fermenting tub, where it is mixed with the yeast and left to work for 24 or 30 hours. It is then run into barrels to cleanse, a few gallons being reserved for filling up the casks as the yeast works over.

Of course when the yeast is worked out it must be bunged. If one-half a pint of this was taken each meal by men, and half that amount by females, and no other spirits, tea nor coffee, during the day, I hesitate not in saying that I firmly believe it would conduce to health. I know that this, which a man makes himself, or some of the wines mentioned in this work, home-made, are all that any person ought to allow themselves to use in these days when dollars and cents are the governing influences of all who deal in such articles.

Dr. Chase's Recipes, 1869

PORTER, ALE, OR WINE. TO PREVENT FLATNESS IN PARTS OF BOTTLES FOR THE INVALID: Sick persons who are recommended to use ale, porter, or wine, and can only take a small glass at a time, nearly always find the last of the bottle flat or stale.

To prevent this put in the cork firmly, and turn the cork-end downwards, in a large tumbler or other vessel nearly filled with water.

This plan prevents communication with the external air.

TO BREW ALE IN SMALL FAMILIES: A bushel

and three quarters of ground malt, and a pound of hops, are sufficient to make 18 gallons of good family ale. That the saccharine matter of the malt may be extracted by infusion, without the farina, the temperature of the water should not exceed 155 or 160 deg. Fahrenheit's thermometer. The quantity of water should be poured on the malt as speedily as possible, and the whole being well mixed together by active stirring, the vessel should be closely covered over for an hour; if the weather be cold, for an hour and a half. If hard water be employed, it should be boiled, and the temperature allowed, by exposure to the atmosphere, to fall to 155 or 160 degrees Fahrenheit; but if rain water is used, it may be added to the malt as soon as it arrives to 155 degrees. During the time this process is going on, the hops should be infused in a close vessel, in as much boiling water as will cover them, for two hours. The liquor may then be squeezed out, and kept closely covered.

The hops should then be boiled for about ten minutes, in double the quantity of water obtained from the infused hop, and the strained liquor, when cold, may be added with the infusion, to the wort, when it has fallen to the temperature of 70 deg. The object of infusing the hop in a close vessel previously to boiling, is to preserve the essential oil of the hop, which renders it more sound, and, at the same time, more wholesome. A pint of good thick yeast should be well stirred into the mixture of wort and hops, and covered over in a place of the temperature of 65 deg. Fahrenheit; and when the fermentation is completed, the liquor may be drawn off into a clean cask previously rinsed with boiling water. When the slow fermentation which will ensue has ceased, the cask should be loosely bunged for two days, when, if the liquor be left quiet, the bung may be properly fastened. The pale malt is the best, because, when highly dried, it does not afford so much saccharine matter. If the malt be new, it should be exposed to the air, in a dry room, for two days previously to its being used; but if it be old, it may be used in 12 or 20 hours after it is ground. The great difference in the flavour of ale, made by different brewers, appears to arise from their employing different species of the hop.

Mackenzie's 5000 Receipts, 1829

LONDON ALE: Almost every country in England has its variety of ale, but the difference consists chiefly (the same quantity of malt and hops being used) in the preparation of the malt. Water may, in some cases, vary in quality, the boiling may be longer or shorter, or the liquor may be turned on at a different heat; but these varieties being considered, one general process serves for the whole. For good ale, the malt and hops should be of the best quality. For immediate use, the malt should be all pale; but if brewed for keeping, or in warm weather, one fourth should be amber malt. Six pounds of Kentish hops should be used to the quarter, or ten pounds for keeping ale.

Mackenzie's 5000 Receipts, 1829

BEER FOR THE FAMILY: Beer is a good family drink. A handful of hops, to a pailful of water, and a half-pint of molasses, makes good hop beer. Spruce mixed with hops is pleasanter than hops alone. Roxberry, fever-bush, sweet fern, and horseradish make a good and healthy diet-drink. The winter evergreen, or rheumatism weed, thrown in, is very beneficial to humors. Be careful and not mistake kill-lamb for winter-evergreen; they resemble each other. Malt mixed with a few hops makes a weak kind of beer; but it is cool and pleasant; it needs less molasses than hops alone. The rule is about the same for all beer. Boil the ingredients two or three hours, pour in a half-pint of molasses to a pailful, while the beer is scalding hot. Strain the beer, and when about lukewarm, put a pint of lively yeast to a barrel. Leave the bung loose till the beer is done working; you can ascertain this by observing when the froth subsides. If your family be large, and the beer will be drank rapidly, it may as well remain in the barrel; but if your family be small, fill what bottles you have with it; it keeps better bottled. A raw potato or two, cut up and thrown in, while the ingredients are boiling, is said to make beer spirited.

Ginger beer is made in the following proportions: —One cup of ginger, one pint of molasses, one pail and a half of water, and a cup of lively yeast. Most people scald the ginger in half a pail of water, and then fill it up with a pail full of cold; but in very hot weather some people stir it up cold. Yeast must not be put in till it is cold, or nearly cold. If not to be drank within twenty-four hours, it must be bottled as soon as it works.

Table beer should be drawn off into *stone* jugs, with a lump of white sugar in each, securely corked.

Plate 9. *Plain, undecorated Norton stoneware items. The beer or ale bottle on the left is ten inches high; the jug, four and one-half; and the jar on the right, seven inches. (Courtesy of the Bennington Museum, Bennington, Vermont)*

It is brisk and pleasant, and continues good several months.

American Frugal Housewife, 1833

COMMON BEER: Two gallons of water to a large handful of hops is the rule. A little fresh-gathered spruce or sweet fern makes the beer more agreeable, and you may allow a quart of wheat bran to the mixture; then boil it two or three hours. Strain it through a sieve, and stir in, while the liquor is hot, a teacup of molasses to every gallon. Let it stand till lukewarm, pour it into a clean barrel and add good yeast, a pint, if the barrel is nearly full; shake it well together; it will be fit for use the next day.

The Way To Live Well, 1849

CORN BEER, WITHOUT YEAST: Cold water 5 gals.; sound nice corn 1 qt.; molasses 2 qts.; put all into a keg of this size; shake well, and in 2 or 3 days a fermentation will have been brought on as nicely as with yeast. Keep it bunged tight.

It may be flavoured with oils of spruce or lemon, if desired, by pouring on to the oils one or two quarts of the water, boiling hot. The corn will last five or six makings. If it gets too sour add more molasses and water in the same proportions. It is cheap, healthy, and no bother with yeast.

Dr. Chase's Recipes, 1869

DORCHESTER BEER: To five pails of water put one quart bowl of hops, and one large handful of sage; or if you can procure them, about two quarts of sassafras roots and checkerberry, mixed, instead of the sage. Add a half a pint of rye meal, and let all boil together three hours. Strain it through a sieve, while it is scalding hot, upon two quarts of molasses. There should be about four pails of the liquor when it is done boiling; if the quantity should be reduced more than that, add a little more water. When it is lukewarm, put to it a half pint of good yeast; then turn it into a keg and let it ferment. In two days or less it will be fit to bottle.

The Young Housekeeper's Friend, 1846

ENGLISH BEER, STRONG: Malt 1 peck; coarse brown sugar 6 lbs.; hops 4 oz.; good yeast 1 tea-cup; if you have not malt, take a little over 1 peck of barley, (twice the amount of oats will do, but are not as good,) and put it into an oven after the bred is drawn, or into a stove oven, and steam the moisture from them. Grind coarsely.

Now pour upon the ground malt 3½ gals. of water at 170 or 172 degrees of heat. The tub in which you scald the malt should have a false bottom, 2 or 3 inches from the real bottom; the false bottom should be bored full of gimlet holes, so as not to act as a strainer, to keep back the malt meal. When the water is poured on, stir them well, and let it stand 3 hours, and draw off by a faucet; put in 7 gals. more of water at 180 to 182 degrees; stir it well, and let it stand 2 hours and draw it off. Then put on a gal. or two of cold water, stir it well and draw it off; you should have about 5 or 6 gals. Put the 6 lbs. of coarse brown sugar in an equal amount of water; mix with the wort and boil 1½ to 2 hours with the hops; you should have eight gals. when boiled; when cooled to 80 degrees put in the yeast, and let it work 18 to 20 hours, covered with a sack; use sound iron hooped kegs or porter bottles, bung or cork tight, and in two weeks it will be good sound beer, and will keep a long time; and for persons of a weak habit of body, and especially females, 1 glass of this with their meals is far better than tea or coffee, or all the ardent spirits in the universe. If more malt is used, not exceeding ½ a bushel, the beer, of course, would have more spirit, but this strength is sufficient for the use of families or invalids.

Dr. Chase's Recipes, 1869

ENGLISH GINGER BEER: Take one ounce and a half of ginger, one ounce of cream tartar, one pound of brown sugar, four quarts of boiling water, and two fresh lemons, sliced. It should be wrought twenty-four hours, with two gills of good yeast, and then bottled. It improves by keeping several weeks, unless the weather is hot, and it is a delightful beverage. If made with loaf instead of brown sugar, the appearance and flavour are still finer.

The Young Housekeeper's Friend, 1846

GAS BEER, PATENT: Ginger 2 ozs.; allspice 1 oz.; cinnamon ½ oz.; cloves ¼ oz.; all bruised or ground; molasses 2 qts.; cold water 7½ gals.; yeast 1 pt.

Boil the pulverized articles, for fifteen or twenty minutes, in the molasses; then strain into your keg, and add the water, then the yeast; shake it well together and bung down. If made over night it will be ready for use the next day. There ought to be a little space in the keg not filled with the beer. This beer is ahead of all the pops and mineral waters of the day, for flavor, health or sparkling qualities or speed in making. Be careful you do not burst the keg. In hot weather, draw in a pitcher with ice. I have sold this in the principal towns of Ohio, Indiana and Michigan, traveling with a caravan, and obtained two dollars for the recipe of the man who kept the inside stand, and blowed the head out of the first keg of it which he made.

Dr. Chase's Recipes, 1869

GINGER BEER: To every gallon of spring water add one ounce of sliced white ginger, one pound of common loaf sugar, and two ounces of lemon juice, or three large tablespoonfuls; boil it near an hour, and take off the scum; then run it through a hair sieve into a tub, and when cool (viz. 70 degrees) add yeast in proportion of half a pint to nine gallons; keep it in a temperate situation two days, during which it may be stirred six or eight times; then put it into a cask, which must be kept full, and the yeast taken off at the bung-hole with a spoon. In a fortnight add half a pint of fining (isinglass picked and steeped in beer) to nine gallons, which will, if it has been properly fermented, clear it by ascent. The cask must be kept full, and the rising particles taken off at the bung-hole. When fine (which may be expected in twenty-four hours) bottle it, cork it well, and in summer it will be ripe and fit to drink in a fortnight.

Family Receipt Book, 1819

GINGER BEER: Boil gently, in a gallon of water, three tablespoonsful of cream of tartar, three of ginger, and a lemon cut in slices. When it has boiled half an hour, take it from the fire, strain and sweeten it to your taste—white sugar is the best, but brown sugar or molasses answers very well. Put to it, when lukewarm, half a pint of fresh yeast. Turn it off carefully, when fermented, bottle it, and keep it in a cool place. It will be fit to drink in the course of seven or eight days.

Kitchen Directory, 1846

GINGER BEER: White sugar 5 lbs.; lemon juice 1 gill; honey ¼ lb.; ginger, bruised, 5 ozs.; water 4½ gals.

Boil the ginger thirty minutes in three qts. of the water; then add the other ingredients, and strain; when cold, put in the white of an egg, well beaten, with one tea-spoon of lemon essence—let stand four days, and bottle. It will keep for months—much longer than if yeast was used; the honey, however, operates mildly in place of yeast.

Dr. Chase's Recipes, 1869

GINGER BEER (QUICKLY MADE): A gallon of boiling water is poured over three quarters of a pound of loaf sugar, one ounce of ginger, and the peel of one lemon; when milk-warm, the juice of the lemon and a spoonful of yeast are added. It should be made in the evening, and bottled next morning, in stone bottles, and the cork tied down with twine.

Good brown sugar will answer, and the lemon may be omitted if cheapness is required.

The Way to Live Well, 1849

GINGER BEER, BOTTLED: One gallon of boiling water; one pound of loaf-sugar; one ounce of best ginger, bruised; one ounce of cream of tartar (or a lemon sliced). Stir them up until the sugar is dissolved, let it rest until the heat falls to the warmth of new milk; then add one table-spoonful of good yeast, poured on to a bit of bread, and set in the middle of the pan floating in the mixture. Cover with a cloth, and stand for twenty-four hours; then strain and put into bottles, filling each only about three parts. Cork tightly, and tie down; in warm weather it will be ready to drink in two days. The above will make fifteen to eighteen bottles, and costs 8d. or 10d.

Practical Housewife, 1860

GINGER BEER, SIMPLE: One great spoonful of ginger and one of cream tartar. One pint of home-brewed yeast and one pint of molasses. Six quarts of water. When it begins to ferment bottle it, and it will be ready for use in eight hours.

Beecher's Receipt Book, 1857

GINGER BEER, SUPERIOR: Ten pounds of sugar. Nine ounces of lemon juice. Half a pound of honey. Eleven ounces bruised ginger root. Nine gallons of water. Three pints of yeast. Boil the ginger half an hour in a gallon and a half of water, then add the rest of the water and the other ingredients, and strain it when cold, add the white of one egg beaten, and half an ounce of essence of lemon. Let it stand four days then bottle it, and it will keep good many months.

Beechers' Receipt Book, 1857

GOOD, WHOLESOME SMALL BEER: Take two

Plate 10. *Brown slip-covered stoneware mugs made at the Norton Pottery measuring four, six, and four and seven-eighths inches in height, respectively. The one on the left has a Gothic design. (Courtesy of the Bennington Museum, Bennington, Vermont)*

ounces of hops, and boil them, three or four hours, in three or four pailfuls of water; and then scald two quarts of molasses in the liquor, and turn it off into a clean half-barrel, boiling hot; then fill it up with cold water; before it is quite full, put in your yeast to work it; the next day you will have agreeable, wholesome small beer, that will not fill with wind, as that which is brewed from malt or bran; and it will keep good till it is all drank out.

American Economical Housekeeper, 1850

HOP BEER: Put to six ounces of hops five quarts of water, and boil them three hours—then strain off the liquor, and put to the hops four quarts more of water, a tea-cup full of ginger, and boil the hops three hours longer. Strain and mix it with the rest of the liquor, and stir in a couple of quarts of molasses. Take about half a pound of bread, and brown it very slowly—when very brown and dry, put it in the liquor, to enrich the beer. Rusked bread is the best for this purpose, but a loaf of bread cut in slices, and toasted till brittle, will do very well. When rusked bread is used, pound it fine, and brown it in a pot, as you would coffee, stirring it constantly. When the hop liquor cools, so as to be just lukewarm, add a pint of new yeast, that has no salt in it. Keep the beer covered in a temperate situation, till it has ceased fermenting, which is ascertained by the subsiding of the froth—turn it off carefully into a beer keg, or bottles. The beer should not be corked very tight, or it will burst the bottles. It should be kept in a cool place.

Kitchen Directory, 1846

INSTANTANEOUS BEER: Put to a pint and a half of water four tea-spoonsful of Ginger, a table-spoonful of lemon juice—sweeten it to the taste with syrup or white sugar, and turn it into a junk bottle. Have ready a cork to fit the bottle, a string or wire to tie it down, and a mallet to drive in the cork. Then put into the bottle a heaping tea-spoonful of the super-carbonate of soda, cork it immediately, tie it down, then shake the whole up well, cut the string, and the cork will fly out. Turn it out, and drink immediately.

Kitchen Directory, 1846

LEMON BEER: Water 30 gals.; ginger root bruised 6 ozs.; cream of tartar ¼ lb.; coffee sugar 13 lbs.; oil of lemon 1 oz.; or ½ oz. of the oil may be used, and 6 good sized lemons, sliced; yeast 1½ pts.

Boil the ginger and cream of tartar, about twenty to thirty minutes, in two or three gallons of the water; then strain it upon the sugar and oils or sliced lemons, which have been rubbed together, having warm water enough to make the whole thirty gallons just so you can hold your hand in it without burning, or about seventy degrees of heat; then work up the yeast into a paste, as for the cider, with five or six ounces of flour. Let it work over night, skimming off the yeast, or letting it work over as the cider, then strain and bottle for use. This will keep fifteen or twenty days. The Port Huronites think it a splendid drink.

Dr. Chase's Recipes, 1869

MAPLE BEER: To four gallons of boiling water, add one quart of maple molasses, and a small table spoonful of essence of spruce. When it is about milk warm, add a pint of yeast; and when fermented, bottle it. In three days it is fit for use.

The Young Housekeeper's Friend, 1846

PHILADELPHIA BEER: Water 30 gals.; brown sugar 20 lbs.; ginger, bruised, 1¼ lbs.; cream of tartar ¼ lb.; super carbonate of soda 3 oz.s; oil of lemon, put in a little alcohol, 1 teaspoon; whites of 10 eggs, well beaten; hops 2 ozs.; yeast 1 qt.

The ginger root and hops should be boiled twenty or thirty minutes in enough of the water to make all milk warm, then strained into the rest, and the yeast added and allowed to work over night; skimmed and bottled.

Dr. Chase's Recipes, 1869

SPRING BEER: Take a small bunch of all, or part of the following: Sweet fern, sarsaparilla, winter-green, sassafras, prince's pine, and spice wood. Boil them with two or three ounces of hops to three or four gallons of water, and two or three raw potatoes, pared and cut in slices. The strength of the roots and hops is obtained more thoroughly by boiling them in two waters—for, when the liquor is strongly saturated with the hops, it will rather bind up the roots than extract their juices. The roots should be boiled five or six hours—the liquor should then be strained,

Plates 11 and 12. *Front and side views of toby pitchers, used for ale. All five of these are Bennington-made, having flat rather than highly concave bottoms usually found on toby pitchers from other potteries. All five measure between five and three-fourths and six inches in height. The one on the left has a Ben Franklin design with a boot handle; the second, also having a Ben Franklin design, possesses a grapevine handle; the third is a standard toby; the fourth, with a General Stark design, is rare; while the last one has the figure in a sitting position and is marked 1849. (Courtesy of the Bennington Museum, Bennington, Vermont)*

and a quart of molasses put to three gallons of the beer. If you wish to have the beer very rich, brown half a pound of bread, and put it into the liquor. If the liquor is too thick, dilute it with cold water. When just lukewarm, put in a pint of fresh lively yeast, that has no salt in it. The salt has a tendency to keep it from fermenting. Keep it in a temperate situation, covered over, but not so tight as to exclude the air entirely, or it will not work. When fermented, keep it in a tight keg, or bottle and cork it up.

Kitchen Directory, 1846

SPRUCE BEER: Take three gallons of water, lukewarm, three half-pints of molasses, a tablespoonful of essence of spruce, and the same quantity of sugar; mix all together, and add a gill of yeast; let it stand over night, and bottle it in the morning. It will be ready for use in twenty-four hours.

American Economical Housekeeper, 1850

SPRUCE OR AROMATIC BEER: For 3 gals. water put in 1 qt. and ½ pt. of molasses, 3 eggs well beaten, yeast 1 gill. Into 2 qts. of the water boiling hot put 50 drops of any oil you wish the flavor of; or mix 1 oz. each, oils sassafras, spruce and wintergreen, then use 50 drops of the mixed oils.

Mix all, and strain; let it stand two hours, then bottle, bearing in mind that yeast must not be put in when the fluid would scald the hand. Boiling water cuts oil for beers, equal to alcohol.

Dr. Chase's Recipes, 1869

SPRUCE BEER: Allow an ounce of hops and a spoon-ful of ginger to a gallon of water. When well boiled, strain it, and put in a pint of molasses and half an ounce or less of the essence of spruce; when cool, add a teacup of yeast, and put into a clean tight cask, and let it ferment for a day or two, then bottle it for use. You can boil the sprigs of spruce fir in room of the essence.

The Way To Live Well, 1849

TABLE BEER (EXCELLENT SUBSTITUTE): As small beer is apt to become sour in warm weather, a pleasant beer may be made, by adding to a bottle of porter ten quarts of water, and a pound of brown sugar or molasses. After they have been well mixed, pour the liquor into bottles, and place them, loosely corked, in a cool cellar. In two or three days it will be fit for use. A spoonful of ginger, added to the mixture, renders it more lively and agreeable to the taste. This might be adopted in the navy instead of grog.

Family Receipt Book, 1819

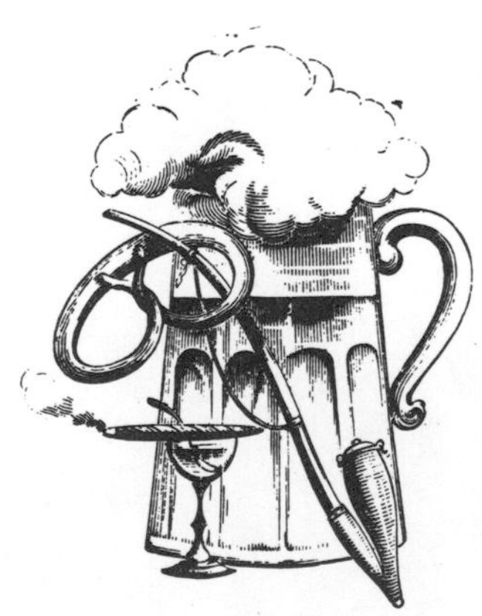

CHAPTER TWO

Cider and Perry

I William McDermott lives here,
I sells good porter, ale, and beer,
I've made my sign a little wider
To let you know I sell good cider.

The source of the following direcitons is *Mackenzie's 5000 Receipts,* 1829.

TO MAKE CIDER: After the apples are gathered from the trees, they are ground into what is called *pommage,* either by means of a common pressing stone, with a circular trough, or by a cider mill, which is either driven by the hand, or by horse power. When the pulp is thus reduced to a great degree of fineness, it is conveyed to the cider press, where it is formed by pressure into a kind of cake, which is called the *cheese.*

This is effected by placing clear sweet straw, or hair cloths, between the layers of pommage, till there is a pile of ten or twelve layers. This pile is then subjected to different degrees of pressure in succession, till all the *must,* or *juice,* is squeezed from the pommage. This juice, after being strained in a coarse hair-sieve, is then put either into open vats or close casks, and the pressed pulp is either thrown away, or made to yield a weak liquor called washings.

After the liquor has undergone the proper fermentation in these close vessels, which may be best effected in a temperature of from forty to sixty degrees of fahrenheit, and which may be known by its appearing tolerably clear, and having a vinous sharpness upon the tongue, any farther fermnetation must be stopped by racking off the pure part into open vessels, exposed for a day or two in a cool situation. After this the liquor must again be put into casks, and kept in a cool place during winter. The proper time for racking may always be known by the brightness of the liquor, the discharge of the fixed air, and the appearance of a thick crust formed of fragments of the reduced pulp. The liquor should always be racked off anew, as often as a hissing noise is heard, or as it extinguishes a candle held to the bung-hole.

When a favourable vinous fermentation has been obtained, nothing more is required than to fill up the vessels every two or three weeks, to supply the waste by fermentation. On the beginning of March, the liquor will be bright and pure, and fit for final racking, which should be done in fair weather. When the bottles are filled, they should be set by uncorked till morning, when the corks must be driven in tightly, secured by wire or twine and melted rosin, or any similar substance.

TO MAKE DEVONSHIRE CIDER: Prefer the bitter sweet apples, mixed with mild sour, in the proportion of one-third. Gather them when ripe, and lay them in heaps in the orchard. Then take them to the crushing engine, made of iron rollers at top and of stone beneath; after passing through which, they are

Plate 13. *"Cider Making on Long Island" is the title of this oil on canvass painted by William M. Davis in 1871. (Courtesy of the New York State Historical Association, Cooperstown, New York)*

received into large tubs or cives, and are then called pommage. They are afterwards laid on the vat in alternate layers of the pommage and clean straw, called reeds. They are then pressed, the juice running through a hair sieve. After the cider is pressed out, it is put into hogsheads, where it remains for two or three days previously to fermenting. To stop the fermentation, it is drawn off into a clean vessel; but if the fermentation be very strong, two or three cans of cider are put into a clean vessel, and a match of brimstone burnt in it: it is then agitated, by which the fermentation of that quantity is completely stopped. The vessel is then nearly filled, the fermentation of the whole is checked, and the cider becomes fine: but if, on the first operation, the fermentation is not checked, it is repeated till it is so, and continued from time to time till the cider is in a quiet state for drinking.

Some persons, instead of deadening a small quantity with a match, as above directed, put from one to two pints of an article called *stum* (bought of the wine coopers) into each hogshead: but the system of racking as often as the fermentation appears, is generally preferred by the cider manufacturers of Devonshire.

About six sacks, or twenty-four bushels of apples, are used for a hogshead of sixty-three gallons. During the process, if the weather is warm, it will be necessary to carry it on in the shade, in the open air, and by every means keep it as cool as possible.

In nine months it will be in condition for bottling or drinking; if it continues thick, use some isinglass finings, and if at any time it ferments and threatens acidity, the cure is to rack it and leave the head and sediment.

SCOTCH METHOD: The apples are reduced to muscilage, by beating them in a stone trough (one of those used at pumps for watering horses) with pieces of ash—poles, used in the manner that potatoes are mashed. The press consists of a strong box, three feet square, and twenty inches deep, perforated on each side with small auger or gimblet holes. It is placed on a frame of wood, projecting three inches beyond the base of the box. A groove is cut in this projection one inch and a half wide, and one inch deep, to convey the juice when pressed out of the box into a receiving pail. This operation is performed in the following manner. The box is filled alternately with strata of fresh straw and mashed fruit, in the proportion of one inch of straw to two inches of mucilage: these are piled up a foot higher than the top of the box; and care is taken in packing the box itself, to keep the fruit and straw about one inch from the sides of the box, which allows the juice to escape freely. A considerable quantity of the liquor will run off without any pressure. This must be applied gradually at first and increased regularly towards the conclusion. A box of the above dimensions will require about two tons weight to render the residuum completely free from juice.

(The residuum is excellent food for pigs, and peculiarly acceptable to them).

The necessary pressure is obtained very easily, and in a powerful manner, by the compound lever pressing upon a lid or sink, made of wood about two inches thick, and rendered sufficiently strong by two cross-bars. It is made to fit the opening of the box exactly; and as the levers force the lid down, they are occasionally slacked or taken off, and blocks of wood are placed on the top of the lid, to permit the levers to act, even after the lid has entered the box itself. Additional blocks are repeated, until the whole juice is extracted. The pressure may be increased more or less, by adding or diminishing the weight suspended at the extreminty of the lever.

The liquor thus obtained is allowed to stand undisturbed twelve hours, in open vessels, to deposit sediment. The pure juice is then put into clean casks, and placed in a proper situation to ferment, the temperature being from fifty-five to sixty degrees. The fermentation will commence sooner or later, depending chiefly on the temperature of the apartment where the liquor is kept; in most cases, during the first three or four days; but sometimes it will require more than a week to begin this process. If the fermentation begins early and proceeds rapidly, the liquor must be racked off, and put into fresh casks in two or three days; but if this does not take place at an early period, and proceeds slowly, five or six days may elapse before it is

Plate 14. *"Cider Making in the Country" is the title of this oil on canvas painted by George Henry Durrie (1820–1863), signed and dated 1863. Currier and Ives made this painting popular with their 1866 lithograph, "Autumn in New England—Cider Making." (Courtesy of the New York State Historical Association, Cooperstown, New York)*

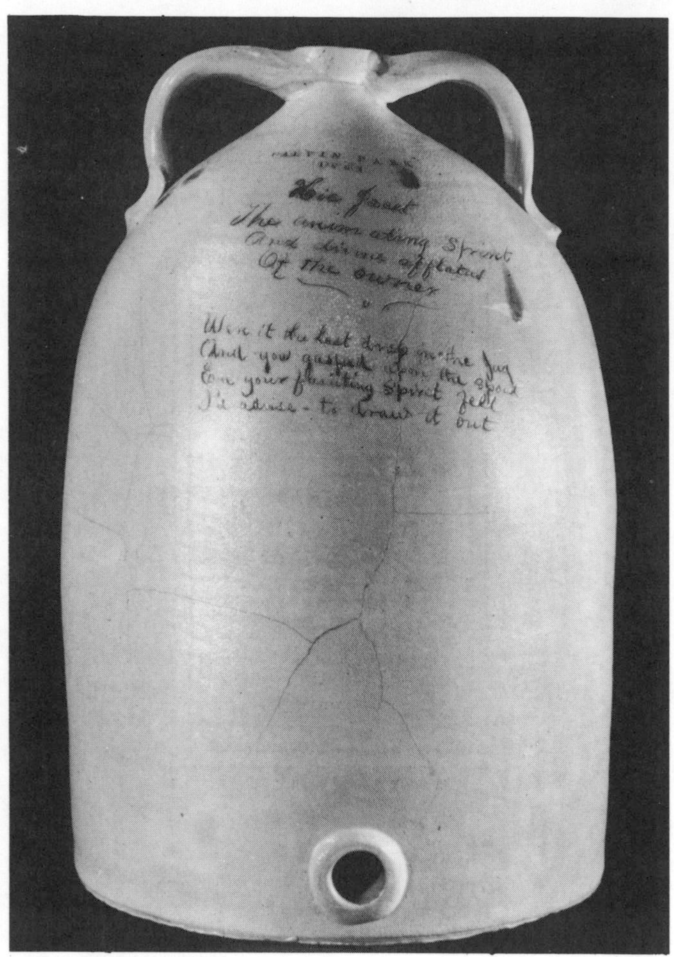

Plate 15. *This presentation stoneware cider jug with cobalt decoration was made in 1864 for Calvin Park upon the occasion of his election to the Vermont State Legislature. (Courtesy of the Bennington Museum, Bennington, Vermont)*

racked. In general, it is necessary to rack the liquor at least twice. If, notwithstanding, the fermentation continues briskly, the racking must be repeated; otherwise the vinous fermentation, by proceeding too far, may terminate in acetous fermentation, when vinegar would be the result.

In racking off the liquor it is necessary to keep it free of sediment, and the *scum* or yeast produced by the fermentation. A supply of spare liquor must be reserved to fill up the barrels occasionally, while the fermentation continues. As soon as this ceases, the barrels should be bunged up closely, and the bungs covered with rosin, to prevent the admission of air. If the cider is weak, it should remain in the cask about nine months; if strong, twelve or eighteen months is necessary before it should be bottled.

TO MANAGE CIDER AND PERRY: To fine and improve the flavour of one hogs-head, take a gallon of good French brandy, with half an ounce of cochineal, one pound of alum, and three pounds of sugar-candy; bruise them all well in a mortar, and infuse them in the brandy for a day or two; then mix the whole with the cider and stop it close for five or six months. After which, if fine, bottle it off.

Cider or perry, when bottled in hot weather, should be left a day or two uncorked, that it may get flat; but if too flat in the cask, and soon wanted for use, put into each bottle a small lump or two of sugarcandy, four or five raisins of the sun, or a small piece of raw beef; any of which will much improve the liquor, and make it brisker.

Cider should be well corked and waxed, and packed upright in a cool place. A few bottles may always be kept in a warmer place to ripen and be ready for use.

TO MAKE CHEAP CIDER FROM RAISINS: Take fourteen pounds of raisins with the stalks; wash them out in four or five waters, till the water remains clear; then put them into a clean cask with the head out, and put six gallons of good water upon them; after which cover it well up, and let it stand ten days. Then rack it off into another clean cask, which has a brass cock in it, and in four or five days time it will be fit for bottling. When it has been in the bottles seven or eight days, it will be fit for use. A little colouring should be added when putting into the cask the second time. The raisins may afterwards be used for vinegar.

TO MAKE PERRY: Perry is made after the same manner as cider, only from pears, which must be quite dry. The best pears for this purpose are such as are least fit for eating, and the redder they are the better.

OBSERVATIONS ON CIDER: From the great diversity of soil and climate in the United States of America, and the almost endless variety of its apples,

Plate 16. *"The Cider Mill," an oil on canvas, was painted by William T. Carleton (1816–1888). (Courtesy of the New York State Historical Association, Cooperstown, New York)*

it follows that much diversity of taste and flavour will necessarily be found in the cider that is made from them.

To make good cider the following general, but *important* rules should be attended to. They demand a little more trouble than the ordinary mode of collecting and mashing apples of all sorts, rotten and sound, sweet and sour, dirty and clean, from the tree and the soil, and the rest of the slovenly process usually employed; but in turn they produce you a wholesome, high flavoured, sound and palatable liquor, *that always commands an adequate price,* instead of a solution of "villainous compounds," in a poisonous and acid wash, that no man in his senses will drink. The finest cider I ever tasted, was made of an equal portion of *ripe, sound,* pippin and crab apples, *pared, cored,* and

pressed, & c. with the utmost nicety. It was equal in flavour to any champagne that ever was made.

GENERAL RULES FOR MAKING CIDER: 1. Always choose perfectly ripe and sound fruit. 2. Pick the apples by hand. An active boy, with a bag slung over his shoulders, will soon clear a tree. Apples that have lain any time on the soil, contract an earthy taste, which will always be found in the cider. 3. After *sweating,* and before being ground, *wipe them dry,* and if any are found bruised or rotten, put them in a heap by themselves, for an inferior cider to make vinegar. 4. Always use hair cloths, instead of straw, to place between the layers of pommage. The straw when heated gives a disagreeable taste to the cider. 5. As the cider runs from the press, let it pass through a hair sieve into a large open vessel, that will hold as much juice as can be expressed in one day. In a day, or sometimes less, the pumice will rise to the top, and in a short time grow very thick: when little white bubbles break through it, draw off the liquor by a spigot, placed about three inches from the bottom, so that the lees may be left quietly behind. 6. The cider must be drawn off into very clean sweet casks, and closely watched. The moment the white bubbles before mentioned are perceived rising at the bung-hole, rack it again. When the fermentation is completely at an end, fill up the cask with cider, in all respects like that already contained in it, and bung it up tight; previous to which a tumbler of *sweet oil* may be poured into the bung-hole.

Sound, well made cider, that has been produced as described, and without any foreign mixtures excepting always that of good cognac brandy, (which added to it in the proportion of one gallon to thirty, greatly improves it) is a pleasant, cooling and useful beverage. While on the contrary, the acid and nasty wash that has passed through leaden pipes, and been otherwise carelessly and unskillfully made, is a perfect poison, producing colic, and not unfrequently, incurable obstructions.

CHAPTER THREE

Liqueurs and Cordials

Mynheer Vandunck, though he never was drunk, Sipped brandy *and water gayly.*

GEORGE COLMAN, *Mynheer Vandunck*

ANISETTE: Oil of anise-seed, ten drops; alcohol, three pints; sugar, two pounds; pure water, one and a half pounds. Make the syrup with the sugar and water cold, and mix the liquors.

ANOTHER ANISETTE: Star anise-seed, eight ounces; bitter almonds pounded, and coriander, each, eight ounces; powdered Florence iris, four ounces; alcohol, five gallons. Macerate in the alcohol for five days; distil in the water-bath, and add twelve pounds of sugar dissolved in seven pints of distilled water.

The Art of Confectionery, 1866

ANISETTE DE BOURDEAUX: Take of sugar, 9 oz.; oil of aniseed, 6 drops. Rub them together, and add by degrees, spirit of wine, 2 pints; water, 4 pints. Filter.

Mackenzie's 5000 Receipts, 1829

ANISETTE DE BOURDEAUX: Green anise-seed, ten ounces; hyson tea, two ounces; star anise-seed, four ounces; coriander, one ounce; fennel, one ounce. Macerate for fifteen days in three and a half gallons of alcohol; distil in the water-bath; then make a syrup with ten pounds of sugar and seven pints of water; mix well, and filter.

ANOTHER ANISETTE DE BOURDEAUX: Dill, one pound; green aniseseed, eight ounces; fennel, four ounces; coriander, four ounces; sassafras-wood cut fine, four ounces; pearl gunpowder tea, four ounces; musk-seed, one ounce. Macerate all these substances in three and a half gallons of alcohol for six days; then distil in the waterbath; add a syrup made with twenty-eight pounds of fine sugar, two and a half gallons of distilled water, one quart of double-distilled orange-flower water, and one quart of pure water.

The Art of Confectionery, 1866

ANNISEED CORDIAL: Melt a pound of loaf-sugar in two quarts of water. Mix it with two quarts of white brandy, and add a tablespoonful of oil of an-nissed. Let it stand a week; then filter it through white blotting paper, and bottle it for use.

Clove or Cinnamon Cordial may be made in the same manner, by mixing sugar, water and brandy, and adding oil of cinnamon or oil of cloves. You may colour any of these cordials red by stirring in a little powdered cochineal that has been dissolved in a small quantity of brandy.

Miss Leslie's Complete Cookery, 1839

BALM OF MANKIND: Peruvian balsam, one

ounce; cashew-nuts, eight ounces; coriander, four drachms; dried heads of wormwood, one ounce; yellow rinds of six lemons. Macerate these in two gallons of alcohol for eight days; distil the liquor in the water-bath to nearly one-half; add a syrup made with five and a half pounds of sugar; filter, and color green.

The Art of Confectionery, 1866

BLACKBERRY CORDIAL: Take the ripest blackberries. Mash them, put them in a linen bag and squeeze out the juice. To every quart of juice allow a pound of beaten loaf-sugar. Put the sugar into a large preserving kettle, and pour the juice on it. When it is all melted, set it on the fire, and boil it to a thin jelly. When cold, to every quart of juice allow a quart of brandy. Stir them well together, and bottle it for use. It will be ready at once.

Seventy-five Receipts, 1838

BRANDY SHRUB: Take 8 oz. of citric acid,—1 gallon of porter,—3 gallons of raisin wine,—2 quarts of orange flower water, —7 gallons of good brandy, —5 ditto of water. This will produce 16 gallons. First, dissolve the citric acid in the water, then add to it the brandy: next, mix the raisin wine, porter, and orange flower water together; and lastly, mix the whole: and in a week or ten days, it will be ready for drinking, and of a very mellow flavour.

Mackenzie's 5000 Receipts, 1829

CHERRY BOUNCE: Mix together six pounds of ripe morellas and six pounds of large black heart cherries. Put them into a wooden bowl or tub, and with a pestle or mallet mash them so as to crack all the stones. Mix with the cherries three pounds of loaf-sugar, or of sugar candy broken up, and put them into a demijohn, or into a large stone jar. Pour on two gallons of the best double rectified whiskey. Stop the vessel closely, and let it stand three months, shaking it every day during the first month. At the end of the three months you may strain the liquor and bottle it off. It improves by age.

Miss Leslie's Complete Cookery, 1839

CHERRY BRANDY: Get equal quantities of morello and common black cherries; fill your cask, and pour on (to a ten gallon cask) one gallon of boiling water; in two or three hours, fill it up with brandy—let it stand a week, then draw off all, and put another gallon of boiling water, and fill it again with brandy—at the end of the week, draw the whole off, empty the cask of the cherries, and pour in your brandy with water, to reduce the strength; first dissolving one pound of brown sugar in each gallon of your mixture. If the brandy be very strong, it will bear water enough to make the cask full.

Virginia Housewife, 1856

CHERRY CORDIAL: Take Black Cherries, large and full ripe, plucking off their Stalks only, 12 Pounds; put them into a large Stone Bottle, to which put choice Brandy six Quarts, Double Refined Loaf Sugar, 3 pounds in Powder, Lime Juice a Pint and a half, Cinamon bruised, Cloves slit, Nutmegs bruised, of each a quarter of an Ounce; stop them up close, shaking the Bottle once every Day: After three weeks you may use it: Two, three, or four Spoonfuls, will be an extraordinary Cordial, at any time upon any Fainting, or Illness, especially in a Morning fasting.

Dr. Salmon's Recipes, 1710

CHERRY SHRUB: Gather ripe morello cherries, pick them from the stalk, and put them in an earthen pot, which must be set into an iron pot of water; make the water boil, but take care that none of it gets into the cherries; when the juice is extracted, pour it into a bag made of tolerably thick cloth, which will permit the juice to pass, but not the pulp of your cherries; sweeten it to your taste, and when it becomes perfectly clear, bottle it—put a gill of brandy into each bottle, before you pour in the juice—cover the corks with rosin. It will keep all summer, in a dry cool place, and is delicious mixed with water.

Virginia Housewife, 1856

CORDIAL EXCELLENT: Take two Ounces of dried Clove Gilliflowers, and put them into a Bottle of Canary; add three Ounces of fine Sugar, and half a Scruple of Ambergrise in Powder; put them into a Stone Bottle, and stop it close, often shaking it; and when it has stood 10 Days, then strain it through a Gelly Bag; and putting it up for use, take two or three Spoonfuls of it at a time, and it will greatly strengthen the Heart, and restore Health again, & c.

Dr. Salmon's Recipes, 1710

CURRANT SHRUB: Your currants must be quite ripe. Pick them from the stalks, and squeeze them through a linen bag. To each quart of juice allow a pound of loaf-sugar. Put the sugar and juice into a preserving kettle, and let it melt before it goes on the fire. Boil it ten minutes, skimming it well. When cold, add a jill of the best white brandy to each quart of the juice. Bottle it, and set it away for use; sealing the corks. It improves by keeping.

Miss Leslie's Complete Cookery, 1839

CITRONELLE: Zests of lemons, sixty; zests of oranges, eight; nutmeg and cloves, each, one drachm. Macerate the whole in seven quarts of alcohol for fifteen days; distil in the water-bath, and add a syrup made with five pounds of sugar. Color yellow.

The Art of Confectionery, 1866

CURACOA: Surface of the zests of oranges, thirty-six; cinnamon, two drachms; mace, one drachm. Macerate in two gallons of alcohol for fifteen days; distil in the water-bath, and add a syrup made with seven pounds of sugar and two quarts of water. Color with carmel. *The Art of Confectionery,* 1866

CURRANT SHRUB: Take white currants, when quite ripe, pick them off the stalks, and bruise them; strain out the juice through a cloth, and to two quarts of the juice put 2 lbs. of loaf sugar; when it is dissolved add to it a gallon of rum, then strain it through a flannel bag that will keep in the jelly, and it will run off clear; then bottle it for use.

Mackenzie's 5000 Receipts, 1829

DRINK FOR THE SUMMER: Take one bottle of sherry, (but Madira is preferable,) two bottles of cyder, one of perry, and one gill of brandy; and after those ingredients are mixed, take two lemons, pare the rind as thin as possible; then slice the lemons, and put the rind and lemons into a cup; to these add a little grated nutmeg and powdered sugar, to make it palatable; stir them together; then toast a biscuit very brown, and throw it hot into the liquor. It is generally found a pleasant draught at dinner, and produces no bad effects on those who drink it in moderation.

Family Receipt Book, 1819

EASTERN BEVERAGE, CALLED SHERBET: This liquor is a species of negus without the wine. It consists of water, lemon or orange juice, and sugar, in which are dissolved perfumed cakes, made of the best Damascus fruit, and containing also an infusion of some drops of rose-water; another kind is made of violets, honey, juice of raisins, &c. It is well calculated for assuaging thirst, as the acidity is agreeably blended with sweetness. It resembles, indeed, those fruits which we find so grateful when one is thirsty.

Family Receipt Book, 1819

EAU DE BARBADES: Take of fresh orange peel, 1 oz.; fresh lemon-peel, 4 oz.; cloves, ½ drachm; coriander, 1 do.; proof spirit, 4 pints. Distil in a bath heat and add white sugar in powder.

Mackenzie's 5000 Receipts, 1829

EAU DIVINE: Take of spirit of wine, 1 gallon; essence of lemons, and essence of bergamot, each 1 drachm: Distil in a bath heat: add sugar 4 lbs. dissolved in 2 gallons of pure water: and, lastly, orange flower water, 5 oz.

Mackenzie's 5000 Receipts, 1829

ELEPHANT'S MILK: Take of benjamin, 2 oz.; spirit of wine, 1 pint, boiling water, 2½ pints. When cold, strain; and add sugar, 1½ lbs.

Mackenzie's 5000 Receipts, 1829

FOX GRAPE SHRUB: Gather the grapes when they are full grown, but before they begin to purple. Pick from the stems a sufficient quantity to nearly fill a large preserving kettle, and pour on them as much boiling water as the kettle will hold. Set it over a brisk fire, and keep it scalding hot till all the grapes have burst. Then take them off, press out and strain the liquor, and allow to each quart a pound of sugar stirred well in. Dissolve the sugar in the juice; then put them together into a clean kettle, and boil and skim them for ten minutes, or till the scum ceases to rise. When cold, bottle it; first putting into each bottle a jill of brandy. Seal the bottles, and keep them in a warm closet.

You may make gooseberry shrub in this manner.

Miss Leslie's Complete Cookery, 1839

GERMAN LIQUOR MUM: Mum is made of various sorts of grain, in the following proportions:

to seven bushels of wheaten malt, add one bushel of oatmeal, one bushel of ground beans, and a variety of other articles, as the tops of fir, wild thyme, & c.; also ten new laid eggs. These articles ought to be infused into sixty-three gallons of water boiled down to forty-one. *Family Receipt Book,* 1819

HUILE DE VENUS: Take of flowers of the wild carrot, picked, 6 oz. —spirit of wine, 10 pints. Distil in a bath heat. To the spirit add as much syrup of capillaire; it may be colored with cochineal.
Mackenzie's 5000 Receipts, 1829

LEMON CORDIAL: Cut six fresh lemons in thin slices, put them into a quart and a half of milk, boil it until the whey is very clear, then pass it through a sieve; put to this whey, one and a half quarts of French brandy, and three pounds of powdered loaf sugar; stir it till the sugar is dissolved—let it stand to refine, and bottle it; pare some of the yellow rind of the lemons very thin, and put a little in each bottle.
Virginia Housewife, 1856

LEMON SHRUB Pare a thin rind off from fresh lemons; squeeze out and strain the juice; put to a pint of it, a pound of sugar broken in small pieces; take for each pint of the sirup three spoonfuls of brandy, and soak the rind of the lemon in it. Let all stand one day, frequently stirring up the lemon juice and sugar. Next day pour off the sirup, and mix it with the brandy and lemon rinds. Keep it under sealed corks, in dry sand, in a cool place.
Book of Receipts, 1858

LIQUODILLA: Take the thin peel of six oranges and 6 lemons, steep them in a gallon of brandy or rum, close stopped, for two or three days; then take 6 quarts of water, and 3 lbs. of loaf sugar clarified with the whites of three eggs. Let it boil a quarter of an hour, then strain it through a fine sieve, and let it stand till cold; strain the brandy from the peels, and add the juice of 5 oranges and 7 lemons to each gallon. Keep it close stopped up six weeks, then bottle it.
Mackenzie's 5000 Receipts, 1829

MARASQUIN, A NEW LIQUEUR: Advantage has not hitherto been taken of the fruit of the St. Lucian tree, (prunus mahaleb, Lin.) This small black fruit is of a very disagreeable taste, but it may produce an excellent liqueur. M. Cadet de Vaux, recognizing in this little cherry an aromatic savour, thought it would serve to make a kind of kirschwasser. In effect, it ferments and furnishes by distillation a Prussic alcohol; but by putting it first to infuse in brandy for some time, there is obtained, by distillation in a bath heat, a spirit of a very agreeable aromatic, and which, properly sweetened, forms a liqueur comparable to the best marasquin of Italy. It is necessary to bruise the fruit and the nuts before infusing them in brandy. The spirit must also be brought back to 21 degrees before sweetening it. Then add nearly 12 oz. of sugar to every quart of liqueur.—*Journal de Pharmacie,* 1821.
Mackenzie's 5000 Receipts, 1829

MARASQUIN DE GROSEILLES: Take of gooseberries, quite ripe, 102 lbs. black cherry leaves, 12 lbs. Bruise and ferment; distil and rectify the spirit. To each pint of this spirit add as much distilled water, and sugar, 1 lb.
Mackenzie's 5000 Receipts, 1829

METHEGLIN: For a half a barrel of metheglin, allow forty-eight or fifty pounds of fresh honey. Boil it an hour in a third of a barrel of spring water. Skim it well. It should be so strong with honey that when cold an egg will not sink in it. Add a small dessert spoonful of ginger, and as much of powdered clove and mace; also a spoonful of yeast. Leave the bung of the cask loose till the fermentation has ceased; then stop it close. At the end of six months, draw off and bottle it. It improves until three or four years old, and has a fine color. It is a very healthful cordial.
The Young Housekeeper's Friend, 1846

MINT CORDIAL: Pick the mint early in the morning while the dew is on it, and be careful not to bruise it; pour some water over it, and drain it—put two handsful into a pitcher, with a quart of French brandy, cover it, and let it stand till next day; take the mint carefully out, and put in as much more, which must be taken out next day—do this the third time; then put three quarts of water to the brandy, and one pound of loaf sugar powdered; mix it well together—and when perfectly clear, bottle it.
Virginia Housewife, 1856

Plate 17. *Peddlers' carts were a familiar sight at many inns and taverns. P. T. Barnum may have used one similar to this when he engaged at an early age in a career as a peddler of gingerbread, molasses candy, and cherry rum on Training Days. (Courtesy of the New York State Historical Association, Cooperstown, New York)*

NECTAR: White honey, four ounces; coriander, two ounces; fresh zests of lemon, one ounce; storax calamite, benzoin, and cloves, each, one ounce; tincture of vanilla, half a drachm; tincture of orange-flower water, four ounces; highly rectified spirits, five quarts. Pulverize the substances which require it, and macerate them for fifteen days in the alcohol; then distil the liquor to four quarts in the water bath; add a syrup made with six pounds of fine sugar, with the tincture of vanilla. Color a deep red.

The Art of Confectionery, 1866

NOYAU: Blanch and break up a pound of shelled bitter almonds or peach kernels. Mix with them the grated rinds of three large lemons, half a pint of clarified honey that has been boiled and skimmed, and three pounds of the best double-refined loaf-sugar. Put these ingredients into a jar or demijohn; pour in four quarts of the best white brandy or proof spirit; stop the vessel, and let it stand three months, shaking it every day for the first month. Then filter it, dilute it with rose water to your taste, (you may allow a quart of rose water to each quart of the liquor,) and bottle it for use.

This and any other cordial may be coloured red by mixing with it (after it is filtered) cochineal, powdered, dissolved in a little white brandy, and strained through fine muslin.

Miss Leslie's Complete Cookery, 1839

OLD MEN'S MILK: Double-distilled orange-flower water, eight ounces; Peruvian balsam, sixteen drops; alcohol, five quarts. Make a syrup with four pounds of sugar and two pounds of water, and mix with the liquor. This is not colored.

The Art of Confectionery, 1866

ORGEAT: To make orgeat paste, blanch, mix together, and pound in a mortar till perfectly smooth, three quarters of a pound of shelled sweet almonds, and one quarter of a pound of shelled bitter almonds; adding frequently a little orange-flower or rose water, to keep them from oiling; and mixing with them, as you proceed, a pound of fine loaf-sugar that has been previously powdered by itself. When the whole is thoroughly incorporated to a stiff paste, put it into little pots and close them well. It will keep five or six months, and, when you wish to use it for a beverage, allow a piece of orgeat about the size of an egg to each half pint or tumbler of water. Having well stirred it, strain the mixture through a napkin.

To make liquid orgeat for present use; blanch and pound in a mortar, with rose water, a quarter of a pound of sweet and an ounce and a half of bitter almonds. Then sweeten three pints of rich milk with half a pound of loaf-sugar, and stir the almonds gradually into it. Boil it over hot coals; and as soon as it comes to a boil, take it off and stir it frequently till it gets cold. Then strain it, add a glass of brandy, and put it into decanters. When you pour it out for drinking, dilute it with water.

Miss Leslie's Complete Cookery, 1839

PEACH CORDIAL: Take a peck of cling-stone peaches; such as come late in the season, and are very juicy. Pare them, and cut them from the stones. Crack about half the stones and save the kernels. Leave the remainder of the stones whole, and mix them with the cut peaches; add also the kernels. Put the whole into a wide-mouthed demi-john, and pour on them two gallons of double-rectified whiskey. Add three pounds of rock-sugar candy. Cork it tightly, and set it away for three months; then bottle it, and it will be fit for use. It will be improved in clearness by covering the bottom of a sieve with blotting paper (secured with pins) and straining the cordial through it.

Seventy-five Receipts, 1838

PERFECT LOVE: Zests of lemon, two ounces; zests of lime, four ounces; cloves, two drachms; alcohol, two and a half gallons; sugar, ten pounds; water, five quarts. Macerate ten days in the alcohol; then distil.

ANOTHER PERFECT LOVE: Lemon zests, two pounds; cinnamon, half a pound; rosemary-leaves, quarter of a pound; orange-flowers, three-eights of a pound; pinks, one ounce and a half; mace, one ounce; cardamom, one ounce. Macerate in thirty quarts of spirits and fifteen quarts of water; then distil the liquor to twenty-seven quarts; add a syrup made of thirty pounds of sugar in thirteen quarts of water, and color with cochineal.

The Art of Confectionery, 1866

PERSICOT: Bitter almonds pounded, ten ounces; cinnamon, one ounce. Macerate fifteen days in two and a half gallons of alcohol; distil in the water-bath, and add a syrup made with six pounds of fine sugar. Color with cochineal or caramel.

The Art of Confectionery, 1866

QUINCE CORDIAL: Take the finest and ripest quinces you can procure, wipe them clean, and cut out all the defective parts. Then grate them into a tureen or some other large vessel, leaving out the seeds and cores. Let the grated pulp remain covered in the tureen for twenty-four hours. Then squeeze it through a jelly-bag or cloth. To six quarts of the juice allow a quart of cold water, three pounds of loaf-sugar, (broken up), and a quart of white brandy. Mix the whole well together, and put it into a stone jar. Have ready three very small flannel or thick muslin bags, (not larger than two inches square), fill one with grated nutmeg, another with powdered mace, and the third with powdered cloves; and put them into the jar that the spice may flavour the liquor without mixing with it. Leave the jar uncorked for a few days; reserving some of the liquor to replace that which may flow over in the fermentation. Whenever it has done working, bottle it off, but do not use it for six months. If not sufficiently bright and clear, filter it through fine muslin pinned round the bottom of a sieve, or through a white blotting paper fastened in the same manner.

Miss Leslie's Complete Cookery, 1839

RASPBERRYBRANDY: Pick fine dry fruit, put into a stone jar, and the jar into a kettle of water, or on a hot hearth, till the juice will run; strain, and to every pint add half a pound of sugar, give one boil, and skim it; when cold, put equal quantities of juice and brandy, shake well, and bottle. Some people prefer it stronger of the brandy.

Domestic Cookery, 1807

RASPBERRY CORDIAL: To each quart of raspberries allow a pound of loaf-sugar. Mash the raspberries and strew the sugar over them, having first pounded it slightly, or cracked it with the rolling-pin. Let the raspberries and sugar set till next day, keeping them well covered, then put them in a thin linen bag and squeeze out the juice with your hands. To every pint of juice allow a quart of double-rectified whiskey Cork it well, and set it away for use. It will be ready in a few days.

Seventy-five Receipts, 1838

RASPBERRY SHRUB: Raspberry shrub mixed with water is a pure, delicious drink for summer; and in a country where raspberries are abundant, it is a good economy to make it answer instead of Port and Catalonia wine. Put raspberries in a pan, and scarcely cover them with strong vinegar. Add a pint of sugar to a pint of juice; (of this you can judge by first trying your pan to see how much it holds); scald it, skim it, and bottle it when cold.

American Frugal Housewife, 1833

ROSE BRANDY: Gather leaves from fragrant roses without bruising, fill a pitcher with them, and cover them with French Brandy; next day, pour off the brandy, take out the leaves, and fill the pitcher with fresh ones, and return the brandy; do this till it is strongly impregnated, then bottle it; keep the pitcher closely covered during the process. It is better than distilled rose water for cakes, & c.

Virginia Housewife, 1856

ROSE CORDIAL: Put a pound of fresh rose leaves into a tureen, with a quart of lukewarm water. Cover the vessel, and let them infuse for twenty-four hours. Then squeeze them through a linen bag till all the liquid is pressed out. Put a fresh pound of rose leaves into the tureen, pour the liquid back into it, and let it infuse again for two days. You may repeat this till you obtain a very strong infusion. Then to a pint of the infusion add half a pound of loaf-sugar, half a pint of white brandy, an ounce of broken cinnamon, and an ounce of coriander seeds. Put it into a glass jar, cover it well, and let it stand for two weeks. Then filter it through a fine muslin or a blotting paper (which must be white) pinned on the bottom of a sieve; and bottle it for use.

Miss Leslie's Complete Cookery, 1839

RUM SHRUB: Leave out the brandy and porter, and add 1 gallon more raisin wine, 6 lbs. of honey, and 10 gallons of good flavoured rum. (Note: see Mackenzie's *Brandy Shrub*)

Mackenzie's 5000 Receipts, 1829

STRAWBERRY CORDIAL: Hull a sufficient quantity of ripe strawberries, and squeeze them through a linen bag. To each quart of the juice allow a pint of white brandy, and half a pound of powdered loaf-sugar. Put the liquid into a glass jar or a demijohn, and let it stand a fortnight. Then filter it through a sieve, to the bottom of which a piece of fine muslin or blotting paper has been fastened; and afterwards bottle it.

Miss Leslie's Complete Cookery, 1839

WHITE CURRANTSHRUB: Strip the fruit, and prepare in a jar as for jelly; strain the juice, of which put two quarts to one gallon of rum, and two pounds of lump sugar; strain through a jellybag.

Domestic Cookery, 1807

ABSINTHE OR WORMWOOD CREAM: In seven pints of common brandy infuse, for two days, half a pound of the heads of wormwood and the zests of two lemons, or, which is better, two oranges thinly sliced; distil the liquor to half the quantity; dissolve six pounds of fine sugar in three pints of common water; let it cool, and mix it well with brandy; strain it, and put in bottles tightly corked.

Wormwood, ½ lb.; oranges, 2; brandy, 7 pts.; sugar, 6 lbs.; water, 3 pts. Infuse two days.

The Art of Confectionery, 1866

BARBADOES CREAM: Infuse for five or six days, in two quarts of brandy, two drachms each of mace and cinnamon and the zests of two limes; distil the liquor to one-half over a gentle fire; dissolve three pounds of sugar in a quart of water over the fire, let it cool, mix the whole together, add half a pound of orange-flower water, strain it, and keep it in tightly corked bottles.

Mace, 2 drs.; cinnamon, 2 drs.; zests of limes, 2; brandy, 2 qts.; sugar, 3 lbs.; water, 1 qt.; orange-flower water, ½ lb. Infuse six days.

The Art of Confectionery, 1866

CHERRY-WATER CREAM: Distil seven pints of cherry-water to nearly one-half; add four ounces of orange-flower water. Dissolve over the fire four pounds of sugar in a quart of spring-water; let it cool; add it to the cherry-water, and strain the whole. This is a delicious beverage, which may be kept in tightly corked bottles for a long time without the slightest deterioration.

Cherry-water, 7 pts.; orange-flower water, 4 oz.; sugar, 4 lbs.; water, 1 qt.

The Art of Confectionery, 1866

CHOCOLATE CREAM: Take six pounds of pure Caraccas chocolate, six drachms of ground cinnamon, and two gallons of alcohol; distil to one-half; add ten pounds of sugar dissolved in four quarts of distilled water, and four drachms of tincture of vanilla, and filter.

Chocolate, 6 lbs.; cinnamon, 6 drs.; alcohol, 2 gals.; sugar, 10 lbs.; distilled water, 4 qts.; tincture of vanilla, 4 drs.

The Art of Confectionery, 1866

COCOA CREAM: Pound two pounds of roasted cocoa-nuts in a stone mortar; mix with them two quarts of brandy; add two drachms of cinnamon, and let it steep for eight days; then distil the liquor to one-half. Dissolve two and a half pounds of sugar in a quart of water over the fire; mix the whole, let it cool, then add one and a half drachms of tincture of vanilla; filter, and bottle for use.

Cocoa-nuts, 2 lbs.; cinnamon, 2 drs.; brandy, 2 qts.; sugar, 2½ lbs.; water, 1 qt.; vanilla, 1½ drs.

The Art of Confectionery, 1866

CREME DES BARBADES: Take 2 dozen middling sized lemons; 6 large citrons; loaf sugar, 28 lbs.; fresh balm leaves, ½ lb.; spirit of wine, 2½ gallons; water 3½ ditto. This will produce about 7 gallons, full measure. Cut the lemons and citrons in thin slices, and put them into a cask; pour upon them the spirit of wine, bung down close, and let it stand ten days or a fortnight; then break the sugar, and boil it for half an hour in the three gallons and a half of water, skimming it frequently; then chop the balm-leaves, put them into a large pan, and pour upon them the boiling liquor, and let it stand till quite cold; then strain it through a lawn sieve, and put it to the spirits, & c. in the cask; bung down close, and in a fortnight draw it off; strain it through a jelly bag, and let it remain to fine; then bottle it.

Mackenzie's 5000 Receipts, 1829

CREME D'ORANGE OF SUPERIOR FLAVOUR: Take 3 dozen middling sized oranges, orange flower water, 2 quarts, loaf sugar, 18 lbs. spirit of wine, 2 gallons, tincture of saffron, 1½ oz. water, 4½ gallons. This will produce 7½ gallons.

Cut the oranges in slices, put them into a cask, add the spirit and orange flower water, let it stand a fortnight, then boil the sugar in the water for half an hour, pour it out, and let it stand till cold, then add it to the mixture in the cask, and put in the tincture of saffron. Let it remain a fortnight longer; then strain, and proceed as directed in the receipt for *cremes de Barbades,* and a very fine cordial will be produced.

Mackenzie's 5000 Receipts, 1829

CREME DE NOYEAU DE MARTINIQUE: Take 20 lbs. of loaf sugar,—3 gallons of spirit of wine, —3 pints of orange flower water,—1¼ lb. of bitter almonds—2 drachms of essence of lemon, and 4½ gallons of water. The produce will exceed 8 gallons.

Put 2 lbs. of the loaf sugar into a jug or can, pour upon it the essence of lemon, and 1 quart of the spirit of wine; stir it till the sugar is dissolved, and the essence completely incorporated.

Bruise the almonds, and put them into a 4 gallon stone bottle or cask, add the remainder of the spirit of wine, and the mixture from the jug or can: let it stand a week or ten days, shaking it frequently.

Then add the remainder of the sugar, and boil it in the 4½ gallons of water, for three quarters of an hour, taking off the scum as it rises.

When cold, put it in a cask; add the spirit, almonds, & c. from the stone bottle; and lastly, the orange flower water. Bung it down close, and let it stand three weeks or a month; then strain it through a jelly bag, and when fine bottle it off. When the pink is wanted, add cochineal, in powder, at the rate of half a drachm, or two scruples, to a quart.

Mackenzie's 5000 Receipts, 1829

CREAM OF ROSES: Macerate three pounds of rose-leaves in two quarts of good brandy for five or six days; distil the liquor to one-half in the water-bath; mix it thoroughly with one pound of sugar dissolved in a quart of water, or, which is better, in rose-water enough to dissolve it; color with a little cochineal, and filter.

Rose-leaves, 3 lbs.; brandy, 2 qts.; sugar, 1 lb.; water, 1 qt. Infuse six days.

The Art of Confectionery, 1866

FRUIT CREAM: Cut very thin the rind and zests of two bergamots, two Seville oranges, two limes, two lemons, and three oranges; macerate the whole for eight days in seven pints of fourth-proof brandy; then distil the liquor to nearly one-half. Dissolve four pounds of sugar in three pints of water; let it cool; mix the whole thoroughly; filter, and bottle for use.

Bergamot, 2; oranges, 2; limes, 2; lemons, 2; oranges, 3; brandy, 7 pts.; sugar, 4 lbs.; water, 3 pts. Steep eight days. *The Art of Confectionery,* 1866

JASMINE CREAM: Dissolve over the fire two pounds of double-refined sugar in a quart of water; let it cool, and add three ounces of double-distilled tincture of jasmine, four drachms of orange-flower water, and one and a half pints of alcohol; mix the whole well, filter, and bottle for use.

Sugar, 2 lbs.; water, 1 qt.; jasmine, 3 oz.; orange-flower water, 4 drs.; alcohol, 1½ pts.

The Art of Confectionery, 1866

LAUREL CREAM: Distil seven ounces of laurel-leaves, five ounces of myrtle-blossoms, half a nutmeg couarsely grated, and twenty-four cloves which have been first infused for ten hours in two gallons of brandy; distil to half the liquor. Dissolve over a gentle fire twelve pounds of sugar in seven pints of water; let it cool; mix the whole well, filter it, and preserve it in tightly corked bottles.

Laurel-leaves, 7 oz.; myrtle-flowers, 5 oz.; cloves, 24; brandy, 2 gals.; nutmeg, ½; sugar, 12 lbs.; water, 7 pts.

The Art of Confectionery, 1866

MINT CREAM: Take one pound of freshly gathered mint, and the zests of five lemons; cut fine; macerate them for eight days in seven pints of brandy; distil to one-half, then add half a drachm of essence of peppermint. Dissolve four pounds of sugar in three pints of water, let it cool; mix it thoroughly with the distilled liquor, filter, and keep it in bottles in a cool and shady place.

Mint, 1 lb.; zests of lemons, 5; brandy, 7 pts.; essence peppermint, 2 drs.; sugar, 4 lbs.; water, 3 pts. Steep eight days.

The Art of Confectionery, 1866

MOCHA CREAM: Roast one pound of good Mocha coffee slightly without letting it brown, grind it quickly without giving it time to grow cold, and infuse it, with the yellow rind of an orange cut fine, in seven pints of brandy, for five or six days; then distil it nearly to one-half in the water-bath. Dissolve four pounds of sugar over the fire in three pints of water, let it cool, mix it with the coffee mixture, filter, and preserve in well-corked bottles.

Mocha coffee, 1 lb.; zest of orange, 1; brandy, 7 pts.; sugar, 4 lbs.; water, 3 pts. Infuse six days.

The Art of Confectionery, 1866

MYRTLE CREAM: Macerate six ounces of myrtle-blossoms or leaves, one ounce of peach-leaves, and one-quarter of a nutmeg coarsely grated, in seven pints of brandy, for two days; distil to one-half; mix it thoroughly with four pounds of sugar dissolved over the fire in three pints of water; filter, and bottle for use. This cream, which is very bitter at first, becomes a delightful beverage with age.

Myrtle-leaves, 6 oz.; peach-leaves, 1 oz.; nutmeg, ¼; brandy, 7 pts.; sugar, 4 lbs.; water, 3 pts. Infuse two days. *The Art of Confectionery*, 1866

ORANGE-FLOWER CREAM WITH MILK AND CHAMPAGNE WINE: Put three pints of new milk over the fire; add fourteen ounces of orange-blossoms; let it boil up once or twice, then pour it into a porcelain vessel to cool. As soon as it is quite cold, add a quart of rectified brandy; stir the mixture, and filter it to separate the orange-flowers, which are now deprived of their aroma, and contain nothing but bitterness. Dissolve four pounds of double-refined sugar in three pints of water over the fire; let it cool, and mix with it seven pints of good champagne; add the milk, and filter again. This process is far preferable to making a simple infusion of the orange-flowers in the liquor, which is always bitter and acrid; or to distilling it in order to obtain what is called the *spirit*, in which case it loses the greater part of its taste and aroma.

Milk, 3 pts.; orange-flowers, 14 oz.; brandy, 1 qt.; sugar, 4 lbs.; water, 3 pts.; champagne, 7 pts.

The Art of Confectionery, 1866

VANILLA CREAM: Infuse four drachms of tincture of vanilla and half a drachm of tincture of amber in seven pints of alcohol; dissolve five pounds of sugar over the fire in a quart of pure water; let it cool; mix the whole, and filter. This may be colored red or violet.

Tincture of vanilla, 4 drs.; tincture of amber, ½ dr.; alcohol, 7 pts.; sugar, 4 lbs.; water, 1 gal.

The Art of Confectionery, 1866

ELIXIRS

ELIXIR OF GARUS: Myrrh and aloes, each, two drachms; cloves and nutmeg, each, 3 drachms; saffron, one ounce; cinnamon, five drachms. Macerate the whole for fifteen days in four quarts of alcohol; distil in the water-bath, and add a syrup made with six pounds of sugar. This liquor can also be made without distillation.

The Art of Confectionery, 1866

ELIXIR OF VIOLETS: Syrup of violets, ten ounces; filtered raspberry-juice, four ounces; alcohol, two quarts. Make a syrup with four pounds of sugar, and mix the whole thoroughly.

The Art of Confectionery, 1866

JUNIPER-BERRY ELIXIR: Macerate two ounces of juniper-berries in two quarts of alcohol for one month; strain the liquor, and add a syrup made with three pounds of sugar and a pound and a half of water.

The Art of Confectionery, 1866

TABOUREY ELIXIR: Aloes, two drachms; cinnamon, clove, and nutmeg, each, one ounce; zests of orange and lemon, each, two. Macerate for fifteen days in five quarts of alcohol, then distil, and add to the product a syrup made cold with six pounds of powdered sugar, two pounds of orange-flower water, and one pound of rose water. Color red.

The Art of Confectionery, 1866

TROUBADOURS' ELIXIR: Musk roses, two pounds; jasmine blossoms, twelve ounces; orange-blossoms, eight ounces; ravenzaranuts, one ounce; mace two drachms. Macerate the whole for fifteen days in three and a half gallons of alcohol; distil, and add to the product a syrup made with ten pounds of sugar. Color with cochineal.

The Art of Confectionery, 1866

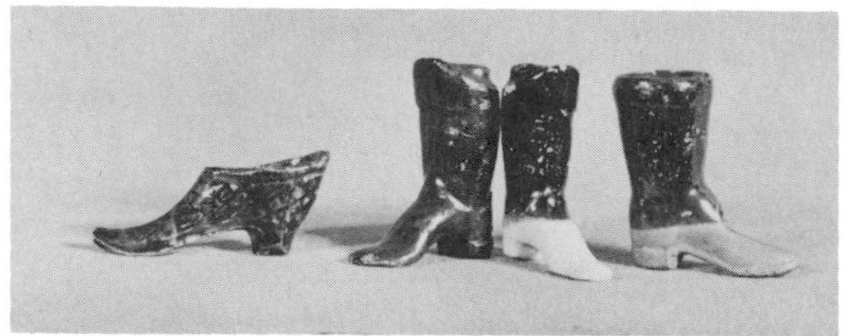

Plate 18. *Rockingham boot and shoe spirit flasks, 1849–1858. These were all made by the Bennington potter, William Leake. The one on the left is seven-eighths of an inch high and the others, two inches high. (Courtesy of the Bennington Museum, Bennington, Vermont)*

RATAFIAS

ABSINTHE OR WORMWOOD RATAFIA: Steep four pounds of bruised wormwood leaves, eight ounces of juniper berries, and two ounces of ground cinnamon, in four drachms of angelica rum and seventeen pounds of brandy, for fifteen days; distil the mixture to twelve pounds of liquor, and redistil this upon the residuum to ten pounds; then add two and a half pounds of powdered sugar, two pounds of pure water, and eight ounces of double-distilled orange-flower water.

Wormwood leaves, 4 lbs.; juniper berries, 8 oz.; cinnamon, 2 oz.; angelica rum, 4 drs.; brandy, 17 lbs.; sugar, 2½ lbs.; water, 2 lbs.; orange-flower water, 8 oz. Steep fifteen days.

The Art of Confectionery, 1866

ANGELICA RATAFIA: Take four ounces of fresh angelica stalks, one ounce of angelica seed, one drachm of nutmeg, half a drachm of Ceylon cinnamon, and one drachm of coriander; bruise the seeds in a mortar, and steep the whole for eight days in seven pints of alcohol; then pass it through a sieve; add a syrup made with four and a quarter pounds of sugar and two and a half pints of water, and filter.

Angelica stalks, 4 oz.; angelica seed, 1 oz.; nutmeg, 1 dr.; cinnamon, ½ dr.; coriander, 1 dr.; sugar, 4½ lbs.; water, 2½ pts. Steep eight days.

The Art of Confectionery, 1866

ANISE-SEED RATAFIA: Take two ounces of green anise-seed and four ounces of star anise-seed; bruise the seed, and steep them in seven quarts of alcohol for eight days; then pass it through a sieve; add a syrup made with six and a half pounds of sugar and two quarts of spring water, and filter.

Green anise-seed, 2 oz.; star anise-seed, 4 oz.; alcohol, 7 qts.; sugar, 6½ lbs.; water, 2 qts. Steep eight days.

The Art of Confectionery, 1866

BLACK-CURRANT RATAFIA: Take six pounds of fully ripe black currants, four ounces of black-currant leaves, half a drachm of cloves, half a drachm of Ceylon cinnamon, and half a drachm of coriander; bruise the berries, and steep the whole for one month in ten quarts of brandy; then express the liquor; add a syrup made with seven pounds of sugar and three and a half pints of water, and filter.

Black currants, 6 lbs.; black-currant leaves, 4 oz.; cloves, ½ dr.; cinnamon, ½ dr.; coriander, ½ dr.; sugar, 7 lbs.; water, 3½ pts. Steep one month.

The Art of Confectionery, 1866

GRENOBLE RATAFIA: Take eight quarts of black wild-cherry juice, two drachms of cinnamon, one drachm of cloves, one drachm of mace, twelve ounces of cherry-leaves, and four pounds of black cherries;

Plate 19. *Pair of Rockingham boot spirit flasks with laces on opposite sides, measuring five inches in height and six inches in length. These date back to the mid-19th century. (Courtesy of the Bennington Museum, Bennington, Vermont)*

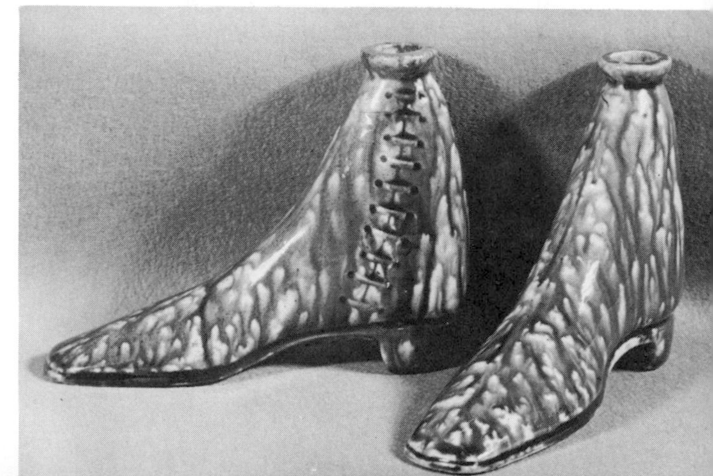

steep the whole in seven quarts of alcohol for twenty days; squeeze through a cloth; add nine pounds of crushed sugar, and filter as soon as it is dissolved.

Wild-cherry juice, 8 qts.; cinnamon, 2 drs.; cloves, 1 dr.; mace, 1 dr.; cherry leaves, 12 oz.; wild cherries, 4 lbs.; sugar, 9 lbs. Steep twenty days.

The Art of Confectionery, 1866

JUNIPER-BERRY RATAFIA: Take eight ounces of juniper berries, one drachm of cinnamon, two drachms of coriander, and half a drachm of mace; bruise the whole, and steep them for fifteen days in fourteen pints of brandy; squeeze through a cloth, and add a syrup made with seven pounds of sugar, and filter.

Juniper-berries, 8 oz.; cinnamon, 1 dr.; coriander, 2 drs.; mace, ½ dr.; brandy, 14 pts.; sugar, 7 lbs. Steep fifteen days.

The Art of Confectionery, 1866

NEUILLY RATAFIA: Steep five pounds of sour cherries, two pounds of black cherries, and one pound of the petals of red pinks, in fourteen pints of brandy, for fifteen days; strain, and add one-fourth of a pound of sugar to every quart of liquor.

Sour cherries, 5 lbs.; black cherries, 2 lbs.; pink petals, 1 lb.; brandy, 14 pts.; sugar according to quantity. Steep fifteen days.

The Art of Confectionery, 1866

ORANGE-FLOWER RATAFIA: Steep two pounds of bruised orange blossoms in ten and a half pints of alcohol for fifteen days; add a syrup made with four pounds of sugar and seven gills of water, and filter.

Orange flowers, 2 lbs.; alcohol 10½ pts.; sugar, 4 lbs.; water, 7 gills. Steep fifteen days.

The Art of Confectionery, 1866

PINK RATAFIA: Take two pounds of the petals of red pinks, one drachm of cinnamon, and one drachm of cloves; steep the whole in seven pints of alcohol for fifteen days; strain; add a syrup made with two pounds of sugar, and filter.

Pinks, 2 lbs.; cinnamon, 1 dr.; cloves, 1 dr.; alcohol, 7 pts.; sugar, 2 lbs. Steep fifteen days.

The Art of Confectionery, 1866

POMEGRANATE RATAFIA: Steep fifteen fully ripe pomegranates, cut in slices, in four quarts of brandy, for fifteen days; squeeze through a cloth; add a syrup made with three pounds of sugar, and filter.

Pomegranates, 15; brandy, 4 qts.; sugar, 3 lbs. Steep Fifteen days.

The Art of Confectionery, 1866

RASPBERRY RATAFIA: Steep eight pounds of raspberries for fifteen days in two gallons of brandy; add a syrup made with seven pounds of sugar and filter.

Raspberries, 8 lbs.; brandy, 2 gals.; sugar, 7 lbs.; water, 3 pts. Steep fifteen days.

The Art of Confectionery, 1866

RATAFIA A LA VIOLETTE: Take of Florentine orris root, 2 dr.—archel, 1 oz.—spirit of wine, 4 pints. Digest, strain, and add sugar, 4 lbs. Liqueurs are also made by adding Hungary-water, honey-water, eau de Cologne, and several other spirits, to an equal quantity of simple syrup, or common capillaire.

Mackenzie's 5000 Receipts, 1829

RATAFIA D'ANGELIQUE: Take of angelica seeds, 1 drachm; stalks of angelica, bitter almonds, blanched, each 4 oz.; proof spirit, 12 pints; white sugar, 2 lbs. Digest, strain, and filter.

Mackenzie's 5000 Receipts, 1829

RATAFIA DE CAFE: Take of roasted coffee, ground 1 lb.; proof spirit, 1 gallon; sugar, 20 oz. Digest for a week.

Mackenzie's 5000 Receipts, 1829

RATAFIA DE CASSIS: Take of ripe black currants, 6 lbs.; cloves, ½ drachm; cinnamon, 1 ditto; proof spirit, 18 pints; sugar, 3½ lbs. Digest for a fortnight.

Mackenzie's 5000 Receipts, 1829

RATAFIA DES CERISES: Take of morello cherries, with their kernels, bruised, 8 lbs.; proof spirit, 8 pints. Digest for a month, strain with expression, and then add 1½ lbs. of sugar.

Mackenzie's 5000 Receipts, 1829

RATAFIA DE CHOCOLAT: Take of Caracca cocoa nuts, roasted, 1 lb.; West India ditto, roasted ½ lb.; proof spirit, 1 gallon. Digest for a fortnight, strain, and then add sugar, 1½ lbs.; tincture of vanilla, 30 drops. *Mackenzie's 5000 Receipts*, 1829

Plate 20. *Among the Rockingham and flint enamel objects displayed here are pint, quart and gallon book flasks. These frequently had titles impressed on the spine, such as* Battle of Bennington, Hermit's Delight, Suffering and Death, Life of Kossuth, *and many others. (Courtesy of the Bennington Museum, Bennington, Vermont)*

RATAFIA D'ECORES D'ORANGES: Take of fresh peel of Seville oranges, 4 oz.—proof spirit, 1 gallon,—sugar, 1 lb. Digest for 6 hours.

Mackenzie's 5000 Receipts, 1829

RATAFIA DE FLEURS D'ORANGES: Take of fresh flowers of orange-tree, 2 lbs., proof spirit, 1 gallon,—sugar, 1½ lbs. Digest for 6 hours.

Mackenzie's 5000 Receipts, 1829

RATAFIA DE GRENOBLE: Take of small wild black cherries, with their kernels, bruised, 12 lbs.; proof spirit, 6 gallons. Digest for a month, strain, and then add 12 lbs. of sugar. A little citron peel may also be added at pleasure.

Mackenzie's 5000 Receipts, 1829

RATAFIA DE NOYEAU: Take of peach or apricot kernels, with their shells bruised, in number, 120, proof spirit, 4 pints, sugar, 10 oz. Some reduce the spirit of wine to proof with the juice of apricots or peaches, to make this liqueur.

Mackenzie's 5000 Receipts, 1829

RATAFIA OF RED FRUITS: Infuse one pound of sour cherries, one pound of black cherries, one pound of wild cherries, one pound of raspberries, one pound of red currants, and three pounds of strawberries, in two and a half gallons of brandy for fifteen days; add a syrup made with eight pounds of sugar, and filter.

Sour cherries, 1 lb.; black cherries, 1 lb.; wild cherries, 1 lb.; raspberries, 1 lb.; red currants, 1 lb.; strawberries, 1 lb.; brandy, $2\frac{1}{2}$ gals.; sugar, 8 lbs. Steep fifteen days.

The Art of Confectionery, 1866

SEED RATAFIA: Take one ounce each of dill, angelica, fennel, caraway, carrot, coriander, and green anise seed; pound them, and steep them for a month in six quarts of alcohol; strain, and add a syrup of eight pounds of sugar with one quart of water; then filter.

Dill, angelica, fennel, caraway, carrot, coriander, and anise seeds, 1 oz. each; alcohol, 6 qts.; sugar, 8 lbs.; water, 1 qt. Steep one month.

The Art of Confectionery, 1866

USQUEBAUGH: Usquebaugh is a strong compound liquor, chiefly taken by way of dram; it is made in the highest perfection at Drogheda in Ireland. The following are the ingredients, and the proportions in which they are to be used.

Take of best brandy, 1 gallon,—raisins, stoned, 1 lb. —cinnamon, cloves, nutmeg, and cardamoms, each 1 oz. crushed in a mortar, —saffron, half an ounce,— rind of 1 Seville orange, and brown sugar candy, 1 lb. Shake these well every day, for at least 14 days, and it will, at the expiration of that time, be ready to be fined for use.

ANOTHER METHOD: Take of nutmegs, cloves, and cinnamon, each 2 ounces; of the seeds of anise, caraway, and coriander, each 4 ounces; liquorice root, sliced, half a pound; bruise the seeds and spices, and put them together with the liquorice, into the still, with 11 gallons of proof spirit, and 2 gallons of water; distil with a pretty brisk fire. As soon as the still begins to work, fasten to the nozel of the worm 2 ounces of English saffron, tied up in a cloth, that the liquor may run through it, and extract all its tincture. When the operation is finished, sweeten with fine sugar.—This liqueur may be much improved by the following additions; Digest 4 pounds of stoned raisins 3 pounds of dates, and 2 pounds of sliced liquorice root, n 2 gallons of water, for 12 hours. When the liquor is strained off, and has deposited all sediment, decant it gently into the vessel containing the usquebaugh.

Mackenzie's 5000 Receipts, 1829

USQUEBAUGH: Steep one ounce of saffron, half a drachm of mace, and the yellow rinds of four oranges and two lemons, in two gallons of alcohol, for one month; strain; add a syrup made with nine pounds of sugar and one quart of water, and filter.

Saffron, 1 oz.; mace, $\frac{1}{2}$ dr.; zests of oranges, 4; zests of lemon, 2; alcohol, 2 gals.; sugar, 9 lbs.; water, 1 qt. Steep one month.

ANOTHER USQUEBAUGH: Saffron, one ounce; dates and nuts without stones and seeds, each, two ounces; juniper-berries, four drachms; pounded jujubes, four drachms; pounded cinnamon, two drachms; green anise, mace, coriander, and cloves, each, one ounce; alcohol, four quarts; syrup boiled to a bead, three quarts. Macerate fifteen days, then strain and add the syrup.

The Art of Confectionery, 1866

WALNUT RATAFIA: Steep sixty freshly cracked walnuts with thirty-seven grains of clove and an equal quantity of mace and cinnamon in five quarts of alcohol for two months; express the juice, and add a syrup made with five pounds of sugar. This ratafia improves with age.

The Art of Confectionery, 1866

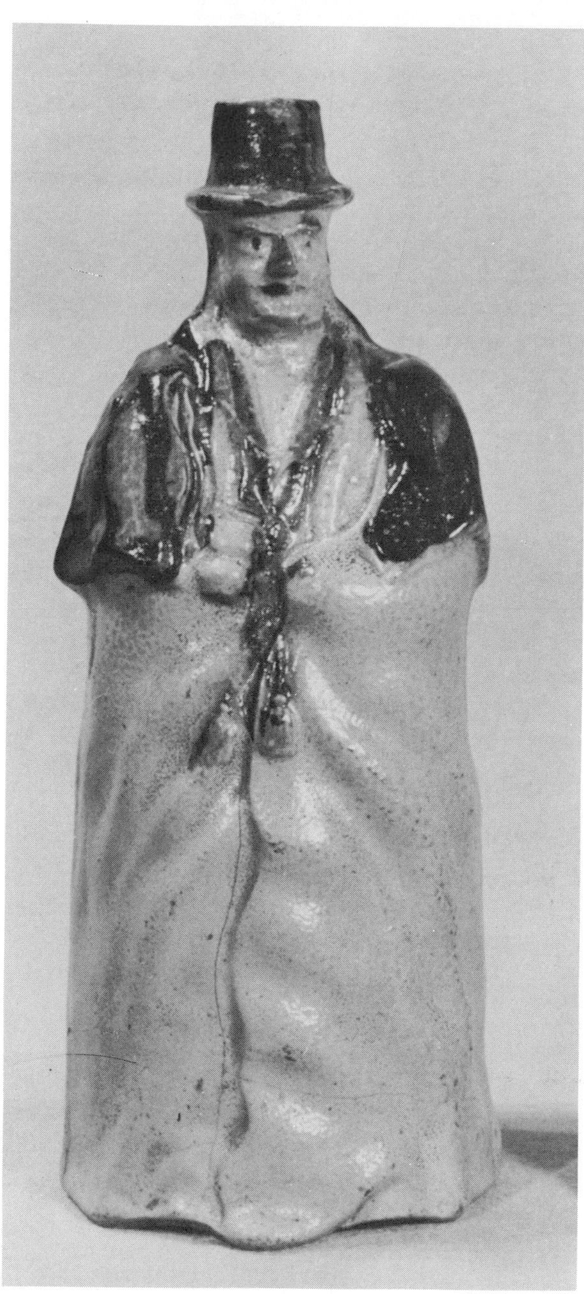

Plate 21, opposite page. *A bottomless, flint enamel "change cover," three and three-fourths inches high, the purpose of which was to protect a host from any further exploitation by those whom he was treating.* Plate 22, above. *A toby or coachman stoneware bottle, nine and one-fourth inches tall, cobalt decorated and dated 1849.*

SPIRITUOUS WATERS

ALMOND WATER: Macerate four ounces of bitter almonds, with four ounces each of apricot, peach, and cherry stones, in seven pints of alcohol, for one month; distil as before; add a syrup made with three pounds of sugar, and filter.

Bitter almonds, 4 oz.; peach stones 4 oz.; apricot-stones, 4 oz.; cherry-stones, 4 oz.; brandy, 7 pts.; sugar, 3 lbs. Steep one month.

The Art of Confectionery, 1866

ANDAYE BRANDY: Macerate an ounce each of green and star anise seed, two ounces of coriander, and one ounce of powdered iris, with the yellow rinds of four oranges, in ten pints of Spanish brandy, for eight days; then distil in a water-bath; add a syrup made with five pounds of sugar and filter.

Green and star anise seed, each, 1 oz.; coriander, 2 oz.; iris, 1 oz.; Spanish brandy, 10 pts.; sugar, 5 lbs.; zests of 4 oranges. Macerate eight days.

The Art of Confectionery, 1866

ANISE-SEED WATER (COMPOUND): Rub four ounces each of green anise, angelica, and star anise seed, to a very fine powder in a mortar; macerate the whole in five pints of alcohol for five or six days; then distil in a water-bath.

Green anise, angelica, and star anise seed, each, 4 oz.; alcohol, 5 pts. Macerate six days.

The Art of Confectionery, 1866

AROMATIC WATER: Macerate one ounce of pounded cinnamon, three drachms of cardamom, four drachms of sassafras, and one drachm of ginger, for eight days, in five pints of alcohol; then distil in a water-bath.

Cinnamon, 1 oz.; cardamom, 3 drs.; sassafras, 4 drs.; ginger, 1 dr.; alcohol, 5 pts. Macerate eight days.

The Art of Confectionery, 1866

BERGAMOT WATER: Macerate the yellow rinds of four bergamots, four oranges, and two lemons, in ten pints of alcohol, for eight days; then distil to one-half the quantity in the water-bath, and add a syrup made with four pounds of fine sugar and three pints of water.

Zests of bergamot, 4; zests of orange, 4; zests of lemon, 2; alcohol, 10 pts.; sugar, 4 lbs.; water, 3 pts. Macerate eight days.

The Art of Confectionery, 1866

CARAWAY WATER: Macerate four ounces of pounded caraway-seeds in seven pints of alcohol for eight days; then distil in the water-bath, and add a syrup made with four pounds of sugar and three pints of water. Filter, and color green.

Caraway, 4 oz.; alcohol, 7 pts.; sugar, 4 lbs.; water, 3 pts. Macerate eight days.

The Art of Confectionery, 1866

CINNAMON WATER: Macerate two ounces of pounded cinnamon, ten drops of essence of lemon, and the yellow rind of two oranges, in seven quarts of alcohol, for eight days; then distil in the water-bath, and add a syrup made with eight pounds of sugar and two quarts of water. Color yellow.

Cinnamon, 2 oz.; essence of lemon, 10 drops; zests of orange, 2; alcohol, 7 qts.; sugar, 8 lbs.; water, 2 qts. Steep eight days.

The Art of Confectionery, 1866

CLOVE WATER: Take one ounce of pounded cloves, one drachm of mace, seven pints of alcohol, and four pounds of sugar. Proceed as in Eau Divine, and color yellow.

The Art of Confectionery, 1866

EAU DIVINE: Macerate the zests of three limes and four lemons with four ounces of fresh orange-flowers, one ounce of fresh heads of balm, and six ounces of white hoarhound, in seven pints of alcohol, for ten days; distil in the water-bath, and add a syrup made with three pounds of sugar and one quart of distilled water.

Zests of limes, 3; zests of lemons, 4; orange-flowers, 4 oz.; balm, 1 oz.; hoarhound, 6 oz.; alcohol, 7 pts.; sugar, 3 lbs.; distilled water, 1 qt. Steep ten days.

The Art of Confectionery, 1866

MALTA WATER: Macerate the zests of six oranges with four ounces of fresh orange-flowers in seven pints of brandy for eight days; distil in the water-bath; add a syrup made with four pounds of sugar and three pints of water, and filter.

Zests of oranges, 6; orange-flowers, 4 oz.; brandy, 7 pts.; sugar, 4 lbs.; water, 3 pts. Steep eight days.

The Art of Confectionery, 1866

MINT WATER: Steep two pounds of peppermint-blossoms, with the yellow rinds of four lemons, in six quarts of alcohol, for eight days; distil in the water-bath; add a syrup made with nine pounds of sugar and three pints of water; to which is added half a pint of rose-water, and filter.

Peppermint-flowers, 2 lbs.; zests of lemons, 4; alcohol, 6 qts.; sugar, 9 lbs.; water, 3 pts.; rose-water, ½ pt. Steep eight days.

The Art of Confectionery, 1866

ORANGE WATER: Macerate the yellow rinds of a dozen oranges in ten pints of highly rectified spirits for fifteen days; add one drachm of neroli; distil in the water-bath, and add a syrup made with four pounds of sugar and one quart of water, and filter.

Zests of orange, 12; neroli, 1 dr.; alcohol, 10 pts.; sugar, 4 lbs.; water, 1 qt. Steep fifteen days.

The Art of Confectionery, 1866

ROSEMARY WATER: Macerate eight ounces of rosemary blossoms in three pints of alcohol for ten days; then distil in the water-bath to perfect dryness.

Rosemary, 8 oz.; alcohol, 3 pts.

The Art of Confectionery, 1866

TEA WATER: Distil one ounce of hyson and half an ounce of souchong tea in seven pints of alcohol by means of the water-bath; add a syrup made with two pounds of sugar and a quart of distilled water, and filter. This can also be made by infusion.

Hyson, 1 oz.; souchong, ½ oz.; alcohol, 7 pts.; sugar, 2 lbs.; distilled water, 1 qt.

The Art of Confectionery, 1866

WATER OF PINKS: Macerate one pound of the petals of red pinks and half a drachm of pounded cloves in ten pints of alcohol for eight days; distil in the water-bath; add a syrup made with five pounds of sugar and three pints of water, and color a deep red.

Pinks, 1 lb.; cloves, ½ dr.; alcohol, 10 pts.; sugar, 5 lbs.; water, 3 pts. Steep eight days.

The Art of Confectionery, 1866

CHAPTER FOUR

Miscellaneous Mixed Drinks

At the punch-bowl's brink
Let the thirsty think
What they say in Japan:
"First the man takes a drink,
Then the drink takes a drink,
Then the drink takes the man!"
An Adage from the Orient

ALEBERRY: Mix two large spoonfuls of fine oatmeal in sufficient sweet small beer, two hours previous to using it; strain well, boil, and sweeten according to taste. Pour into a warm jug, add wine, lemon-juice, and nutmeg to taste, and serve hot with thin slips of toast or rusks.

Practical Housewife, 1860

ALE, MULLED: Boil a pint of good sound ale with a little grated nutmeg and sugar. Beat up three eggs, and mix them with a little cold ale; then add the hot ale to it gradually, and pour backwards and forwards from one vessel to the other several times, to prevent its curdling. Warm, and stir till it thickens, then add a table-spoonful of brandy, and serve hot with toast.

Practical Housewife, 1860

ARRACK, MOCK: Take a scruple (twenty grains) of benzoic acid, and add to a quart of rum. Prepare punch with it. *Practical Housewife,* 1860

ATHOL BROSE: Add two wine-glassfuls of Scotch Whisky to a wine-glassful of heather-honey; mix well, and then stir in a well-beaten new-laid egg.

Practical Housewife, 1860

BANG: Take a pint of cider, and add to a pint of warm ale; sweeten with treacle or sugar to taste, grate in some nutmeg and ginger, and add a wine-glassful of gin or whisky.

Practical Housewife, 1860

BEER, TREACLE: Take a pound and a half of hops, and boil in thirty-six gallons of water for an hour, then add fourteen pounds of treacle, and a little yeast to work it; ferment and bottle.

Practical Housewife, 1860

BISHOP: Take three smooth-skinned and large Seville oranges, and grill them to a pale brown colour over a clear slow fire; then place in a small punch-bowl that will about hold them, and pour over them half a pint from a bottle of old Bordeaux wine, in which a pound and a quarter of loaf sugar is dissolved; then cover with a plate, and let it stand for two days. When it is to be served, cut and squeeze the oranges into a small sieve placed above a jug containing the remainder of the bottle of sweetened Bordeaux, previously made very hot, and if when mixed it is not sweet enough, add more sugar. Serve hot in tumblers. Some persons make Bishop with raisin or Lisbon wine, and add mace, cloves, and nutmegs, but it is not the proper way.

Practical Housewife, 1860

BROWN SPRUCE BEER: Pour four gallons of cold water into a nine-gallon barrel, then add four gallons more, quite boiling, and six pounds of molasses, with about eight or nine table-spoonfuls of the essence of spruce, and on its getting a little cooler, the same quantity of good ale yeast. Shake the barrel well, then leave with bung out for three days; bottle in stone bottles, cork well, wire carefully, pack in sand, and it will be fit to drink in two weeks.

Practical Housewife, 1860

CARDINAL: Is made the same way as Bishop, substituting old Rhenish wine for the Bordeaux.

Practical Housewife, 1860

CAUDLE: 1. Make half a pint of fine gruel with "Robinson's Patent Groats," add a piece of butter the size of a large nutmeg, a table-spoonful of brandy, the same of white wine, a little grated nutmeg and lemon-peel, and serve hot. 2. Put three quarts of water into a pot, set over the fire to boil; mix smooth as much oatmeal as will thicken the whole with a pint of cold water, and when the water boils, pour in the thickening, and add about twenty peppercorns finely powdered. Boil till pretty thick, then add sugar to taste, half a pint of good ale, and a wine-glassful of gin, all warmed up together. Serve hot.

Practical Housewife, 1860

CAUDLE, BROWN: Take a quart of water, mix in three table-spoonfuls of oatmeal, a balde of mace, and a small piece of lemon-peel; let it boil about a quarter of an hour, skimming and stirring it well, but taking care that it does not boil over. When done, strain through a coarse sieve, sweeten to taste, add a little grated nutmeg, a pint of good sweet ale, and half a pint of white wine; then serve hot.

Practical Housewife, 1860

CAUDLE, COLD: Boil a quart of spring water, when cold, add the yolk of an egg, the juice of a small lemon, six table-spoonfuls of raisin wine, and sugar to taste.

Practical Housewife, 1860

CAUDLE, FLOUR: Take a dessert-spoonful of fine flour, and rub it into a smooth batter, with five table-spoonfuls of spring water. Put a quarter of a pint of new milk into a saucepan, set over the fire, with two lumps of sugar, and when it boils, stir the flour and water gradually into it, and keep stirring for twenty minutes over a slow fire. Nutmeg or ginger may be grated in, if thought proper.

Practical Housewife, 1860

CAUDLE, FLUMMERY: Put half a pint of fine oatmeal into a quart of spring water, and let it stand all night. In the morning stir it well, and strain through a coarse sieve into a skillet or saucepan, then add two baldes of mace and some grated nutmeg; set on the fire, keep stirring, and let it boil for a quarter of an hour, when if too thick, add a little more water, and let it boil a few minutes longer; then add half a pint of white wine, a tablespoonful of orange-flower water, the juice of a lemon, the same of an orange, sugar to taste, and a piece of butter about the size of a walnut; warm the whole together, thicken with the yolk of a well beaten egg, and drink hot.

Practical Housewife, 1860

CAUDLE, OATMEAL: Take a quart of ale, a pint of stale beer, and a quart of water; mix all together, and add a handful of fine oatmeal, six cloves, two blades of mace, some nutmeg, and eight allspice berries bruised. Set over a slow fire, and let it boil for half an hour, stirring it well all the time; then strain through a coarse sieve, add half a pound of sugar, or to taste, a piece of lemon-peel. Pour into a pan, cover close, and warm before serving.

Practical Housewife, 1860

CAUDLE, TEA: Make a pint of strong green tea, pour it into a saucepan, and set over a slow fire. Beat the yolks of two eggs well, and mix with half a pint of white wine, some grated nutmeg, and sugar to taste; then pour into the saucepan, stir well until hot, and serve.

Practical Housewife, 1860

CAUDLE, RICE: Make the same as flour caudle, using ground rice instead of flour, and when done add cinnamon and sugar to taste, and a wine-glassful of brandy.

Practical Housewife, 1860

Plate 23. *The bottles shown here used to contain such concoctions as Vienna Drink (a mixture of rhubarb, senna, and port wine), antimonial, barley, koumiss, scurvy-grass, and turnip wines. This doctor's office, built in 1829, was first used by Elhanen Jackson whose supplies included various homemade medicines. (Courtesy of the New York State Historical Association, Cooperstown, New York)*

CAUDLE, WHITE: Mix two table-spoonfuls of fine oatmeal in a quart of water, two hours before using it, strain through a sieve and boil it, then sweeten with sugar, and season with lemon-juice and nutmeg.

Practical Housewife, 1860

CLARY, MOCK: Warm a bottle of claret, sweeten with honey, and add allspice and cloves to taste. Serve hot.

Practical Housewife, 1860

COBBLER, SHERRY: Take some very fine and clean ice, break into small pieces, fill a tumbler to within an inch of the top with it, put a table-spoonful of plain syrup, capillaire, or any other flavour—some prefer strawberry—add the quarter of the zest of a lemon, and a few drops of the juice. Fill with sherry, stir it up, and let it stand for five or six minutes. Sip it gently through a straw.

Practical Housewife, 1860

COOL TANKARD: Put into a quart of mild ale a wine-glassful of white wine, the same of brandy and capillaire, the juice of a lemon, and a little piece of the rind. Add a sprig of borage or balm, a bit of toasted bread and nutmeg grated on the top.

Practical Housewife, 1860

CRAMBAMBULL: Take two bottles of light porter or ale, and boil them in a pan. Then put into the liquor half a pint of rum, and from half a pound to a pound of loaf sugar. After this has been boiling for a few minutes, take the whole from the fire, and put into the mixture the whites and the yolks of from six to eight eggs, previously well whisked; stir the whole for a minute or two, and pour it into a punch-bowl, to be drunk out of tumblers. It tastes well hot or cold.

Practical Housewife, 1860

DEVILLED ALE: Cut a slice of bread about an inch

thick, toast and butter it, then sprinkle with cayenne pepper and ginger, and place in the bottom of a jug, add a pint of warm ale, and sugar to taste.

Practical Housewife, 1860

DRINK DIVINE: Mix a bottle of cider, half a bottle of perry, and the same of sherry, with half a gill of brandy, then add a sliced lemon, the rind pared as thin as possible, and a toasted biscuit, which is to be added to the liquor as hot as possible. Drink iced, or cooled.

Practical Housewife, 1860

EGG FLIP: To make a quart of flip, put the ale on the fire to warm, and beat up three or four eggs with four ounces of moist sugar; remove the froth of the ale, while on the fire, until it begins to boil, mix the froth with the sugar and eggs, add grated nutmeg or ginger to taste, and a gill of rum. When the ale boils, stir it gradually into the eggs and rum, until quite smooth, then serve.

Practical Housewife, 1860

FLAP: Put a little brandy in a tumbler, and add a bottle of soda-water.

Practical Housewife, 1860

GINGER BEER, INDIAN: To ten quarts of boiling water, add two ounces of pounded ginger, one ounce of cream of tartar, two limes, and two pounds of sugar. Stir until cold, then strain through flannel until quite clear, adding a pint of beer, and four wine-glassfuls of good toddy. Bottle, tie down the corks, shake each bottle well for some time, place them upright, and they will be fit to drink the next day. This does not keep long.

Practical Housewife, 1860

HOT PURL: Put a quart of mild ale into a saucepan, add a table-spoonful of grated nutmeg, and place over a slow fire until it nearly boils. Mix a little cold ale with sugar to taste, and, gradually, two eggs well beaten; then add the hot ale, stirring one way to prevent curdling—and a quarter of a pint of whisky. Warm the whole again, and then pour from one vessel into another till it becomes smooth.

Practical Housewife, 1860

JINGLE: Roast three apples, grate some nutmeg over them, add sugar to taste, and place in a quart jug, with some slices of toasted plumcake; make some ale hot, and fill up the jug, then serve.

Practical Housewife, 1860

NORFOLKPUNCH: Pare six lemons and three Seville oranges very thin, squeeze the juice into a large teapot, put to it two quarts of brandy, one of white wine, and one of milk, and one pound and a quarter of sugar. Let it be mixed, and then covered for twenty-four hours, strain through a jellybag till clear; then bottle it.

Domestic Cookery, 1807

OXFORD NIGHTCAP: Take half a tumbler of tea, made as usual with sugar and milk, add a slice of lemon, a wine-glass of new milk, and the same of rum or brandy; beat up a new-laid egg, and add to the whole while warm.

Practical Housewife, 1860

POSSET, ALE: Boil a pint of new milk with a slice of toasted bread, sweeten a bottle of mild ale, and pour it into a basin with nutmeg or other spice, add the boiling milk to it, and when the head rises, serve.

Practical Housewife, 1860

POSSET, COLD: Take a pint of cream, half a pint of white wine, the juice of half a lemon, and the peel rasped into it. Sweeten the cream and wine, put the latter into a basin, and then pour the cream from a height into the basin, stirring both well all the time; remove the froth, let it remain for a day in lukewarm water if the weather is cold, and then serve.

Practical Housewife, 1860

POSSET, JELLY: Take eight eggs, leave out the whites of four, and beat all the remainder well together in a basin; then add half a pint of white wine, a little strong ale (to taste), and sugar: put into a saucepan, and set over a slow fire, stirring all the time. Boil a pint of milk with a little nutmeg and cinnamon, just enough to flavour it, and, when the eggs and wine are hot, add the boiling milk to it; then remove from the fire, pour into a punch-bowl, cover with a plate for half an hour, then sprinkle the top with pounded sugar and serve.

Practical Housewife, 1860

POSSET, LEMON: Steep the rind of a lemon pared thin, in a pint of sweet white wine two hours before required, add the juice of one lemon, and sugar to taste; put it in a bowl with a quart of milk or cream, and whisk one way till very thick. This will fill twenty glasses, which may be filled the day before required.

Practical Housewife, 1860

POSSET, ORANGE: Take the crumb of a penny loaf grated fine, and put it into a pint of water, with half the peel of a Seville orange grated, or sugar rubbed upon it. Boil all together, till it looks thick and clear; then take the juice of half a Seville orange, three ounces of sweet, and one of bitter almonds, beat well with a table-spoonful of brandy, add sugar to taste, and a pint of white or raisin wine; mix well, add to the posset, and serve.

Practical Housewife, 1860

POSSET, POPE'S: Blanch and pound four ounces of sweet almonds, and half an ounce of bitter ones; add boiling water, and strain, sweeten, and make hot half a bottle of white wine; mix.

Practical Housewife, 1860

POSSET, ROYAL: Take half a pint of ale, mix a pint of cream with it; then add the yolks of four eggs and the whites of two well beaten, sweeten to taste and flavour with nutmeg. Pour into a saucepan, set over the fire, stir well until thick, and before it boils, remove; pour into a basin and serve hot.

Practical Housewife, 1860

POSSET, SACK: Put a quart of new milk into a saucepan, and place it over a slow clear fire. When it boils, crumble four Damascus biscuits into it; give it one boil, remove from the fire, add grated nutmeg and sugar to taste, stir in half a pint of sack (canary wine), and serve. French roll will answer instead of the biscuits.

Practical Housewife, 1860

POSSET, SNOW: Boil a stick of cinnamon, and a quarter of a nutmeg, with a quart of new milk, and when it boils remove the spice. Beat the yolks of ten eggs well, and mix gradually with the milk until thick; then beat the whites of the eggs with sugar and canary wine into a snow. Put a pint of canary (sack) into a saucepan, sweeten to taste, set over a slow fire, and pour the milk and snow into the saucepan, stirring all the time it is over the fire; when warm, remove from the fire, cover close, and set aside for a little time before being used.

Practical Housewife, 1860

POSSET, TREACLE: Boil a pint of milk, add sufficient treacle to curdle it; allow the curd to settle,

Plate 24. *Included on the shelves of a typical early 19th century kitchen cupboard such as this in the Lippitt farmhouse kitchen were such utensils for the preparing and serving of beverages as a teapot, mug, wine glass, hand-blown glass pitcher, and a 1796 States pitcher, being similar to the Liverpool jug of 1815. A greenish brown flavoring bottle contains a mixture of lemon juice, rind, and brandy for cooking. (Courtesy of the New York State Historical Association, Cooperstown, New York)*

Plate 25. *Hound-handled pitchers used for various kinds of beverages both at home and at taverns. The six-quart size on the left stands eleven and one-fourth inches high and the two-quart one on the right, eight and three-fourths inches. (Courtesy of the Bennington Museum, Bennington, Vermont)*

strain off the liquid, and drink it as hot as possible.
Practical Housewife, 1860

POSSET, WINE: Boil some slices of white bread in a quart of milk; when quite soft take it off the fire, add sugar and grated nutmeg to taste. Pour it into a basin, add a pint of raisin or other sweet wine by degrees, and serve with toasted bread.
Practical Housewife, 1860

PUNCH, COLD: Pour half a pint of gin on the rind of a lemon; add a table-spoonful of lemon-juice, a wine-glassful of maraschino, a pint and a half of water, and two bottles of iced water.
Practical Housewife, 1860

PUNCH, COMMON: Take two large fresh lemons with rough skins and full of juice. Rub some large lumps of white sugar over the lemons till they have acquired the oil from the rind, then put them into a bowl with as much more as is necessary to sweeten the punch to taste; then squeeze the lemon-juice upon the sugar, and bruise the sugar in the juice, add a quart of boiling water and mix well; then strain through a fine sieve, and add a quart of rum, or a pint of rum and brandy, or a pint and a half of rum and half a pint of porter; then add three quarts more water, and mix well. About half a pound of sugar is usually required, but it is impossible to fix a limit to sugar, spirits, or lemon-juice, as they depend upon taste.
Practical Housewife, 1860

PUNCH MILK—FOR CHRISTMAS-DAY: Add the peel and juice of twenty-four lemons, and three pounds and a half of loaf-sugar, to five bottles of cold water, and four bottles of rum; when these are well mixed, add two bottles of boiling milk, and mix the whole well. Let it stand for twenty-four hours, strain well, bottle, and cork tight; it is then ready for use. N.B. The finer the strainer is, the better the punch. This is the best receipt we have ever seen or used.
Practical Housewife, 1860

PUNCH, MILK, ORDINARY: Pare six oranges and six lemons as thin as you can; grate them over with sugar, to get the flavour. Steep the peels in a bottle of rum or brandy stopped close twenty-four hours. Squeeze the fruit on two pounds of sugar, add to it four quarts of water and one of new milk boiling hot; stir the rum into the whole, run through a jelly-bag till clear, bottle, and cork close immediately.
Practical Housewife, 1860

PUNCH, REGENT'S: Take a bottle of champagne, a quarter of a pint of brandy, the juice of a lemon, a Seville orange, and a wine-glassful of Martinique, with this mix a pint or more of a strong infusion of the best green tea strained, and syrup or sugar to taste.
Practical Housewife, 1860

PUNCH A LA ROMAINE: Take a quart of lemon ice, add the whites of three eggs well beaten, with rum and brandy, till the ice liquefies, in the proportion of three parts of rum to one of brandy, and water to taste. Then add a teacupful of strong green tea infusion, strained, and a little champagne.
Practical Housewife, 1860

PUNCH, TEA: Infuse two ounces of hyson tea, and an ounce of black tea, in three quarts of boiling water; then add four pounds of loaf sugar, citric acid and spirit of citron, of each six drachms, rum one pint, and five pints of brandy; mix well, and serve.
Practical Housewife, 1860

PUNCH, AFTER THE FASHION OF THE WEST INDIAN PLANTERS: "He made his appearance with a respectably sized bowl, an enormous jug of boiling water, and a large paper bag filled with sugar. Our punch-maker then commenced operations, and having extracted from his secret store a bottle of his matchless rum, his limes, and a small pot of Guave Jelly, he brewed about a pint of green tea (two ounces); and, the infusion finished, two-thirds of the sugar was dissolved in it. After the tea leaves had been thrown aside, the remainder of the sugar was rubbed on the rind of the limes, Mr. Hamilton observing that the essential oil which conveyed the exquisite flavour was thus more strongly diffused throughout the compound than when the skin was peeled: then the delicious acid of the fruit was added to the already impregnated sugar, and as soon as the several lumps had imbibed the proportion required, the Guava Jelly (and without this confection no punch can be pronounced perfect) was dissolved in a pint or so of boiling water. This done, the tea, the sweets and acids were commingled, and the foundation or sherbet tasted by the experienced palate of the grand compounder; six glasses of cognac, two of madeira, and the bottle of old rum were added, and over all about a quart more of boiling water, and, as a finishing touch, the slightest possible sprinkling of nutmeg. Here was the punch! and oh! what punch! it outnectared nectar! I have, in the West Indies, since the period I am recording, drunk some very luscious and fascinating mixtures nearly resembling it; but I never knew it surpassed, if equalled, even in the tropical regions."—From TOPLEY, *Sportsman in Canada*

Practical Housewife, 1860

SCOTCH PUNCH, OR WHISKY TODDY: The Duke of Athol's receipt: Pour about a wine-glassful of *boiling* water into a half-pint tumbler, and add sugar according to taste. Stir well up, then mix a wine-glassful of whisky, and add a wine-glassful and a half more boiling water. *Be sure the water is boiling.* Never put lemon into toddy. the two in combination, in almost every instance, produce acidity on the stomach. If possible, store your whisky *in the wood,* not in bottles, as the keeping it in the barrel mellows it, and takes away the coarser particles.

Practical Housewife, 1860

TODDY, BUTTERED: Mix a glass of rum-grog pretty strong and hot, sweeten to taste with honey, flavour with nutmeg and lemon-juice, and add a piece of fresh butter about the size of a walnut.

Practical Housewife, 1860

VERDER, OR MILKPUNCH: Pare six oranges, and six lemons as thin as you can, grate them after with sugar to get the flavour. Steep the peels in a bottle of rum or brandy stopped close twenty-four hours. Squeeze the fruit on a pound and a half of sugar, add to it four quarts of water, and one of new milk boiling hot; stir the rum into the above, and run it through a jellybag till perfectly clear. Bottle, and cork close immediately.

Domestic Cookery, 1807

Plate 26. *This elaborate stoneware water cooler was made for a Bennington, Vermont hostelry by J. & E. Norton sometime between 1850 and 1859. Note the spicket holes at the bottom. It was equipped with a removable cover and stands 33½ inches high. (Courtesy of the Bennington Museum, Bennington, Vermont)*

Plate 27, above. *As a by-product from the churning of butter, buttermilk provided a delicious and healthful beverage. (Courtesy of the New York State Historical Association, Cooperstown, New York)*

Plate 28. *Skimming off the cream from fresh milk used to be a daily chore. In this photo a shell-shaped skimmer is being used. (Courtesy of the New York State Historical Association, Cooperstown, New York)*

CHAPTER FIVE

Temperance Drinks

HISTORICAL BACKGROUND

Among the social reforms of the first half of the nineteenth century was the temperance crusade which had its roots in the colonial period. Dr. Benjamin Rush did much to stimulate the temperance movement. Goodrich in his *Lives of the Signers of the Declaration of Independence* (1832) writes of Rush:—

He powerfully, and to some extent successfully, employed his pen against some of the habits and vices of mankind. His 'Inquiry into the effects of ardent spirits upon the human body and mind,' has been more read than any of his works. All the medical philosophy that was pertinent to the subject, was incorporated with it. Striking descriptions of the personal and family distress occasioned by that vice, and of its havoc on the minds, bodies and estates of its unhappy votaries, were given, and the means of prevention and cure pointed out. The whole was illustrated by a scale, graduated like a thermometer, showing at one view the effects of certain enumerated liquors on the body, mind, and the condition in society of those who are addicted to them. In the last year of Dr. Rush's life, he presented to the general assembly of the Presbyterian church in the United States, one thousand copies of this popular pamphlet, to be given away among the people of their respective congregations. About the same time, that numerous and respectable body passed a resolution, enjoining on their members to exert themselves in counteracting this ruinous vice.

Another leader who did much to stimulate temperance reform was Rev. Lyman Beecher, a charter member of the Connecticut Moral Society which was started to combat "Sabbath-breakers, rum-selling, tippling folk, infidels, and rugg-scruff," among the Protestant clergy.

One of those who had been duly influenced by Rev. Beecher's views regarding temperance was his son, Henry Ward Beecher. Harriet Beecher Stowe in her *Men of Our Times* writes, in 1868, "Mr. Beecher had received from family descent what might be called a strictly temperance organization. In no part of his life did he ever use, or was he ever tempted to use tobacco or ardent spirits in any shape. All his public labors, like those of his father before him, have been performed by the strict legal income of ordinary nervous investment; they have not been those deep ruinous drafts on the reserved principal of vital force, which are drawn by the excitements of extra stimulants."

Activities of the General Conference of the Methodist Church in 1780 and 1816; the American Temperance Society founded as the Nation's first temperance organization in 1826 whose first national convention was a decade later; and the Washingtonian Temperance Society whose members were reformed drunkards, 1840, all contributed significantly to the support of the temperance crusade.

Thirteen states and one territory, Minnesota, passed state-wide prohibition laws between 1846 and 1855.

The First national temperance group was founded, February 13, 1826. Rev. William Collier, a Baptist missionary, established the first temperance journal, *The National Philanthropist,* that year, also.

Within seven years, national interest was aroused in the whole gamut of temperance when the nation's Congressmen formed an organization in Washington, D. C. entitled, The Congressional Temperance Society. Its purpose was to discourage "the use of ardent spirit and the traffic in it, by example and by kind moral influence."

This society lacked any dynamic sustaining qualities until a dedicated temperance lecturer, named John H. W. Hawkins, resparked interest in it, in 1833. Hawkins was a fire-and-brimstone sort of crusader and in his first decade of lecturing, he traveled over 100,000 miles and gave a minimum of 2500 speeches.

Drinking was so widespread by 1835, that Rev. Charles Giles estimated that 56,000 was the death toll each year from drink and that "500,000 drunkards are now living in our blessed America, all moving onward to the dreadful verge. What a scene of immolation."

One gathers that even the ministers were not exempt from the national urge to drink. Otherwise, why would 300,000 of them take a pledge of total abstinence in 1836?

This was the year that Cold Water societies became an important part of the temperance movement. Rev. Thomas P. Hunt contacted children attending Sunday School, distributed pledge cards among them, and sent them on their way to obtain the signatures of any remaining nonabstainers.

On December 15, 1838 the *New York Mirror* resorted to one of Benjamin Franklin's nuggets of wisdom in his *Poor Richard's Almanac* by referring to the following quotation: "Keep your head cool by temperance, your feet warm by exercise, rise early and go soon to bed; and if you are inclined to get fleshy, keep your eyes open and your mouth shut."

On the other hand, in Mississippi a law was passed in 1839 forbidding the sale of any alcoholic beverage "in quantities less than a gallon."

The forerunner of Alcoholics Anonymous made its appearance in 1840 with the beginning of the Washington Temperance Society, in Baltimore. Six devotees of Bacchus were captivated by the dynamic oratory of a temperance lecturer in a nearby community hall. The membership in this organization consisted of former heavy drinkers who gathered to tell of their experiences prior to and after taking their oath of abstinence. By 1843, there are said to have been one half million "intemperate drinkers" and 100,000 "habitual drunkards" now reformed by this temperance society. In the words of one convert to abstinence, "A few leaders in the ranks of intemperance having signed the Pledge, it appeared to be a signal for the mass to follows; and on they came, like a torrent sweeping everything before it. It was for weeks the all-absorbing topic." But, with his use of the word "torrent", he is still thinking in terms of liquids.

In New York City, the Sons of Temperance was established at Teetotaler's Hall, in 1842. This organization had as its objectives: to help its members from being intemperate; to raise their characters to a higher plane; and to offer mutual assistance in the event of illness. Dues and an initiation fee were its means of financial support. Its rituals were secret. To this, great opposition was voiced by John Marsh of the American Temperance Union. His objection was especially based on the fact that non-members were not allowed to attend meetings of the association.

Within three years another combined temperance and fraternal society was founded in New York City. Its name was the Temple of Honor and only Protestants could become members. In 1849, the Temple was reported to be "all that is excellent in older associations with additional advantages," by the Most Worthy Templar of the National Temple, Mr. William L. Stacey. To become a member, one had to accept the existence of God. "Unceasing and universal abstinence" was to be constantly practiced. Although the Temple of Honor was established in the North, it was received even more enthusiastically in the South in the locale of the large plantations, where elaborate, colorful costumes became an important part of the ceremonies and passwords were an additional embellishment.

But not everyone took the "pledge". Two, who did not, appear in a report by Amelia Bloomer, in *Lily* Magazine, in an item concerning two bar partners who engaged in a drinking contest in Auburn, New York, in 1850. They attempted what easily could become fatal, i.e. rapidly drinking three pints of whisky. With the last gulp, the defending champion sank to the bar room floor and expired.

By 1851, there was such mounting concern over the evils of overindulgence, that temperance stories appeared more and more frequently. A series of those written by Lucius Manlius Sargent were collected that year into a single volume. The preface states: "The perusal of some of these narratives is well known to have turned the hearts of many persons of intemperate habits, from drunkenness and sloth, to temperance and industry. Many years have passed since their first publication, in separate numbers. It may not be uninteresting to the children of parents, once intemperate, to cast their eyes upon these pages, whose influence, under the blessing of Heaven, has preserved them from a miserable orphanage."

Even the temperance theme was a popular one for dramatists. In 1854, *Little Katy; or,*

The Hot Corn Girl was a successful temperance theatrical production. The plot centered around a husband in what had been a happy, harmonius family. Turning to drink, he then began to gamble; suffered great losses. To recover, he turned to thievery and was caught. The wife, too, began to imbibe, "the rum destroying her maternal feelings." The victim is their little girl, Katy, who is pushed from her home onto the dirty street to sell "hot corn" to support the family. There, undernourished and poorly clad, she catches pneumonia and dies.

The following year witnessed the publication of *Ten Nights in a Bar-Room and What I Saw There* by T. S. Arthur. Within twenty-five years, about 100,000 copies had been sold. Dramatizations based on Arthur's book were presented for many years.

But during the first half of the nineteenth century when temperance agitation was active, there were still those who stressed the medicinal properties of alcoholic beverages, and many still followed the time worn adage expressed in *Troilus and Cressida* "Be moderate, be moderate."

This explains why directions for the making of beverages during this period are for "temperance drinks." These were purposely designed to offset the popularity of alcoholic drinks.

The earliest reference to tea by the British so far as the author has been able to ascertain was in 1615 in a letter kept by the East India Company; but it was nearly one hundred years before tea was introduced in the colonies. It was much too costly, at first, to be used extensively in New England. Only one reference is made to tea in Judge Sewall's diary when in 1709 tea was served at a Thursday lecture at Madam Winthrop's. No comment is made as to its being considered a particular rarity, however. Perhaps this is due to the fact that as early as 1690, a license had been granted in Boston to Daniel Vernon and Benjamin Harris for the sale of tea "in publique." Those who could afford it, no doubt purchased it. Apothecary Zabdiel Boylston listed "green and ordinary teas" in his 1712 apothecary's list. The following year Bohea tea was introduced, and by 1715 one could purchase tea in the coffee-houses.

A curious discovery was made when it was learned that tea was not always used as a beverage, but as food. Often, it was the cooked tea leaves that were eaten, and the liquid was thrown out. In Salem, the leaves were salted, buttered, and eaten, while the tea, boiled so long that it had a strong bitter taste, was drunk without adding sugar or milk.

Strange labels were attached to this new Oriental drink. Often, it was referred to as a "detestable weed," a "dammed weed," a "rank poison far-fetched and dear bought," a "base exotick," a "base and unworthy Indian drink," and all sorts of physical ailments were attributed to its use, such as the loss of memory, and tooth decay. But there were those who upheld its virtues. Abbe Robin said it was due to the drinking of tea that Revolutionary soldiers could physically endure their military flogging at the hands of the British. Others used tea as a medicinal alleviant for indigestion or to cure the spleen.

Chocolate was exceedingly popular when made into a beverage. In 1697, chocolate was served with a breakfast of venison at the Lieutenant Governor's. Sewall was one of the guests on this occasion. Winthrop refers to its scarcity, the following year. When Madam Knight made her journey to New York in 1704, she took along some of it and writes in her journal, "I told her I had some chocolate if she would prepare it, which, with the help of some milk and a little clean brass kettle, she soon effected to my satisfaction."

The Boston *News Letter* advertised mills in which to grind cocoa.

Chocolate remained the favorite nonalcoholic beverage for quite some time, and coffee was drunk only occasionally. The new era of European expansion was responsible for the use of tea, coffee, and chocolate which had been drunk long before the first English settlers had even arrived. Cortes, in 1520, introduced cocoa with vanilla and sugar added, after cacao beans had been discovered in Mexico.

It was not until 1652 that coffee arrived in England by way of Europe from Turkey. Edwards, a trader, had introduced it to the English.

Coffee houses originated probably in Boston, in 1670, when the officials, according to Dr. Lyon, gave Dorothy Jones a license to sell "Coffe and chuchaletto".

Over a period of years, other innkeepers were entitled to sell coffee, and coffee houses were well established by the beginning of the 18th. Century. An examination of the estate inventories of the day reveals frequent reference to such items as coffee-pots, coffee-dishes, and coffee-mugs. Since whole beans were sometimes boiled for hours, one is not convinced that coffee always was delectable either as a food or a beverage. Lest "instant coffee" be considered an innovation of recent years, Earle reports that "after a few years coffee-powder' was offered for sale."

From 1821 to c. 1835, coffee drinking came to be a matter of great concern to many people, who worried about its increasing use as an aphrodisiac. Temperance movements mobilized all their resources to battle its use. Heavy campaigns against coffee were widespread.

Examination of the recipes for Temperance Drinks, which follow, discloses beers of spruce and ginger. Renewed interest in coffee and how to improve its flavor appear. Methods of brewing it are suggested; the Turkish or Arabian Mode of its preparation is recommended; fish skin is mentioned as an additive. One recipe gives directions for coffee which is "more healthy and better flavored, for one-fourth the expense of Common." And cheap and valuable substitutes are numerous.

New terminology for "beverages" emerges, including ade, as in Apple-, Orange-, or Lemonade; water, such as Barley, Currant, Lemon Waters; pop, especially Ginger Pop; nectar, plain or supreme; and "drink", such as Apricot Effervescing, Cherry, Cranberry, and Tamarind Drinks.

Drink from the well!
In rapture rang the Temperance bell.
G. W. Bungay, *The Creeds of the Bells*

RECIPES

APPLEADE: Cut two large apples in slices, and pour a quart of boiling water on them, strain well and sweeten. To be drunk when cold or iced.

Practical Housewife, 1860

APRICOT EFFERVESCING DRINK: Take a pint of the juice of bruised apricots, filter until clear, and make into a syrup with half a pound of sugar, then add one ounce of tartaric acid, bottle, and cork well. For a tumbler three parts full of water, add two table-spoon-fulls of the syrup, and a scruple of carbonate of soda, stir well, and drink while effervescing.

Practical Housewife, 1860

BARLEY WATER: 1. Pick clean, and wash well a handful of common barley, then simmer gently in three pints of water with a bit of lemon-peel. Prepared thus, it does not nauseate like pearl-barley water. 2. Take two ounces and a half of pearl-barley: wash well, then add half a pint of water, and boil for a little time, throw away the liquor, pour four imperial pints of boiling water on the barley, boil down to two pints, strain, flavour with sugar, and lemon-peel, if wished.

Practical Housewife, 1860

BARLEY WATER, COMPOUND: Boil two pints of barley-water, and a pint of water together, with two ounces and a half of sliced figs, half an ounce of liquorice root sliced and bruised, and two ounces and a half of raisins. Reduce to two pints, and strain.

Practical Housewife, 1860

CAPILLAIRE: Take one pound of loaf sugar, quarter of a pound of moist sugar, one egg well beaten, one pint of water. Simmer it one hour, skim it while boiling, let it get cold, then again boil and skim, and add one ounce of orange-flower water and two table-spoonfuls of brandy. Strain through a jelly-bag, and bottle for use. A spoonful in a tumbler of water makes a pleasant beverage.

Godey's Lady's Book, August, 1866

CAPILLAIRE, MOCK: 1. Take three pounds and a half of loaf sugar, three-quarters of a pound of coarse sugar, two whites of eggs well beaten with the shells, boil together in a pint and a half of water, and skim carefully. Then add an ounce of orange-flower water, strain and put into *perfectly dry* bottles. When cold, mix a table-spoonful or two of this syrup in a little warm or cold water. 2 Mix two teasponfuls of curacoa with a pint of syrup. 3. Boil a quart of water well, add three pounds of white sugar, the white of an egg; skim, and boil to a syrup; then add, while warm, four table-spoonfuls of orange-flower water, strain, and use the same as the others.

Practical Housewife, 1860

CAPILLAIRE, TRUE: Take forty-eight grains of Canadian maiden-hair (adiantum pedatum), six drams of boiling water, and an ounce and twenty grains of white sugar. Infuse two-thirds of the maiden-hair in the water, strain, dissolve the sugar in the infusion. Clarify with the white of egg, pour it over the remainder of the maiden-hair, placed in a water-bath, digest for two hours, and strain the syrup. For large quantities the proportions are: Maiden-hair, 192 parts. Boiling water, 1500 parts. White sugar, 2000 parts.

Practical Housewife, 1860

CHERRY DRINK: Prepare the same as apricot, substituting the cherry juice for the other fruit.

Practical Housewife, 1860

CURDS AND WHEY (CHEAP METHOD): Add six grains of citric acid to a wine-glassful of milk, and the result will be a pleasant acidulous whey, and a fine curd.

Practical Housewife, 1860

CURRANT ICE WATER: Press the juice from ripe currants, strain it, and put a pound of sugar to each pint of juice. Put it into bottles, cork and seal it, and keep it in a cool, dry place. When wanted, mix it with ice water for a drink. Or put water with it, make it *very* sweet, and freeze it. Freezing always takes away much of the sweetness.

The juices of other acid fruits can be used in the same way.

Beecher's Receipt Book, 1857

CURRANT WATER: Take a pound of currants,

Plate 29. *Getting ready for tea. The Swedish scientist, Peter Kalm (1716–1779), observed when visiting New York that the Dutch generally had plain tea, without milk, for breakfast. For sweetening they put a small lump of sugar in their mouth while they drank, instead of adding it directly to the beverage. The fireplace shown here is in the Lippett farmhouse at the Farmers' Museum at Cooperstown, New York. (Courtesy of the New York State Historical Association, Cooperstown, New York)*

and squeeze into a quart of water; put in four or five ounces of pounded sugar. Mix well, strain, and ice, or allow to get cold.

Practical Housewife, 1860

EAU SUCRE: Dissolve lump sugar in water. This is a beverage much used in France. It is considered wholesome and refreshing, particularly just before going to bed.

Godey's Lady's Book, August, 1866

EFFERVESCING LEMONADE: Boil two pounds of white sugar with a pint of lemon-juice, bottle and cork. Put a table-spoonful of the syrup into a tumbler about three parts full of cold water, add twenty grains of carbonate of soda, and drink quickly.

Practical Housewife, 1860

GINGER BEER POWDERS: Powdered lump-sugar, four ounces; carbonate of soda, five drachms; powdered ginger, one drachm. Mix these ingredients well together, divide into twelve equal parts—put each into a *blue* paper. Tartaric acid, one ounce; divide into twelve equal parts—put each into a *white* paper. Dissolve the contents of one of the blue and one of the white papers, each in half a glass of spring water. Pour one into the other, and drink while effervescing. ("I have used this for many years, and have given it to many of my messmates."—T. J. L., Midshipman, R. N.). The tartaric acid may (if Preferred) be thrown into the glass of the other mixture, which should then be nearly full. This plan prolongs the effervescence. Cost, 7d.

Practical Housewife, 1860

GINGER BEER POWDERS, AND SODA POWDERS: Put into blue papers, thirty grains to each paper, of bicarbonate of soda, five grains of powdered ginger, and a drachm of white powdered sugar. Put into white papers, twenty-five grains to each, of powdered tartaric acid.

Put one paper of each kind to half a pint of water. The common soda powders of the shops are like the above, when the sugar and ginger are omitted.

Soda powders can be kept on hand, and the water in which they are used can be flavored with any kind of syrup or tincture, and thus make a fine drink for hot weather.

Beecher's Receipt Book, 1857

GINGER LEMONADE: Boil twelve pounds and a half of lump-sugar for twenty minutes in ten gallons of water; clear it with the whites of six eggs. Bruise half a pound of common ginger, boil with the liquor, and then pour it upon ten lemons pared. When quite cold, put it in a cask, with two table-spoonfuls of yeast, the lemons sliced, and add half an ounce of isinglass. Bung up the cask the next day. It will be ready to bottle in three weeks, and to drink in another three weeks.

Practical Housewife, 1860

GINGER POP: Water $5\frac{1}{2}$ gals.; ginger root, bruised, $\frac{1}{4}$ lb.; tartaric acid $\frac{1}{2}$ oz.; white sugar $2\frac{1}{2}$ lbs.; whites of 3 eggs, well beaten; lemon oil 1 tea-spoon; yeast 1 gill.

Boil the root for thirty minutes in one gallon of the water, strain off, and put the oil in while hot; mix. Make over night, and in the morning skim and bottle, keeping out sediments.

Dr. Chase's Recipes, 1869

IMITATION LEMON SYRUP: Four ounces tartaric acid, powdered. Two drachms oil of lemon. This can be kept in a vial for a month, and then must be renewed. A tablespoonful put to water sweetened with loaf sugar, makes six glasses of lemondae.

Beecher's Receipt Book, 1857

IMPERIAL GINGER POP: Take cream tartar one pound; ginger one and a half ounce; white sugar seven pounds; essence lemon one drachm; water six gallons; yeast half a pint. Mix. Tie the corks down.

Family Keepsake, 1849

LAIT SUCRE: Take one pint of milk, add loaf sugar, and flavor with lemon. Drink cold.

Godey's Lady's Book, August, 1866

LEMONADE OF A DELICIOUS FLAVOR: Dissolve one pound of loaf sugar in two quarts of water, grate over it five large lemons. Then mix in twelve drops of essential oil of sulphur. When going to mix your liquid, cut thin some slices of lemon. Keep cool and covered.

Demorest's Monthly Magazine, November, 1869

LEMON BUR: To one gallon of warm water add one pound of sugar, half ounce of ginger root, one lemon, one cup of yeast. Let it stand twelve hours. Bottle, and cork tight.

Demorest's Monthly Magazine, November, 1869

LEMON WATER:—is also a delightful drink. Put two slices of lemon, thinly peeled, into a teapot, a little bit of the peel and a large spoonful of capillaire; pour in a pint of boiling water, and stop it close two hours.

Gody's Lady's Book, April, 1865

LEMON WATER ICE: Half a pint of lemon-juice, and the same of water, to which put one pint of syrup, the peels of six lemons rubbed off on sugar; strain, mix, and freeze. Then mix up the whites of three eggs to a strong broth, with a little sugar. When the ice is beginning to set, work this well into it, and it will be very soft and delicious.

Godey's Lady's Book, August, 1866

ORANGEADE: Squeeze out the juice of an orange, pour boiling water on a little of the peel, and cover it close. Boil water and sugar to a thin syrup, and skim it. When all are cold, mix the juice, the infusion, and the syrup, with as much more water as will make a rich drink. Strain through a jelly-bag, and ice.

Practical Housewife, 1860

ORANGE, OR LEMON SYRUP: Put a pound and a half of white sugar to each pint of juice, add some of the peel, boil ten minutes, then strain and cork it. It makes a fine beverage, and is useful to flavor pies and puddings.

Beecher's Receipt Book, 1857

PORTABLE LEMONADE: Tartaric or citric acid, one ounce; finely powdered lump-sugar, half a pound; essence of lemon, twenty drops. Mix. Two or three tea-spoonfuls make a capital glass of lemonade. Cost, 8d.; with tartaric acid; 1s. with citric acid.

Practical Housewife, 1860

SARSAPARILLA MEAD: One pound of Spanish sarsaparilla. Boil it in four gallons of water five hours, and add enough water to have two gallons. Add sixteen pounds of sugar, and ten ounces of tartaric acid.

To make a tumbler of it, take half a wine-glass of the above, and then fill with water, and put in half a teaspoonful of soda.

Beecher's Receipt Book, 1857

SHAM CHAMPAGNE: One lemon sliced. A tablespoonful of tartaric acid. One ounce of race ginger. One pound and a half of sugar.

Two gallons and a half of boiling water poured on to the above. When blood warm, add a gill of distillery yeast, or twice as much of home-brewed. Let it stand in the sun through the day. When cold in the evening, cork and wire it. In two days it is ready for use.

Beecher's Receipt Book, 1857

SODA POWDERS: Carbonate of soda, thirty grains in each blue paper; tartaric acid, twenty-five grains in each white paper. Mix as ginger beer powders.

Practical Housewife, 1860

SUMMER BEVERAGE: Ten drops of oil of sassafras. Ten drops of oil of spruce. Ten drops of oil of wintergreen. Two quarts of boiling water poured on to two great spoonfuls of cream tartar. Then add eight quarts of cold water, the oils, three gills of distillery yeast (or twice as much home-brewed), and sweeten it to the taste. In twenty-four hours, bottle it, and it is a delicious beverage.

Beecher's Receipt Book, 1857

TAMARIND DRINK: Boil three pints of water with an ounce and a half of tamarinds, three ounces of currants, and two ounces of stoned raisins, till about a third has evaporated. Strain, add a bit of lemon-peel, which is to be removed in half an hour, then cool.

Practical Housewife, 1860

WHITE SPRUCE BEER: Take six pounds of white sugar, four ounces of essence of spruce, ten gallons of boiling water, and an ounce of yeast. Work the same as in making ginger-beer, and bottle immediately in half pints. Brown spruce beer is made with treacle instead of sugar.

Practical Housewife, 1860

CHOCOLATE: To each square of chocolate, scraped off fine, and put in the pot, allow a pint (less if you like it strong) of water. Stir it while boiling; and let it be uncovered. Let it boil about fifteen minutes, or half an hour, then pour in your cream or rich milk, and let it boil up. Nutmeg grated over a cup of chocolate improves the flavor.

The Way to Live Well, 1849

CHOCOLATE: For those who use a great deal of chocolate, the following is an economical method.

Plate 30. *Flint enamel cow creamers such as these were made at many potteries back around 1849–1858. The one on the left is colored a rare light yellow and that on the right, dark browns and blues. (Courtesy of the Bennington Museum, Bennington, Vermont)*

Cut a cake into small bits and put them into a pint of boiling water. In a few minutes set it off the fire and stir it well till the chocolate is dissolved; then boil it again gently a few minutes, pour it into a bowl, and set it in a cool place. It will keep good eight or ten days. For use, boil a spoonful or two in a pint of milk, with sugar.

Young Housekeeper's Friend, 1846

CHOCOLATE: Many people boil chocolate in a coffee-pot; but I think it is better to boil it in a skillet, or something open. A piece of chocolate about as big as a dollar is the usual quantity for a quart of water; but some put in more, and some less. When it boils, pour in as much milk as you like, and let them boil together three or four minutes. It is much richer with the milk boiled in it. Put the sugar in either before or after, as you please. Nutmeg improves it. The chocolate should be scraped fine before it is put into the water.

American Frugal Housewife, 1833

COMMON MODE OF MAKING CHOCOLATE: Shave fine an inch of a cake of chocolate; pour on it a quart of boiling water; boil it twenty minutes, add milk in such proportion as you like, and boil it up again.

Young Housekeeper's Friend, 1846

COCOA: Boil two large spoonfuls of ground cocoa in a quart of water half an hour; skim off the oil, pour in three gills of milk, and boil it up again. It is the best way to make it the day before it is used, as the oily substance can be more perfectly removed when the cocoa is cold.

Young Housekeeper's Friend, 1846

COCOA AND SHELLS: Dry the nut in a warm oven after bread is drawn, pound it, and put an ounce to each pint of water. Boil an hour, and do not add milk till it is used. If shells are used, soak them over night, then boil them an hour in the same water. Put in as much as you like. Boil cocoa and chocolate the day before, cool and take off the oil, and then heat for use, and it is as good, and more healthful.

Beecher's Receipt Book, 1857

TO MAKE COFFEE: Take fresh-roasted coffee, (a quarter of a pound for three persons is the rule, but *less* will do); allow two table-spoonfuls for each person, grind it just before making, put it in a basin and break into it an egg, yolk, white, shell and all. Mix it up with the spoon to the consistence of mortar, put in a warm not *boiling* water in the coffee pot; let it boil up and *break* three times; then stand a few minutes, and it will be as clear as amber, and the egg will give it a rich taste.

TO MAKE COFFEE WHEN MUCH IS REQUIRED: In the morning, pour upon a quarter of a pound of fresh-ground coffee about two quarts of boiling water; stir it for three or four minutes; cover it closely, and let it remain till the evening; pour it off quite clear, and boil it up for use.

Practice of Cookery, 1830

TO MAKE COFFEE: For a two-quart coffee-pot, put in a tea-cup of ground coffee, a small piece of fish-skin; fill the coffee-pot nearly full of boiling water, boil it from three quarters to one hour, then fill it up and let it settle ten minutes.

Peas, roasted and ground, are an excellent substitute for coffee, and you would hardly know which was best.

American Economical Housekeeper, 1850

ANOTHER WAY TO MAKE COFFEE: Pour hot water into your coffee pot, and then stir in your coffee, a spoonful at a time, allowing three to every pint of water; this makes *strong* coffee. Stir it to prevent the mixture from boiling over, as the coffee swells, and to force it to combine with the water. This will be done after it has boiled gently a few minutes. Then let it stand and boil slowly for half an hour; remove it from the fire, and pour in a tea-cup of cold water, and set it in the corner to settle. As soon as it becomes clear, it is to be poured, gently, into a clean coffee pot for the table.

Made in this manner it may be kept two or three days in summer, and a week in winter; you need only heat it over when wanted.

The grounds and sediment may be boiled over and used once for coffee.

Fish skin is often used to settle coffee, and will answer tolerably well, if rightly prepared. Pull off the skin from a salted cod; scrape, wash and dry it in the

Plate 31. *A "Victorian Dairy Farm" is depicted in this anonymous oil on canvas study in green, painted c. 1875. (Courtesy of the New York State Historical Association, Cooperstown, New York)*

oven, after removing the bread; then divide it in pieces about an inch square, and put it in a paper bag for use. It will require one big for every pint of water; put in when you make the coffee. Several subsitutes for coffee are used by those who cannot afford the real berry—rye, peas, & c. None of these are very healthy, and certainly are not good. The best substitute is toasted crust of bread, but it is cheaper to drink water, and if taken for a little time will be as palatable.

The Way to Live Well, 1849

BREWING COFFEE: Old Java and Mocha coffee are the best kinds. Coffee should be put in an iron pot, and dried over a moderate fire for several hours, before it is roasted. It should be put at such a distance from the fire, as to be in no danger of burning. When it has dried three or four hours, set the pot on a hot bed of coals, and stir it constantly, until sufficiently roasted, which is ascertained by biting one of the lightest colored kernels—if it is brittle, the whole is done. Turn it out of the pot immediately, into a box —cover it tight, to keep in the steam. A coffee-roaster is better than a pot to roast coffee in, as it preserves the fine aromatic flavor of the coffee, which in a great measure escapes with the steam of the coffee, when roasted in an open pot. To make good common coffee, allow a table-spoonful of it, when ground, to each pint of water. Turn on the water boiling hot, and boil the coffee in a tin pot, from twenty to twenty-five minutes—if boiled longer, it will not taste fresh and lively. Let it stand, after being taken from the fire, four or five minutes to settle, then turn it off carefully from the grounds, into a coffee-pot or urn.

When the coffee is put on the fire to boil, a piece of fish-skin or isinglass, of the size of a nine-pence, should be put in, or else the white and shell of half an egg, to a couple of quarts of coffee. Many persons dislike to clear coffee with fish-skin, thinking that it imparts an unpleasant taste to coffee, but it will not, if properly prepared. The skin should be taken from mild codfish, that has not been soaked, as the skin loses its clearing properties by soaking. Rinse it in cold water and dry it perfectly. When dried, cut it into pieces of the size of a nine-pence. If torn off, as it is wanted for use, too much is apt to be put in at once, and give the coffee a bad taste. A piece of the size of a twelve and half cent piece, is sufficient to settle a couple of quarts of water. French coffee is made in a German filter, the water is turned on boiling hot, and one-third more coffee is necessary than when boiled in the common way. Where cream cannot be procured for coffee, the coffee will be much richer to boil it with a less proportion of water than the above rule, and weaken it with boiling hot milk, when served out in cups.

Kitchen Directory, 1846

AN IMPROVED METHOD OF MAKING THE COFFEE BEVERAGE: To an ounce of coffee add a common teaspoonful of the best flour of mustard seed, previous to the boiling. To those unacquainted with the method, it is inconceivable how much it improves the fragrancy, fineness, transparency, and gratefully quick flavour of the beverage, and probably too it adds to its wholesomeness.

Family Receipt Book, 1819

TURKISH OR ARABIAN MODE OF PREPARING COFFEE: The coffee ground or beaten to an impalpable powder is preserved, by closely pressing it down in a wooden box; and the quantity required for use is scraped from the surface by means of a wooden spoon. Two small coffee-pots are employed; in one is boiled the water, generally mixed with the remaining coffee of a former meal; in the other is put the fresh powder, which is sometimes placed near the fire, to become heated before the boiling water is added to it. The mixture is then boiled two or three times, taking care to pour a few drops of cold water upon it the last time, or to place a cloth dipped in cold water over it; then it is allowed to subside, and afterwards poured into the coffee-pot which contained only the boiling water.

N. B. The quantity of coffee powder necessary to make a fine strong tincture of coffee may be estimated as one coffee-cup of coffee powder, to three dishes of proper coffee liquor for the table.

Family Receipt Book, 1819

COFFEE SUBSTITUTES: As substitutes for coffee, some use dry brown bread crusts, and roast them; others soak rye grain in rum, and roast it; others roast peas in the same way as coffee. None of these are very good; and peas so used are considered unhealthy. Where there is a large family of apprentices and workmen, and coffee is very dear, it may be worth while to use the substitutes, or to mix them half and with coffee; but, after all, the best economy is to go without.

French coffee is so celebrated, that it may be worth while to tell how it is made; though no prudent housekeeper will make it, unless she has boarders, who are willing to pay for expensive cooking.

The coffee should be roasted more than is common with us; it should not hang drying over the fire, but should be roasted quick; it should be ground soon after roasting, and used as soon as it is ground. Those who pride themselves on first-rate coffee, burn it and grind it every morning. The powder should be placed in the coffee-pot in the proportions of an ounce to less than a pint of water. The water should be poured upon the coffee boiling hot. The coffee should be kept at the boiling point; but should not boil. Coffee made in this way must be made in a biggin. It would not be clear in a common coffee-pot.

A bit of fish-skin as big as a ninepence, thrown into coffee while it is boiling, tends to make it clear. If you use it just as it comes from the salt-fish, it will be apt to give an unpleasant taste to the coffee: it should be washed clean as a bit of cloth, and hung up till perfectly dry. The white of eggs, and even egg shells are good to settle coffee. Rind of salt pork is excellent.

Some people think coffee is richer and clearer for having a bit of sweet butter, or a whole egg, dropped in and stirred, just before it is done roasting, and ground up, shell and all, with the coffee. But these things are not economical, except on a farm, where butter and eggs are plenty. A half a gill of cold water, poured in after you take your coffee-pot off the fire, will *usually* settle the coffee.

If you have not cream for coffee, it is a very great improvement to boil your milk, and use it while hot.

American Frugal Housewife, 1833

BOY'S COFFEE: Crumb bread, or dry toast, into a bowl. Put on a plenty of sugar, or molasses. Put in one half milk and one half boiling water. To be eaten with a spoon, or drank if preferred. Molasses for sweetening is preferred by most children.

Beecher's Receipt Book, 1857

FISH SKIN FOR COFFEE: Take the skin of a mild codfish which has not been soaked, rinse and then dry it in a warm oven, after bread is drawn. Cut it in inch squares. One of these serves for two quarts of coffee, and is put in the first thing.

Beecher's Receipt Book, 1857

CHEAP AND VALUABLE SUBSTITUTE FOR COFFEE: The seeds of the flower de luce, or common yellow water flag, being roasted in the same manner as coffee very much resemble it in colour and flavour, but have something more of a saccharine odour, approaching to that of extract of liquorice. When carefully prepared they possess much more of the aroma of coffee than is to be found in any of the leguminous and gramineous seeds that have been treated in the same manner. Coffee made of these seeds is extremely wholesome and nutricious, in the proportion of half an ounce or an ounce, to a pint of boiling water.

Family Receipt Book, 1819

ANOTHER SUBSTITUTE FOR COFFEE: The seeds of foreign grapes have lately been discovered to be an excellent substitute for coffee. When pressed, they first produce a quantity of oil, and afterwards, when roasted and boiled, furnish a liquid much resembling that produced from coffee. The practice is rapidly becoming general in Germany.

Family Receipt Book, 1819

OCHRA: It is said that the seeds of ochra burnt like coffee, make a beverage almost exactly like it.

Beecher's Receipt Book, 1857

COFFEE: More Healthy and Better Flavored, for One-Fourth the Expense of Common. Coffee, by weight or measure, one-fourth, rye three-fourths.

Look them over separately, to remove bad grains; then wash to remove dust, draining off the water for a moment as you take it with the hands, from the washing water, putting directly into the browning skillet, carefully stirring, all the time, to brown it evenly. Brown each one separately; then mix evenly, and grind only as used; settling with a beaten egg, seasoning with a little cream and sugar as usual.

And I do sincerely say the flavor is better, and it is one hundred per cent more healthy than all coffee.

You may try barley, peas, parsnips, dandelion roots, & c. but none of their flavors are equal to rye. Yet all of them are more or less used for coffee.

Dr. Chase's Recipes, 1869

TEA: Scald the tea-pot, and if the tea is a strong kind, a teaspoonful for a pint of water is sufficient—if it is a weak kind, more will be required. Pour on just

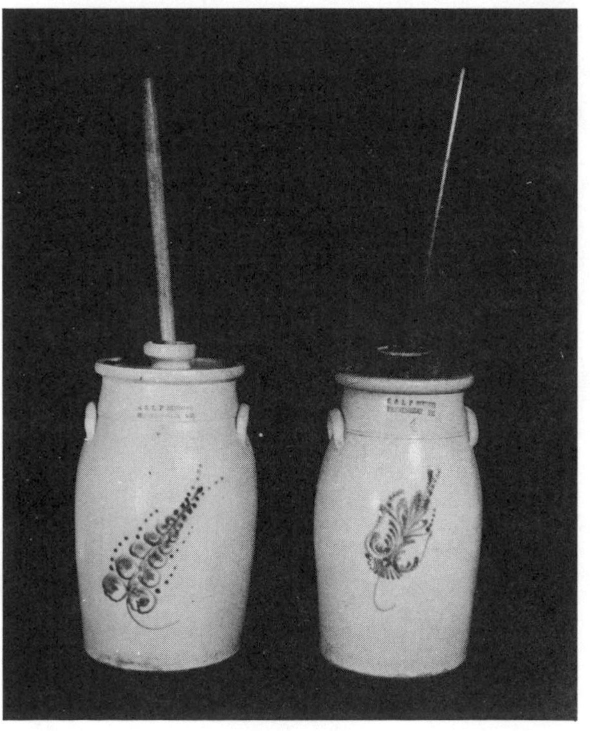

Plate 32. *Norton stoneware churns marked "E. & L. P. Norton" that date back to around 1861–1881. (Courtesy of the Bennington Museum, Bennington, Vermont)*

Plate 33. *Precious china and utensils were arranged on what was known as "pewter racks" or "dressers," such as this in the Lippitt farmhouse kitchen. Lewis, in his* History of Lynn, *records that "when ladies went to visiting parties, each one carried her tea cup, saucer and spoon. The tea cups were of the best china, very small, containing as much as a common wine glass." (Courtesy of the New York State Historical Association, Cooperstown, New York)*

enough boiling water to cover the tea, and let it steep. Green tea should not steep more than five or six minutes before drinking—if steeped longer, it will not be lively. Black tea requires steeping ten or twelve minutes to extract the strength.

Kitchen Directory, 1846

TEA: Young Hyson is supposed to be a more profitable tea than Hyson; but though the *quantity* to a pound is greater, it has not so much *strength*. In point of economy, therefore, there is not much difference between them. Hyson tea and Souchong mixed together, half and half, is a pleasant beverage, and is more healthy than green tea alone. Be sure that water boils before it is poured upon tea. A tea-spoonful to each person, and one extra thrown in, is a good rule. Steep ten or fifteen minutes.

American Frugal Housewife, 1833

TEA: Scald the teapot with boiling water; then put in the tea, allowing three tea-spoonfuls to a pint of water—or for every two persons. Pour on the water. It must be boiling hot, and let the tea steep about ten minutes.

Black tea is healthier than green. Hyson and Souchong mixed together, half and half, is a pleasanter beverage than either alone, and safer for those who drink *strong* tea, than to trust themselves wholly with green.

The Way to Live Well, 1849

TEA: The old-fashioned rule to put one teaspoonful for each person, is not proper, as thus fifty persons would require fifty teaspoonfuls, which is enormous. Every person must be guided by taste in this matter. Tea is spoilt unless the water is boiling when it is made. Black tea improves by boiling, but green is injured by it.

Beecher's Receipt Book, 1857

BEEF TEA: Broil a pound of fresh lean beef ten minutes—then cut it into small bits, turn a pint of boiling water on it, and let it steep in a warm place half an hour—then strain it, and season the tea with salt and pepper to the taste. This is a quick way of making the tea, but it is not so good, when the stomach will bear but a little liquid on it, as the following method: cut the beef into small bits, which should be perfectly free from fat—fill a junk bottle with them, cork it up tight, and immerse it in a kettle of lukewarm water, and boil it four or five hours. This way is superior to the first, on account of obtaining, the juices of the meat, unalloyed with water, a tablespoonful of it being as nourishing as a tea-cup full of the other.

Kitchen Directory, 1846

WHITE TEA: Put two teaspoonfuls of sugar into half a cup of good milk, and fill it with boiling water.

Beecher's Receipt Book, 1857

CHAPTER SIX

Medicinal Beverages

Once Antigonus was told his son was ill, and went to see him. At the door he met some young beauty. Going in, he sat down by the bed and took his pulse. "The fever," said Demetrius, "has just left me." "Oh, yes," replied the father, "I met it going out at the door."

PLUTARCH, *Lives, Demetrius.* (A.D. 46)

HISTORICAL BACKGROUND

When the various reasons for drinking hard liquor were discussed by the writer, it was noted that at times it was a matter of life and death—an attempt to save a desperately ill wife or child—that made a quick resort to an alcoholic beverage necessary. No one can estimate how many fatal illnesses there would have been without the availability of some such drink as brandy, whiskey, or rum.

A rare discovery on the part of the writer was a copy of the first American herbal printed in 1801. This work by Samuel Stearns entitled, *The American Herbal, or Materia Medica,* 1801, contains numerous medicinal, alcoholic remedies, to alleviate various illnesses and discomforts as well as critical emergencies.

A good remedy for rheumatism, as well as for fever and ague, was an ounce of prickly ash bark, pulverized, and "digested in a pint of brandy."

Both internal and external doses of balsam of Peru were recommended. When taken internally in rectified spirits of wine, it helped palsies, dysentery, and "has often done service in coughs."

Beaver tree, which, Stearns writes, "seldom grows further north than Pennsylvania and the Jerseys," when its red berries are "steeped in rum or brandy, cure coughs, consumptions, and other disorders." It is suggested that a decoction of the branches of this tree will cure colds.

For jaundice, Stearns recommends black-cherry bark steeped in rum, wine, brandy, or cyder. When the fruit is disintegrated in rum and water, it makes a popular American drink.

As for brandy, or spirits of wine, Stearns writes:

Brandy is a spirituous inflammable liquor, obtained from wine, and some other liquors by distillation. Wine brandy, made in France, is esteemed the best in Europe, both for drinking and for medicinal purposes. This kind of *brandy,* drunk with moderation, well diluted with water, strengthens the tone of the nervous system, raises the spirits, and braces the fibres; it is good in the gout, and a variety of other complaints; but drank to excess, and that practice being long continued, often proves fatal.

Stearns warns against the use of "Cockle" called by the French, "drunken wheat". He reports, "It is supposed to be generated by corrupted barley or wheat. It is not used in medicine: but it produces speedy drunkenness if taken inwardly, and prevents drunkenness if applied outwardly. It causes a vertigo and torpor."

Arrack, which is frequently referred to in regard to early American drinks, was made by the Indians, according to Stearns, from the "Coco Nut Tree". "From this tree the Indians extract a liquor called *suri,* and from it distil the liquor called *arrac;* also a species of sugar called *jagra.*

In regard to the virtues of cider, Stearns states the following:

Good Pleasant *cyder* is cordial, and antiscorbutic; being a very wholesome liquor for most constitutions. . . . if mixed with and sweetened with sugar, or molasses, it makes a very salutary liquor for people in the heat of summer. Those who drink *cyder,* or water, can live longer in the cold, than those who drink ardent spirits. Some of our physicians have directed *cyder* instead of wine for their patients in fever. . . . On being distilled it produces a spirit called *cyder brandy.* This, by age, becomes a pleasant liquor, which many drink instead of rum or brandy. It appears to me, that *cyder* is a preventative against various diseases; for I have observed, that families who make it their constant drink, are not so subject to fevers, dysenteries, and other putrid disorders, as those who live without it. Whey, made by turning milk with *cyder,* is a more agreeable drink for patients in fevers, than that turned with wine."

The writer, since very young, has been well informed on the deadly poison of night shade. Stearns' antidote follows:

Give as soon as possible after the poison has been swallowed, a scruple of white vitriol, dissolved in warm water, and repeat it *pro re nata.* When the operation is over, give a spoonful of sharp vinegar in a glass of water, sweetened if most agreeable. Then give purgatives, . . . Cyder, perry, vinegar, and water, may be drank afterwards.

As for the virtues of garget, or stoke, Stearns informs us that "The expressed juice of the berries, mixed with brandy, is extolled by some people for the cure of the rheumatism." He adds, "To a pint and an half of the juice of the berries, add half a pint of brandy, and take from one to two table-spoonfuls of the liquor diluted with brandy and water. According to the *Encyclopedia,* the Portuguese formerly mixed the juice of the berries with their wines, to give them a deeper colour, but it injured the flavour, and proved deleterious, wherefore the king ordered that the plants should all be cut down before they blossomed. The same method of mixing the juice with wine was prohibited in France, on pain of death, by an edict of Louis XVI."

Gooseberries, described by Stearns as an appetizer, "afford an excellent wine.—If they are pressed with the addition of water, then well fermented, and distilled, they make brandy, almost equal to that of the French kind."

Dr. Brookes is quoted by Stearns as saying the *hops* help digestion. According to the herbal author,

> *Hops* are stimulant, balsamic, aperient, and diuretic. They are one of the most agreeable of all the strong bitters. They are used in making malt liquors, which they render glutinous, . . . Their watery infusion, or rum or brandy impregnated with them, is good in the jaundice.

Spearmint, garden mint, and green mint are considered to be stimulant, stomachic, carminative, and restringent. "The leaves boiled in port wine and applied to the wrists and pit of the stomach, are said to stop vomiting."

Similar to the directions for combating the poison of deadly night shade are the instructions for procedures after eating certain mushrooms. At length, adds Stearns, "Continue the vinegar, and let the patient drink cyder, and perry. . . . But I advise all mankind not to eat any part of this very poisonous Vegetable."

The fruit of the pear tree is refrigerant and astringent, according to Stearns. "A liquor is made of their expressed juice, which is called Perry. Those *Pears* make the best *Perry,* which are the most unfit to be eaten; as the *Choak-Pear,* the *Boerland-Pear, the Horse-Pear,* and the *Barberry Pear;* but they ought to be perfectly ripe, before they are ground and pressed for the making of *Perry.*"

Sugar peas, common peas, and white peas are discussed by Stearns as being "softening, nourishing, and laxative." Then, he includes a curious recipe for making a beer out of this vegetable. "Six gallons of water boiled with a bushel of the shells of green peas, till they become insipid: the liquor poured off, and put into a keg, with the addition of a pint of yeast, and two ounces of ginger, is said to make good beer: —If the beer is distilled, it affords a spirit of the colour and taste of whiskey."

Guinea Pepper, a stimulant being used more and more in medical practice according to Stearns, when "Powdered and digested in brandy, (it) has been used externally, and found useful for rheumatic complaints from a cold cause. It has also been taken internally for the same disorder."

Large doses of bits of the Peruvian barktree prove cathartic, Stearns explains. According to his own testimony, "I have taken two ounces of it in a day myself, in an intermitting fever. The best mode of administering of it, is in substance, in wine, brandy, and water, sweetened, or in any other convenient vehicle."

For gouty pains in the stomach and elsewhere, Stearns considers petty morrel highly beneficial. "The berries, when ripe, infused in an equal quantity of brandy and water, make an excellent cordial, which is very palatable and reviving. . . . They cured me of the gout in the stomach, when other remedies failed." As for dosage, "Fill a glass bottle about half full of the ripe berries, immediately after they are gathered, and then fill the bottle with a mixture of half brandy and half water. Take a small glass of the liquor several times in a day, upon an empty stomach."

Stearns' description of "Proof Spirit of Wine" follows:

> It contains 55 parts of alcohol, and 45 of distilled water in 100.—Its specific gravity is to that of distilled water as 930 to 1000. The Edinburgh College direct proof spirit to be made by mixing equal parts of water and rectified spirit. Proof spirit is used in a large number of medicinal compositions.

One of the less appetizing suggestions of Stearns was the taking of "soft soap, dissolved in ale, for the jaundice." He mentions five kinds of soap—almond, black, soft, volatile, and the white Spanish, or Castile soap—all of which he claims have medicinal uses in addition to washing. Soap Berries which come from a small tree in Jamaica tend to help digestion, and the green sickness, when made into a tincture with white wine, "a tincture in spirit, and an extract from a spirituous tincture."

An excellent cure for a cough discovered by the Indians is a mixture of the juice of wood sorrel berries with good rum, and sweetened with brown sugar.

Strawberries are considered cooling, diuretic, and anti-scorbutic. Stearns heartily disapproves of eating them, however, with milk. He heartily endorses the French mode: "I observed when I travelled in France, in the year 1790, that the French ate them with white wine and sugar, which is a very palatable and salutary composition." He adds, "A pound of sugar added to a quart of the expressed juice of strawberries, makes an agreeable wine, if it is kept a year before it is drank."

Sugar cane, writes Stearns, is cultivated in the West Indies for the purpose of making rum, sugar, and molasses. After being cut, bound, ground between "rollers armed with iron plates," it "comes out of the mill almost dry, and the juice runs off into a proper vessel. It is afterwards boiled, made into sugar or molasses, or distilled into rum."

Sulphur, brimstone, is considered an excellent alleviant for the gout, asthmas, catarrhs, and coughs. Stearns adds, "An ounce of sulphur dissolved in a pint of rum, or gin, is called excellent in rheumatic pains, and to cure the itch."

A highly recommended remedy for hysteria, nervous complaints, and similar ailments is wood soot, "Dissolved in water or spirit."

Apricot Beer, or "Ratifia", is admittedly drunk more for pleasaure than for health. Directions for its preparation are as follows:

> 1. By boiling Apricots in white wine, adding to the liquor an equal quantity of brandy with sugar, cinnamon, mace, and the kernels of Apricots; infusing the whole for eight or ten days, straining the liquor, and putting it up for use: or by cutting the fruit in pieces, infusing it a day or two in brandy, straining, and then adding the above ingredients. 2. *Ratifia* is also prepared by bruising cherries, and putting them into a vessel wherein brandy has been kept a long time; then adding the kernels of cherries, with strawberries, sugar, cinnamon, white pepper, nutmegs, cloves, and to twenty pounds of cherries, ten quarts of brandy. The vessel is left open ten or twelve days, and then stopped close for two months before it is tapped.

One of the reasons cited earlier for heavy

drinking was due to prevailing attitudes about water. Stearns who started his research for *The American Herbal, or Materia Medica,* from which the medicinal beverages just mentioned are excerpted, in September 1772 reflects contemporary views regarding the use of water.

Among the many varieties of water discussed by Stearns is rain water which he considers the "best in medicine, cookery, washing, & c. It ought to be thin, clear, and void of taste or smell. That *water* which falls in great towns and cities, is apt to be impregnated with the fumes of the city, & c. and therefore is not so good for use as that which falls in the country."

Snow water, he considers, the softest of all *waters,* except *rain water,* "and therefore more fit for use than that of the rivers."

The herbalist has little regard for spring water, of which he writes, "Springs afford different kinds of waters, some are as soft as that of the rain; but the most of them afford the hardest and most impure waters; being impregnated with poisonous qualities, imbibed from the bowels of the earth, as poisonous minerals, & c."

Lake and pond water are "generally stagnant, and therefore unfit for use; nay, their very effluvia generates intermitting fevers and agues, putrid fevers, putrid dysenteries."

But there is little doubt left as to why few drank water in this country during the seventeenth and eighteenth centuries after reading Stearns' comments on "Well Water":

The chief substances found in water are, pure, inflammable, and hepatic airs; acid of chalk, the fixed alkalies, vitriolated, muriated, cretised; the vegetable, oftener intrated; cretised volatile alkali; muriated barytes; lime, and sometimes magnesia, vitriolated, nitrated, and subcretised; sometimes clay, supervitriolated and muriated; iron, vitriolated, muriated, cretised; manganese, muriated; copper, vitriolated; calx of arsenic; petroleum; vegetable and animal putrescent mucilage.

One should not drink water without first boiling it. Stearns warns, this is "to kill the animalculae, which float in it, and may be discovered by the microscope. These animals generate diseases."

Another suggestion is that "water may be freed from impurities by distillation; as the operation goes, about two thirds is to be drawn off, which is much more pure and fit for medicinal and other purposes, than that charged with heterogeneous particles."

Yet, "Wholesome, soft water" is described as being "emollient, diluent, dulcifying, refrigerating, and diuretic." Stearns adds other virtues as, "It assists digestion, renders the chyle fluid, softens and sweetens the animal fluids; dilutes thick humours, quenches thirst, abates acrimony, allays heat, cools fevers, removes rigidities, makes the parts flexible, excites urine, sweat, and other necessary evacuations. It is the natural drink of all animals. . . . It is of great utility both internally and externally in the cure of diseases; but it should not be drank, till it has been boiled, as we observed before; nor should it be taken too warm, nor too cold."

Stearns seems to have high regard for the medicinal properties of sea-water.

Sea water is purgative and antiseptic. It gently purges the belly, promotes the other excretions, warms and strengthens the habit, helps strumous swellings, obstructions of the glands, cutaneous disorders, carious bones, resolves tumours, prevents fresh fluxions, tumours of the liver, mesentery, and other parts; but when pus is formed it must be discharged before this water is used.

The recommended dose for drinking sea-water is "From half a pint to a pint every morning. A large quantity excites vomiting. Fresh water may be made as salt as any part of the sea, by putting a pound of salt into twenty of water."

Even bathing in the sea is admittedly healthful. It is described as being "discutient, antiseptic, and corroborant; good for melancholy, and madness. If the head is bathed with it, it prevents the hair from falling off."

MEDICINAL ATTRIBUTES OF BEVERAGES

Information relative to the medicinal qualities of Beer, Broth, Cedar Wine, Chocolate and Chocolate Nuts, Coffee, Flip, Perry, Punch, Rum, Toddy, and Wine which were included in Stearns' 1801 *American Herbal,* published in Walpole, New Hampshire, follow:

BEER: Common malt beer is made of water, malt and hops. Porter and ale is also made of the same ingredients.—There are likewise other kinds of beer, as pumpkin beer, bran beer, spruce beer, & c.

Porter agrees with some constitutions, but not with others; and the same may be said of other malt liquors. It cured a young woman in Connecticut of the palpitation of the heart when other remedies were tried in vain.

Spruce beer is a very wholesome liquor, which is somewhat purgative, and very beneficial in scorbutic complaints. Different kinds of beer, ale, & c. are often prepared according to the prescriptions of the physicians, all of which, as well as pumpkin and bran beer, partake of the virtues of the ingredients put into such liquors.

BROTH: Broths are made of the lean parts of beef, mutton, & c. They are very nourishing when used as aliment; but it should be observed, that in weak, worn out constitutions, strong broth cannot be easily digested, and that the strength thereof should be always proportioned to the strength of the patient.

CEDAR WINE: Take pieces of wood just cut from the tree, whilst the fruit is upon it, and expose them to the sun or fire to obtain the juice by exudation. Mix a pint of this juice with six pints of wine. Let the mixture stand two months, then decant, and put the liquor into another vessel, and let it stand some days in the sun, and it will be fit for use.

In the same manner wines may be prepared from juniper, pine, cyprus, bay, and some trees.

These wines are very healing, diuretic, and astringent: the bay wine is remarkably so.

Cedar wine is also prepared by mixing half a pound of the bruised berries with six pints of must, which is to stand in the sun forty days, and then it becomes fit to drink.

CHOCOLATE NUTS: These nuts are the product of the chocolate tree, which is small, bearing a large red fruit like a cucumber, which contains thirty or more of these nuts. This tree is found in Mexico, is about 18 inches in diameter, and produces a crop of nuts in June, and another in December. The cream of these nuts is emollient and cordial.

The chocolate is very demulcent, emollient, and nutritious.

The mucilaginous pulp contained in the husks, if pressed, yields a cream that is cordial and grateful to

Plate 34. *The gentlemen's reading room at the Bump Tavern. Included among its furnishings is a hutch table on which stands a rack for wine bitters that contains a mixture of poplar, bayberry, goldenseal, balmony, unicorn, quassia chips, scull-cap, cayenne, sugar, prickly ash berries, various spices, and sweet Malaga wine. This concoction was considered to be very effective in providing relief from dyspepsia, sick headache, heartburn, sinking feelings, and whatever other ailments in which a tonic is indicated. (Courtesy of the New York State Historical Association, Cooperstown, N.Y.)*

the taste: and, as an emollient for external applications is of admirable efficacy.

Chocolate is good in hectic, scorbutic, and catarrhous disorders, atrophies, malignant itch, hooping cough, acrid falineous, acid, and bilious complaints, and for hypochondriac, hysteric, and melancholic patients if made with milk and only a small proportion of aromatics. It is said to make the teeth grow black.

If the drinking of chocolate produces uneasiness in the stomach, drink a tea cup full of cold water.

COFFEE: Coffee is the fruit of an oriental shrub, which is now cultivated in the West Indies.

It is slightly stringent, and antiseptic: also stimulant, and a powerful sedative. It is more used as food than physic. Some call it good for the head-ache, a weak stomach, and disorders arising from intemperance and hard study. It moderates internal fermentation, and does service in corpulent and phlegmatic habits.

In delicate constitutions, it sometimes produces headaches, and other nervous symptoms.

In some it assists digestion, promotes the natural secretions, prevents sleepiness, and relieves the spasmodic asthma.

Dr. Motherby informs, that coffee should be boiled from eight to twelve hours before it is drank, and also mixed with an equal quantity of milk.

Twelve berries of raw coffee, boiled in a quart of water to 8 or 10 ounces with the addition of 20 drops of the *ae herial* spirit of nitre, taken twice in a day for two months, has been recommended for pains in the kidneys and ureters.

Dr. Lewis relates, that coffee is good for the phlegmatic and corpulent, but hurtful to thin habits, the bilious, melancholic, hypochondriac, and those subject to haemorrhages.

FLIP: This kind of liquor is made by putting a spoonful of brown sugar into about five or six jills of malt beer, which is then warmed by putting a hot iron into it, called a logger-head; afterwards, half a pint of rum or brandy is added, and the mixture well stirred with a spoon. Then a little nutmeg is grated on the top, which makes the flip fit for use.

This quantity is enough for four men. It is nourishing and strengthening, but in some constitutions it excites a pain in the head, and also corpulency.

Flip is also made with spruce beer, instead of malt, and then it is called callabogus.

PERRY: This liquor is the expressed juice of pears, and partakes of the nature of the fruit, as much as cyder does of the nature of apples.

PUNCH: Punch is an agreeable liquor, made of water, lemon juice, and fine sugar, and this liquor alone is called sherbet; to which if a proper quantity of rum, or brandy, is added it commences punch. Some instead of lemon juice, use lime juice, which makes what is called punch royal. This is found less liable to affect the head, and more grateful to the stomach, according to the opinion of some people.

Some also make milk punch, by adding as much milk to the sherbet, as there is water.—Others use green tea instead of water: and what is called chamber maid's punch, is made without any water, or lime juice, twice as much white wine as lime juice, and four times as much brandy with augsr.

Punch, made with lemon juice, must be antiscorbutic; but the too frequent use of it may be injurious. Some say it is prejudicial to the brain and nervous system; and also, that it generates a colic in some constitutions.

RUM: *Rum* is an ardent spirit distilled from sugar cane; but in New England, it is often distilled from molasses imported from the West Indies, which is the product of those canes.

Jamaica spirits is generally called the best *rum,* but that distilled in New England, becomes good by age, and by being carried to sea; and this I know by my own observation; for some years ago, I bought two hogsheads of New England rum, that was distilled in Salem; had been carried to the West Indies, and kept upon the water about eighteen months; it appeared colourless, was free from any disagreeable smell, and had a very pleasant taste; whereas, when it is first distilled, the odour and taste is so disagreeable that it is not fit to be drank by the human species.

Good *rum* properly diluted with water, sweetened with sugar, and drank with moderation, strengthens the lax fibres, incrassates the thin fluids, and warms the habit. It proves the most beneficial to those exposed to heat, moisture, corrupted air, and putrid diseases. . . .

Strong grog, poured down a sailor's throat, when he was apparently dead with the yellow fever in the year 1798, restored him to life and health. . . .

TODDY: This liquor is prepared by adding to three half pints of water, one of rum or brandy, a little sugar, and after stirring, a little nutmeg.

It is called a salutary liquor, and especially in the summer season, if it is drank with moderation.

WINE: Wines are considered as cordials.

Red Port is the most astringent.

Rhenish wine is detergent and laxative.

Canary is nutritious.

And the Spanish white wine, is strengthening.

Wine, according to Dr. Wallis, is stimulant, sedative, expectorant, diaphoretic, inspissant, antalkaline, and antiseptic.

Good wine stimulates the stomach, cheers the spirits, warms the habit, promotes perspiration, renders the vessels full and turgid, raises the pulse, and quickens the circulation.

Claret, Madeira, and Port, are often used with great success in fevers of a typhus kind, when the stomach is weak, rejects all food, and the wine agrees with the patient. It is good in languors, debilities, the low stage of fevers, and for resisting putrefaction; for those who are aged, weak, relaxed, and exposed to contagion, and a warm, moist corrupted air.

Some think it is hurtful in gouty and calculous complaints.

Plate 35. *Included among the paints, soaps, and medicines in this old apothecary's shop are such elixirs and other medicinal beverages as those of violets, juniper-berry, tabourey, and troubadours. (Courtesy of the New York State Historical Association, Cooperstown, New York)*

RECIPES

Now let us examine other medicinal beverages which the author's research has uncovered.

BEVERAGE FOR A WEAK CONSTITUTION: Boil as much pearl or Scotch barley, in pure water, as will make about three pints, then straining it off, and having in the mean time dissolved an ounce of gum arabic in a little water, mix them, and just boil the whole up together. The Barley water need not be thick, as the gum will give it sufficient consistence. When used, take it milk warm, the good effect will soon appear. It must be substituted as a common beverage in place of beer, ale, & c. at meals.

The Husbandman and Housewife, 1820

SPRUCE BEER: This cheap and wholesome liquor is thus made: take of water sixteen gallons, and boil the half of it; put the water thus boiled, while in full heat, to the reserved cold part, which should be previously put into the barrel or other vessel; then add 16 pounds of treacle or molasses, with a few tablespoonfuls of the essence of spruce, stirring the whole well together; add half a pint of yeast, and keep it in a temperate situation, with the bung hole open, for two days, till the fermentation be abated; then close it up, or bottle it off, and it will be fit to drink in a few days afterwards. In North America, and perhaps in other countries, where the black and white spruce firs abound, instead of adding the essence of the spruce at the same time with the molasses, they make a decoction of the leaves and small branches of these trees, and find the liquor equally good.

It is a powerful antiscorbutic, and may prove very useful in a long sea voyage.

Family Receipt Book, 1819

BUTTERMILK: If made of sweet cream, is delicious and most wholesome food. Those who can relish sour buttermilk, find it still more light; and it is reckoned more beneficial in some cases.

Domestic Cookery, 1807

CORDIAL PEPPERMINT: Take of spirits of wine two ounces; English oil of peppermint, half an ounce; mix them together; then add the spirit to a syrup made by boiling lump sugar, two pounds, in one gallon of water: good for flatulence, and to prevent the griping of aperient medicines.

Godey's Lady's Book, October 1859

SASSAFRAS COCOA: The fruit of the sassafras-tree is highly esteemed in many parts of South America, as a nutritious article of diet.

Its substance is the same as that of cocoa; and, by means of heat, is convertible into chocolate; but in this process, its aromatic quality is dissipated. This nut, in a ground state, is employed in the same manner as cocoa or coffee, by boiling it in water or milk: but, on account of its aromatic quality being very volatile, it requires to be boiled in a pot with a close cover, and not for so long a time as is requisite for cocoa. Its aromatic virtue renders it very pleasant to the palate, and agreeable to the stomach; and, at the same time, possessing the well-known correcting properties of the sassafras root, and the nutritious virtues of cocoa, it becomes a valuable article of diet to a great variety of invalids. It has been found to recruit exhaused strength more rapidly than either cocoa, chocolate, or any farinaceous substances, and to sit lighter on the stomach than either animal or vegetable jellies.

Mackenzie's 5000 Receipts, 1829

VIRTUES OF COFFEE: Coffee accelerates digestion corrects crudities, removes colic and flatulencies. It mitigates headaches, cherishes the animal spirits, takes away listlessness and languor, and is serviceable in all obstructions arising from languid circulation. It is a wonderful restorative to emaciated constitutions, and highly refreshing to the studious and sedentary.

The habitual use of coffee would greatly promote sobriety being in itself a cordial stimulant; it is a most powerful antidote to the temptation of spirituous liquors.

It will be found a welcome beverage to the robust labourer, who would despise a lighter drink.

Family Receipt Book, 1819

FOR IMPROVING COFFEE: To valetudinarians and others, the following method of making coffee for breakfast is earnestly recommended as a most wholesome and pleasant jentacular beverage, first ordered by an able physician.

Let one ounce of fresh ground coffee be put into a clean coffee-pot, or other proper vessel well thinned: pour a pint and a quarter of boiling water upon it, set it on the fire, let it boil thoroughly, and afterwards put by to settle; this should be done on the preceding night, and on the following morning pour off the clear liquor; add to it one pint of new milk; set it again over the fire, but do not let it boil, Sweetened to every person's taste, coffee thus made is a most wholesome and agreeable breakfast, summer or winter, with toast, bread and butter, rusks, biscuits, & c. This process takes off that raw, acidous, and astringent quality of the coffee, which makes it often disagree with weak stomachs. It should not be drank too warm.

A gentleman of the first fortune in the kingdom, after a variety of medical applications in vain, was restored to health by applying to the above beverage morning and afternoon.

Family Receipt Book, 1819

ACORN COFFEE: Take sound and ripe acorns, peel off the shell or husk, divide the kernels, dry them gradually, and then roast them in a close vessel or roaster, keeping them continually stirring; in doing which special care must be taken that they be not burnt or roasted too much, both which would be hurtful.

Take of these roasted acorns (ground like other coffee) half an ounce every other morning and evening, alone mixed with a dram of other coffee, and sweetened with sugar, with or without milk.

This receipt is recommended by a famous German physician, as a much esteemed, wholesome, nourishing, strengthening nutriment for mankind; which, by its medicinal qualities, has been found to cure slimy obstructions in the *viscera,* and to remove nervous complaints when other medicines have failed.

Remark: Since the duty was taken off, West India coffee is so cheap that substitutes are not worth making. On the continent the roasted roots of the wild chicory, a common weed, have been used with advantage.

Family Receipt Book, 1819

COFFEE MILK: Boil a dessert spoonful of ground coffee in about a pint of milk, a quarter of an hour;

then put into it a shaving or two of isinglass, and clear it; let it boil a few minutes, and set it on the side of the fire to fine. This is a very fine breakfast, and should be sweetened with real Lisbon sugar.

Those of a spare habit, and disposed towards affections of the lungs, would do well to make this their breakfast.

Mackenzie's 5000 Receipts, 1829

A DRINK: Boil in a gallon of water two ounces of sarsaparilla and two ounces of Spanish liquorice, until the water is reduced to three pints. This decoction may be taken at any time, even at meals; instead of water, ale, or porter; it is a good purifier of the blood, and slightly aperient.

Godey's Lady's Book, October, 1859

FLAXSEED LEMONADE: Pour one quart of boiling water over four tablespoonfuls of whole flaxseed, and steep three hours. Strain and sweeten to taste, and add the juice of two lemons. Add a little more water if the liquid seems too thick. This is soothing in colds.

The Universal Cookery Book, 1888

IMPERIAL: Take half an ounce of cream of tartar, three ounces of fresh orange or lemon-peel, four ounces of lump sugar, and three pints of boiling water. Mix together; cover the vessel till cold, then pour off the clear part for use. This is a very agreeable drink for hot weather, or in fever.

Godey's Lady's Book, August, 1866

IMPERIAL, BOTTLED: Pour a pint of boiling water on a drachm of cream of tartar, flavour with lemon-peel and sugar, and bottle.

Practical Housewife, 1860

IMPERIAL DRINK: Put half an ounce of cream of tartar, four ounces of white sugar, and three ounces of orange-peel, into a pan; pour three pints of boiling water on, strain, and cool.

Practical Housewife, 1860

INDIAN TEA: Pour a pint of boiling water on a tablespoonful of Indian meal. Add salt. When cool and settled it is transparent. It has a pleasant taste, and will remain in the stomach when other drinks are rejected.

Guide to Health, 1848

MILK-PUNCH, Hot: One quart milk, warm from the cow. Two glasses best sherry wine. Four tablespoonfuls powdered sugar. Four eggs, the yolks only, beaten light. Cinnamon and nutmeg to taste.

Bring the milk to the boiling point. Beat up the yolks and sugar together; add the wine; pour into a pitcher, and mix with it, stirring all the time, the boiling milk. Pour from one vessel to another six times, spice, and serve as soon as it can be swallowed without scalding the throat.

This is said to be an admirable remedy for a bad cold if taken in the first stages, just before going to bed at night.

Breakfast, Luncheon and Tea, 1884

ROOT BEER: For each gallon of water to be used, take hops, burdock, yellow dock, sarsaparilla, dandelion, and spikenard roots, bruised, of each ½ oz.; boil about 20 minutes, and strain while hot, add 8 or 10 drops of oils of spruce and sassafras mixed in equal proportions, when cool enough not to scald your hand, put in 2 or 3 table-spoons of yeast; molasses two-thirds of a pint, or white sugar ½ lb. gives it about the right sweetness.

Keep these proportions for as many gallons as you wish to make. You can use more or less of the roots to suit your taste after trying it; it is best to get the dry roots, or dig them and let them get dry, and of course you can add any other root known to possess medicinal properties desired in the beer. After all is mixed, let it stand in a jar with a cloth thrown over it, to work about two hours, then bottle and set in a cool place. This is a nice way to take alteratives, without taking medicine. And families ought to make it every Spring, and drink freely of it for several weeks, and thereby save, perhaps, several dollars in doctors' bills.

Dr. Chase's Recipes, 1869

ROYAL STRAWBERRY ACID: Take three pound of ripe strawberries, two ounces of citric acid, and one quart of Spring water. Dissolve the acid in the water and pour it on to the strawberries, and let them stand in a cool place twenty-four hours. Then drain the liquid off and pour it on to three pounds more of strawberries, and let it stand twenty-four hours. Then add to the liquid its own weight of sugar, boil it three or four minutes (in a porcelain lined preserve kettle, lest metal may affect the taste), and when cool, cork it in bottles lightly for three days, and then tight, and seal them. Keep it in a dry and cool place, where it will not freeze. It is very delicious for the sick, or the well.

Beecher's Receipt Book, 1857

SEIDLITZ POWDER: Half a drachm of tartaric acid, two scruples carbonate of soda, one drachm of Rochelle salts, five grains of ginger powder.

Godey's Lady's Book, Sept., 1858

SEIDLITZ POWDERS (APERIENT): Tartrate of soda, two drachms; carbonate of soda, two scruples; mix and put it in a *blue* paper; tartaric acid, thirty-five grains, to be put in *white* paper. Mix in half a pint of water.

ANOTHER—(MAY BE KEPT IN ONE BOTTLE): Tartrate of soda, three ounces; carbonate of ditto, one ounce; tartaric acid, one ounce; white sugar, four ounces; all in fine powder, well dried separately; mix well, add five drops essence of lemon; pass through a sieve, and put into a clean dry bottle. A dessert-spoonful to a glass of water. Cost, 1s. 4d., if mixed at home.

Practical Housewife, 1860

SEEDS OF CLIVERS, OR GOOSE GRASS, AS COFFEE SUBSTITUTE: Young geese are very fond of the branches of this plant; the seeds may be used instead of coffee. The expressed juice of the stems and leaves, taken to the amount of four ounces night and morning, is very efficacious in removing many of those cutaneous eruptions, which are called, though improperly, scorbutic: but it must be continued for several weeks.

Family Receipt Book, 1819

SPANISH GINGERETTE: To each gal. of water put 1 lb. of white sugar; ½ oz. best bruised ginger root; ¼ oz. of cream of tartar, and 2 lemons sliced.

Directions: In making 5 gals. boil the ginger and lemons 10 minutes in 2 gals. of the water; the sugar and cream of tartar to be dissolved in the cold water, and mix all, and add ½ pint of good yeast; let it ferment over night, strain and bottle in the morning.

This is a valuable recipe for a cooling and refreshing beverage; compounded of ingredients highly calculated to assist the stomach, and is recommended to persons suffering with Dyspepsia or Sick Headache. It is much used in European countries, and persons having once tested its virtues will constantly use it as a common drink. And for saloons, or groceries, no temperance beverage will set it aside.

Dr. Chase's Recipes, 1869

TAMARINDS OR CRANBERRY JUICE, with double the quantity of water, makes a pleasant drink for an invalid when approaching convalescence.

Godey's Lady's Book, April 1865

VIRTUES OF SAGE: This valuable herb was held in such high esteem among the ancients, that they have left us a Latin verse, which signifies, "Why should a man die whilst he has sage in his garden?"

It is reckoned admirable as a cordial, and to sweeten and cleanse the blood. It is good in nervous cases, and is given in fevers, with a view to promote perspiration. With the addition of a little lemon juice, it is very grateful and cooling; some choose to take it dry, alleging that the surface of the leaves of green sage abound with animalcules, which are very visable through a microscope, and so there are in many articles of common food; but we may be assured, even if this is the case, that as they are nourished with the sage, they are of no harm, and at all events, a little hot water will destroy them.

Family Receipt Book, 1819

COUGH TEA: Make a strong tea of everlasting—strain, and put to a quart of it two ounces of figs or raisins, two of liquorice, cut in bits. Boil them in the tea for twenty minutes, then take the tea from the fire, and add to it the juice of a lemon. This is an excellent remedy for a tight cough—it should be drank freely, being perfectly innocent. It is the most effectual when hot.

Kitchen Directory, 1846

BRITISH HERB TEA: Take of hawthorn leaves, dried two parts, sage and balm one part; mix these well together, and they will make an excellent and pleasant sanative tea, particularly wholesome to nervous people.

Family Receipt Book, 1819

NATIVE TEA: The infusion of good well-made meadow hay in boiling water, in the manner of tea, about three quarters of an ounce for two or three persons, is a beverage for the fasting and evening reflection, as much superior to the dried leaves of China, as gold or silver are superior to copper and lead.

This native tea is as healthful as it is grateful to the palate; it is saccharine and aromatic, instead of bitter and empyreumatic; it is stimulating to the spirits in the morning, and composing to the nerves at night; it is anti-bilious, and acts with a mild, but sensible effect, at first, on all the secretions, promotes digestion and creates appetite.

Mackenzie's 5000 Receipts, 1829

BRITISH SUBSTITUTE FOR FOREIGN TEA: Betony, if gathered when just going to flower, has the taste of tea, and all the good qualities of it, without the bad ones, and moreover, it cures inveterate headaches.

ANOTHER: Make an infusion of ground ivy, which is very agreeable in flavour, especially if you add to it a drop or two of lemon juice. It is reported by many, that the habitual use of this herb will cure the most obstinate consumption. It is certainly a good pectoral, and when green is fragrant; if mixed with a few flowers of lavender, it makes a most agreeable liquor for summer use; and, if gathered at a proper time, has an agreeable taste to many, but wholesome to all, even when dry.

Family Receipt Book, 1819

ANTIMONIAL WINE: Tartrite of antimony, twenty-four grains, Spanish white wine, one pound. Mix them so that the tartrite of antimony may be dissolved.

Tartrite of antimony dissolved in wine, can be preserved longer without decomposition than when dissolved in water; but, even on long keeping, part of the antimonial oxide is deposited. In its employment and effects, the vinous solution of tartar emetic does not differ from one made with water. It is given as an emetic in the dose of one ounce; as a diaphoretic, in a much smaller dose. It contains two grains of tartrite of antimony in the ounce, but it is not of sufficient strength. The formula directed by the London and Doublin Colleges, containing four grains in the ounce, will be found more convenient in practice.

In the old formula for the preparation of *antimonial wine,* vitrified (glass of) antimony was directed to be used; but as the tartarous acid contained in the wine acts on the oxide of antimony, and renders part of it soluble, the quantity must be uncertain, and the wine cannot be uniform in strength. The preparation, therefore, ought to be entirely rejected, since its strength cannot be known.

Thacher's Dispensatory, 1813

BARLEY WINE: Boil half a pound of fresh barley in 3 waters, and save 3 pints of the last water. Mix it with a quart of white wine, half a pint of borage water, as much clary water, a little red rose-water, the juice of 5 or 6 lemons, 3 quarters of a pound of fine sugar, and the thin yellow rind of a lemon. Mix all these well together, run it through a strainer, and bottle it. It is pleasant in hot weather, and very good in fevers.

Mackenzie's 5000 Receipts, 1829

COMPOUND WINE OF GENTIAN (BITTER WINE): Take of Root of gentian sliced and bruised, half an ounce, Red bark of cinchona in powder, one ounce, External rind of Seville oranges, dried and bruised, two drachms, Bark of canella alba in powder, one drachm, Diluted alcohol, four ounces, Spanish white wine, two pounds and a half.

First, pour on the diluted alcohol, and after twenty-four hours, add the wine; then macerate for seven days and filtrate.

This wine is intended to supply the place of the Vinum Amarum, as it was formerly called.

Wine is fully capable of extracting the active power of the different ingredients; and it supplies us with a very useful and elegant stomachic medicine. Its dose is six drachms.

Thacher's Dispensatory, 1813

KOUMISS, A VALUABLE WINE OF THE TARTARS: Take of fresh mare's milk, of one day, any quantity; add to it a sixth-part water, and pour the mixture into a wooden vessel; use then, as a ferment, an eighth-part of the sourest cow's milk that can be got; but at any future preparation, a small portion of old koumiss will better answer the purpose of souring. Cover the vessel with a thick cloth, and set it in place of moderate warmth; leave it at rest twenty-four hours; at the end of which time the milk will have become sour, and a thick substance will be gathered on its top; then, with a stick, made at the lower end in the manner of churn staff, beat it till the thick substance above mentioned be blended intimately with the subjacent fluid. In this situation leave it again at rest for twenty-four hours more; after which, pour it into a higher and narrower vessel, resembling a churn, where the agitation must be repeated as before, till the liquor appear to be perfectly homogeneous; and in this state it is called koumiss: of which the taste ought to be a pleasant mixture of sweet and sour. Agitation must be employed every time before it is used. This wine operates as a cooling antiseptic, an useful stimulant, cordial, and tonic, and may prove a valuable article of nourishment; and it has one excellence, perhaps not the least, that the materials from which it is prepared are cheap, and the mode of preparation simple.

Family Receipt Book, 1819

RHUBARB WINE: Take of sliced rhubarb, 2½ oz.—lesser cardamom seeds, bruised and husked, ½ oz.; saffron 2 drachms; Spanish white wine, 2 pints; proof spirit, ½ pint. Digest for ten days, and strain. This is a warm, cordial, laxative medicine. It is used chiefly in weakness of the stomach and bowels, and some kinds of loosenesses, for evacuating the offending matter and strengthening the tone of the viscera. It may be given in doses of from half a spoonful to three or four spoonsful or more, according to the circumstances of the disorder, and the strength of the patient.

Mackenzie's 5000 Receipts, 1829

SCURVY-GRASS WINE: Scurvy-grass, or spoonwort, is a very sovereign medicinal herb, appropriated chiefly to the health of invalids.

Take the best large scurvy-grass tops and leaves in May, June, or July, bruise them well in a stone mortar, then put them in a well glazed earthen vessel, and sprinkle them over with some powder of crystal of tartar, then smear them with virgin honey, and being covered close, let it stand 24 hours; then set water over a gentle fire, putting to every gallon 3 pints of honey, and when the scum rises, take it off, and let it cool; then put the stamped scurvy-grass into a barrel, and pour the liquor to it, setting the vessel conveniently end-ways, with a tap at the bottom. When it has been infused 24 hours, draw off the liquor, strongly press the juice and moisture out of the herb into the barrel or vessel, and put the liquor up again; then put a little new yeast to it, and suffer it to ferment 3 days, covering the place of the bung or vent with a piece of bread spread over with mustard seed, downward, in a cool place, and let it continue till it is fine and drinks brisk; then draw off the finest part, leaving only the dregs behind: afterwards add more herbs, and ferment it with whites of eggs, flour, and fixed nitre, verjuice, or the juice of green grapes, if they are to be had; to which add 6 pounds of the syrup of mustard, all mixed and well beaten together, to refine it down, and it will drink brisk, but is not very pleasant; being here inserted among artificial wines rather for the sake of health, than for the delightfulness of its taste.

Mackenzie's 5000 Receipts, 1829

TURNIP WINE: Pare and slice a number of turnips, put them into a cider press, and press out all the juice. To every gallon of the juice, add three pounds of lump sugar; have a vessel ready large enough to hold the juice, and put half a pint of brandy to every gallon. Pour in the juice and lay something over the bung for a week, to see if it works; if it does, do not bung it down till it has done working; then stop it close for three months, and draw it off into another vessel. When it is fine, bottle it off.

This is an excellent wine for gouty habits, and is much recommended in such cases in lieu of any other wine.

Mackenzie's 5000 Receipts, 1829

WINE BITTERS: Take poplar 2 lbs., bayberry 1 lb., goldenseal, balmony, unicorn, quassia chips, and scull-cap 4 oz., cayenne 2 oz. Put into water and boil in a covered vessel to 2 quarts. Strain, add 3 lbs. of sugar, scald and skim. Then steep by a gentle heat, prickly ash berries, cinnamon and all-spice, 2 oz. each, in a gallon of sweet malaga wine, strain, and add to the above when cold. *Dose.*—A wine-glassful 2 or 3 times a day.

2nd Formula.—Take balmony, bayberry, cassia buds, and bitter-root 8 oz., golden seal 12 oz., anise seed 4 oz., cloves 2 oz., cayenne 1 oz., brown sugar 3 lbs., pulverized and mixed; put 1 oz. of the powder steeped in hot water to a quart of wine. These are said to be the celebrated wine bitters prepared by Dr. John Thomson. The wine bitters are a very pleasant restorative for debilitated people and convalescents. Very useful in dyspepsia, sick-headache, heart-burn,

Plate 36. *This druggist shop, originally a doctor's office in Hartwick, New York, was built in 1832. The apothecary was often busy preparing herbs and other ingredients. Among those used for medicinal beverages were prickly ash bark, balsam of Peru, beaver tree, black cherry bark, Guinea pepper, petty morrel, wood sorrel berries, and mint. (Courtesy of the New York State Historical Association, Cooperstown, New York.*

sinking, torpid feelings, and when-ever a tonic is required.

Book of Health, 1843

WINE OF IPECACUAN: Take of root of ipecacuan in powder, one ounce, Spanish white wine, fifteen ounces. Macerate for seven days and filtrate through paper.

This medicated wine is preferable to a tincture of ipecacuan, as being less pungent, while it holds the active matter of the root fully dissolved. Its dose, as an emetic, is one ounce to an adult.

Thacher's New Dispensatory, 1813

WINE OF IRON: Take of purified filings of iron, one ounce, Spanish white wine, sixteen ounces. Digest for a month, often shaking the vessel, and then filtrate.

This is merely a solution of tartarized iron in wine; for the iron is only dissolved in the wine by means of the super-tartrite of potass it contains. But a solution of a known proportion of tartarized iron in wine, will give a medicine of more equal powers, and may be made extemporaneously. The dose is from a drachm to half an ounce, twice or thrice a day in chlorotic cases.

Thacher's New Dispensatory, 1813

WINE OF RHUBARB: Take of root of rhubarb sliced, two ounces, bark of canella alba bruised, one drachm, diluted alcohol, two ounces, Spanish white wine, fifteen ounces.

Macerate for seven days and filtrate through paper.

This is a warm, cordial, laxative medicine. It is used chiefly in weakness of the stomach and bowels, and some kinds of loosenesses, for evacuating the offending matter, and strengthening the tone of the vicera. Its dose as a purgative is from half an ounce to an ounce.

Thacher's New Dispensatory, 1813

WINE OF SACRED TINCTURE: Take of gum resin of socotorine aloes in powder, one ounce, lesser cardamom seeds bruised, root of ginger bruised, each one drachm, Spanish white wine, two pounds.

Digest for seven days, stirring now and then, and afterwards filtrate.

This medicine has long been in great esteem, not only as a cathartic, but likewise as a stimulus. It appears, from long experience, to be a medicine of great utility. The dose, as a purgative, is from one to two ounces. It may be introduced into the habit, so as to be productive of excellent effects as an alterant, by giving it in small doses, at proper intervals; thus managed, it does not for a considerable time operate remarkably by stool; but at length proves purgative, and occasions a lax habit of much longer continuance, than that produced by other cathartics.

Thacher's New Dispensatory, 1813

WINE OF TOBACCO: Take of dried leaves of tobacco sliced, one ounce, Spanish white wine, one pound.

Macerate for seven days and filtrate through paper.

We have already, under the article Nicotina in the Materia Medica, offered some observations upon its introduction into practice by Dr. Fowler, as a very useful remedy in the cure of dropsies and dysuries. From his treatise on that subject, the present formula is taken; and we may observe, that while in practice, we have frequently experienced from tobacco those good effects, for which Dr. Fowler recommends it, we are inclined to give the present formula the preference to every other which he has proposed.

Dose, thirty drops, gradually increased to sixty or eighty, twice a day.

Thacher's New Dispensatory, 1813

CHAPTER SEVEN

Wines

HISTORICAL BACKGROUND

THE VARIOUS PREPARATIONS of wines go back to ancient times. Sir Edward Barry in his *Oservations Historical, Critical, and Medical, on the Wines of the Ancients,* 1775, discloses the results of his long and arduous research concerning "previous preparations of the wines of the ancients" in an extensive book which he dedicates to his son, Dr. Nathaniel Barry.

According to Barry, "the custom of cooling Wines with snow was derived from the *Asiatics* and *Greeks* to the *Romans*. In *Dio,* Liber LX, Barry finds evidence that *Plutarch* describes their method of preserving it by covering it with straw and "course cloths unshorn." *Xenophon* is quoted as saying it was necessary to procure snow "to cool the Wines in summer, which otherwise could not be drank with any pleasure." Barry adds, "The *Orientals* more early used it for this purpose, and *Athenaeus* mentions it as an ancient custom, and that they used oak branches for the same purpose." Barry explains that various instances among the eastern nations of this custom of cooling their Wines may be produced, and particularly among the Jews. "In some hot countries it was often difficult to obtain it, and they were obliged to search into the hollow cliffs to collect it. Mount Hebron, which was always covered with snow, plentifully supplied the inhabitants of that country, from whence it was often carried to Tyre."

Barry refers to Atheneus' account of Aristotle's character when his pupils noting his declining health asked him which of the two candidates, Theophrastus of Lesbos, or Menedemus of Rhodes, he would recommend to succeed him in the philosophic school. "He then ordered some *Lesbian* and *Rhodian* Wine to be brought to him, and having tasted and examined both for some time with great attention, he said they were both good; but that the *Lesbian* was most agreeable."

John Heyman, professor of the Oriental languages in the University of Leyden, in

1775, and AEgidius Van Egmont, envoy to the King of Naples, published an account of their observations on the present state of Asia Minor, after extensive travels in that area. As Barry refers to their account, "In their journey from *Ephesus,* they give a curious description of a prospect they enjoyed, of a successive course of hills and mountains extending from Thence, and of a beautiful valley at the bottom of them, through which the river *Cayster* flowed, and emptied itself into the sea. Among these the lofty *Timolus* rises eminent above the rest; but more distinguished for the excellence of its wines; nor was the *Cayster* less celebrated by the poets. . . . " At the bottom of one of the mountains lies Sardis, "the metropolis of *Lydia.*"

Barry describes Lydia as—

This delightful country is now but thinly inhabited by a few poor *Turks,* and some wandering *Arabs;* and few Wines are now made there but by some *Greek* monks, and chiefly for their own use. Some of these, though made with little art and culture, are light, generous, and very agreeable. But these gentlemen give a different account of a town called *Sidonijah,* which was famous for the goodness of its Wines, and the quantities made there.

Barry continued his discussion of Sardis, the metropolis of Lydia.

This town is four hours journey distant from *Damascus,* in the extremity of a fertile extended plain, the see of a bishop, and entirely inhabited by *Greek* Christians. These, particularly the clergy, pretend that if any *Turk,* or person of a different nation, was to inhabit there, some terrible misfortune would attend them. Some of the grapes here are of a remarkable size, as large as a pigeon's egg, and of a very exquisite taste. Great quantities of them are sent into *Europe,* and known by the name of Damask raisins. The Wines are not made from this kind of grapes, which are chiefly cultivated in their gardens, but from the Vines of the adjacent mountains, of which *Herman* and *Lebanon* are most continguous. *Baccius,* observes, that from this last, Wines were made in his time not inferiour to any of *Italy* or *Spain;* and these gentlemen say, that the Wine which they drank there, was indeed incomparable. The best is made by the monks, who have there a celebrated convent. It was of a red colour, very generous, grateful, and so light as not to affect the head, though taken freely.

In a discussion of the medical qualities of the wines of the ancients, Barry concludes that "the rules given by *Hippocrates* are the only true standard, by which the qualities of all Wines, both ancient and modern, can be known." Barry adds, "Hippocrates was the first who applied Wine to medical uses, and has directed *three* different mixtures of the strong Wines, from the first common standard, to another of greater strength, and to a third, which was the extreme degree of strength, which he assigned to those vinous mixtures, which acquired this *increasing* strength, by gradually lessening the quantity of water, though he occasionally varied them. In the same manner . . . he reduced the strength of the Weak Wines . . . to their greatest weakness, . . . "

Barry depicts Hippocrates as being very familiar with the various qualities of "all kinds of ailments of the animal and vegetable kind, and all kinds of liquids, Wine, water, vinegar, oil, milk, honey, and their different combinations. All these," writes Barry, "he (Hippocrates) has particularly described, and thinks the knowledge of them necessary to a physician."

Hippocrates took a strong stand in regard

to the diet. Barry observes, "There is no precept which he more frequently repeats and inculcates, than not to make any rash change in that habitual regimen of diet, to which nature has been long accustomed and *delighted* in; and when from any disease a different regimen is necessary, it ought to be as *similar* to the former, as is consistent with the nature of it."

Barry concludes that "We find therefore that *Hippocrates* made use of but few medicines of the pharmaceutic kind; and his medical dietic regimen, evacuations, and his vinous medicines, were the principal aids on which he chiefly depended in the cure of diseases."

WINEMAKING INSTRUCTIONS

The following instructions on how to make British wines are included in *Mackenzie's 5,000 Receipts* (1829):

TO MAKE BRITISH WINES: The different processes in wine making, range themselves under the following heads:

Gathering the fruit, picking the fruit, bruising the fruit, and vatting the fruit.

Vinous fermentation, flavouring the wine, drawing the wine, drawing the must, pressing the husk, casking the must.

Spirituous fermentation, racking the wine, fining the wine, bottling and corking the wine.

GATHERING THE FRUIT: Fruit of every sort, says Mr. Carnell, in his excellent treatise on wine making, should be gathered in fine weather; those of the berry kind often appear ripe to the eye before they are really so, therefore it is requisite to taste them several times in order to ascertain that they are arrived at the crisis of maturity. If the fruit be not ripe, the wine will be harsh and hard, unpleasant to the palate, and more so the stomach; it will also require more spirit and saccharine, and take a longer time to be fit for the table. If the fruit be too ripe, the wine from it will be faint, low, and vapid; it will not be strong and generous; it will also require more trouble, additional spirit, and expense.

PICKING: Detach the unripe and bad berries: the result, when the wine is drank, will be greatly superior in richness. Pick stalks from grapes, currants, and gooseberries, previously to their being placed in the vat.

BRUISING: The quantity of fruit for making a vintage of domestic wine, is not so large but it may be bruised in a tub, and from thence removed into the vat, or if the quantity be very small, it may be bruised in the vat. While the fruit is picked by one person, another may bruise it, and as it is bruised, remove it into the vat. When Malaga or Smyrna raisins are used, they are to be put into the vat with the water, to soak, and the following day taken out and bruised, then returned into the vat again.

VATTING: The first thing to be done is to place the guard against the tap-hole, to prevent the husks escaping at the time the must or extract is drawn off. When all the fruit is in the vat the water should be added, and the contents stirred with the vat-staff, and left to macerate until the next day, when sugar, tartar, & c. diluted with some of the liquor, is to be put into the vat, and the whole again stirred up. The place where the vat is situated should have a free circulation of air, and a temperature of not less that 58 degrees. If the vinous fermentation do not take place in a reasonable time, the contents must be often stirred, and the place made warmer.

VINOUS FERMENTATION: The time of a vinous fermentation commencing is always uncertain; it depends much on the quality and quantity of the contents of the vat, on its local situation, on the season or weather, and most particularly on the greenness or ripeness of the fruit. To produce a medium vinous fermentation, the vats and contents ought to be placed in a temperature from 60 to 70 degrees. And if this is found not to produce fermentation in a short time, the temperature of the place must be made warmer, and the vat often stirred with the vat-staff.

The commencement of the vinous fermentation may be known by plunging the thermometer into the middle of the vat, for a minute, and when taken out, if a fermentation has commenced, the temperature of the contents will be higher than at the place where the vats are situated. When the vinous fermentation begins, it is very conspicuous, and may be known by its taste, smell, appearance, and effects. The contents will first gently rise, and swell with a slight movement and a little hissing. A considerable motion will take place, and the contents will increase in heat and bulk, while a quantity of air escapes.

It is impossible to lay down an exact time for a vinous fermentation; but for eighteen gallons, two or three days are generally sufficient for white wines; and red wines require a day or two more.

FLAVOURING THE WINE: When the vinous fermentation is about half over, the flavouring ingredients are to be put into the vat and well stirred into the contents. If almonds form a component part, they are first to be beaten to a paste and mixed with a pint or two of the must. Nutmegs, cinnamon, ginger, seeds, & c. should, before they are put into the vat, be reduced to powder, and mixed with some of the must.

DRAWING THE MUST: When the must in the vat gives, by tasting, a strong vinous pungency, that is the period to stop the remaining slight fermentation by drawing off the must, in order to have strong and generous wine.

A cock, or spicket and faucet is to be put into the tap-hole of the vat, and the must drawn off and put into open vessels, there to remain till the pressing is finished.

PRESSING THE HUSK: As soon as all the must is drawn off from the vat, the husks are to be put into hair-bags, and the mouth of the bag is to be well fastened, then put into the press, and the whole pressed without delay. The must that is pressed out is to be mixed with the must that was drawn off from the vat. Many ways may be contrived for pressing a small vintage, for those persons who cannot afford to purchase a proper wine-press; but several wines do not require pressing: and may be strained through a sweet clean, canvass bag, made with a pointed end downwards.

CASKING THE MUST: Each cask is to be filled within about an inch of the bung-hole, which should be covered over lightly with a flat piece of wood. The must now is perfectly cool and calm, and will remain in this state until the spirituous fermentation commences.

SPIRITUOUS FERMENTATION: The spirituous fermentation is essentially necessary to the clarification, goodness, and perfection of the wine. If the vinous fermentation has been well conducted, and the wine cellar be not too cold, a spirituous fermentation will commence in a few days, and abate in six or twelve days, the time depending on circumstances, and on the quality and quantity of the wine. The brandy or spirit assigned should at this time be put to the wine by pouring it in gently without disturbing the wine. The cask now, if not full, must be filled up and bunged with a wooden bugn covered with a piece of new canvass larger than the bung. In about a month after the spirit has been added, the cask will again want filling up, this should be done with the overplus of the vintage, if not with some other good wine, and the cask re-bunged very tight.

The cask should be pegged once a month or oftener to see if the wine be clear and not thick, and as soon as it is fine and bright, it must be racked off its lees.

RACKING THE WINE: This is an operation highly requisite to the keeping wine good; to its purification, strength, colour, brilliancy, richness, and flavour, and is performed by drawing off the wine and leaving the lees in the cask. A siphon should be used: but if not, the cask should be tapped two or three days previously. It may be racked off into another cask, or into a vat or tub, and returned into the same cask again, after it has been well cleaned: and, if requisite, the cask may be slightly fumigated, immediately before the wine is returned into it. If the wine, on being tasted, is found weak, a little spirit is to be given to it, the cask filled up and bunged tight.

The racking off ought to be performed in temperate weather, and as soon as the wines appear clear, a second racking will make them perfectly brilliant, and if so, they will want no fining.

FINING: Many wines require fining before they are racked, and the operation of fining is not always necessary. Most wines, well made, do not want fining; this may be ascertained by drawing a little into a glass, from a peg-hole.

One of the best finings is as follows:—Take one pound of fresh marsh-mallow roots, washed clean, and cut into small pieces; macerate them in two quarts of soft water, for twenty-four hours, then gently boil the liquor down to three half pints, strain it, and when cold mix with it half an ounce of pipe-clay or chalk in powder, then pour the mucilage into the cask, and stir up the wine so as not to disturb the lees, and leave the vent-peg out for some days after.

Or, take boiled rice, two table-spoonsful, the white of one new egg, and half an ounce of burnt alum, in powder. Mix with a pint or more of the wine, then pour the mucilage into the cask, and stir the wine with a stout stick, but not to agitate the lees.

Or, dissolve, in a gentle heat, half an ounce of isinglass in a pint or more of the wine, then mix with it half an ounce of chalk, in powder; when the two are well incorporated, pour it into the cask, and stir the wine, so as not to disturb the lees.

As soon as wines are clear and bright, after being fined down, they ought to be racked into a sweet and clean cask, the cask filled up and bunged tight.

BOTTLING AND CORKING: Fine clear weather is best for bottling all sorts of wines, and much cleanliness is required. The first consideration, in bottling wines, is to examine and see if the wines are in a proper state. *The wines should be fine and brilliant,* or they will never brighten after.

The bottles must be all sound, clean and dry, with plenty of good sound corks.

The cork is to be put in with the hand, and then driven well in with a flat wooden mallet, the weight of which ought to be a pound and a quarter, but however, not to exceed a pound and a half, for if the mallet be too light or too heavy it will not drive the cork in properly, and may break the bottle. The corks must so completely fill up the neck of each bottle as to render them air tight, but leave a space of an inch between the wine and the cork.

When all the wine is bottled, it is to be stored in a cool cellar, and on no account on the bottles' bottoms, but on their sides and in saw-dust.

APPARATUS FOR WINE MAKING: To make wine well, and with facility, persons should have all the requisite apparatus, namely, the vats, vat-staff, fruit-bruiser, strainer, hair-bags, wine-press, thermometer, and bottling machine.

Mackenzie's 5000 Receipts, 1829

COLORING FOR WINES: White sugar 1 lb.; water 1 gill; put into an iron kettle, let boil, and burn to a red black, and thick; remove from the fire and add a little hot water to keep it from hardening as it cools; then bottle for use.

Dr. Chase's Receipes, 1869

TO DISCOVER INJURIOUS METALS IN WINE: The property of liver of sulphur, and of hepatic gas, in precipitating lead of a black colour, has been long known; and that property has been made use of to ascertain the goodness of wine, in the preparation of *liquor probatorius Wurtembergiensis.*

But in trying wines which we suspect to be adulterated, that proof does more harm than good; because it precipitates the iron of the same colour with the pernicious lead; by which means, some dealers of respectable characters have been ruined.

It was wanting, therefore, to find an agent which would discover nothing in wine but what was prejudicial to health. This is accomplished by the following test, which precipitates lead and copper of a black colour, arsenic of an orange colour, & c. but does not iron, which being innocent, or rather salutary, to the human constitution, gets into a great number of different sorts of wine by various accidents.

Family Receipt Book, 1819

dance mehitabel dance
caper and shake a leg
what little blood is left
will fizz like wine *in a keg*

DON MARQUIS, *archy and mehitabel*

RECIPES

AMERICAN WINE: (Originally communicated to the public by Joseph Cooper, Esq. of New Jersey, North America).

"I put a quantity of the comb, from which the honey had been drained, into a tub, and added a barrel of cider, immediately from the press; this mixture was well stirred, and left for one night. It was then strained before a fermentation took place; and honey was added, until the strength of the liquor was sufficient to bear an egg. It was then put into a barrel; and after the fermentation commenced, the cask was filled every day, for three or four days, that the filth might work out of the bung-hole. When the fermentation moderated, I put the bung in loosely, lest stopping it tight might cause the cask to burst. At the end of five or six weeks, the liquor was drawn off into a tub; and the whites of eight eggs, well beat up, with a pint of clean sand, were put into it: I then added a gallon of cider spirit; and after mixing the whole well together, I returned it into the cask, which was well cleaned, bunged it tight, and placed it in a proper situation for racking off, when fine. In the month of April following, I drew it off into kegs, for use; and found it equal, in my opinion, to almost any foreign wine: in the opinion of many judges, it was superior.

"This success has induced me to repeat the experiment for three years; and I am persuaded, that by using clean honey, instead of the comb as above described, such an improvement might be made, as would enable the citizens of the United States to supply themselves with a truly federal and wholesome wine, which would not cost a quarter of a dollar per gallon, were all the ingredients procured at the market price; and would have this peculiar advantage over every other wine hitherto attempted in this country, that it contains no foreign mixture, but is made from ingredients produced on our own farms."

Family Receipt Book, 1819

APPLE WHITE WINE: Take of cold soft water, 2 gallons, apples, well bruised, 3 bushels, honey, 10 lbs., white tartar, 2 ounces, 1 nutmeg, in powder, rum, 3 quarts. This will make 18 gallons.

Mackenzie's 5000 Receipts, 1829

APPLE WINE: To every gallon of apple juice, immediately as it comes from the press, add 2 lbs. of common loaf sugar; boil it as long as any scum rises, then strain it through a sieve, and let it cool; add some good yeast, and stir it well; let it work in the tub for two or three weeks, or till the head begins to flatten, then skim off the head, draw it clear off, and turn it. When made a year, rack it off, and fine it with isinglass; then add ½ a pint of the best rectified spirit of wine, or a pint of French brandy, to every 8 gallons.

Mackenzie's 5000 Receipts, 1829

APPLE RED WINE: Take of cold soft water, 2 gallons, apples, well bruised, 3 bushels. Ferment. Mix, raw sugar, 15 lbs., beet root, sliced 4 lbs., red tartar, in fine powder, 3 oz. then add ginger, in powder, 3 oz. rosemary and lavender leaves, of each two handsful, British spirits, 2 quarts. This will make 18 gallons.

Mackenzie's 5000 Receipts, 1829

APRICOT WINE: Boil together three pounds of sugar, and three quarts of water; and skim it well. Put in six pounds of apricots pared and stoned, and let them boil till they become tender. Then take them up, and when the liquor is cold, bottle it. After taking out the apricots, let the liquor be boiled with a sprig of flowered clary. The apricots will make marmalade, and be very good for present use.

Mackenzie's 5000 Receipts, 1829

BALM WINE: Take 40 pounds of sugar and 9 gallons of water, boil it gently for 2 hours, skim it well, and put it into a tub to cool. Take 2 pounds and a half of the tops of balm, bruise them, and put them into a barrel, with a little new yeast; and when the liquor is cold, pour it on the balm. Stir it well together and let it stand 24 hours, stirring it often. Then close it up, and let it stand 6 weeks. Then rack it off and put a lump of sugar into every bottle. Cork it well, and it will be better the second year than the first.

Mackenzie's 5000 Receipts, 1829

BIRCH WINE: The season for obtaining the liquor from birchtrees, is in the latter end of February, or the beginning of March, before the leaves shoot out, and as the sap begins to rise. If the time is delayed, the juice will grow too thick to be drawn out. It should be as thin and clear as possible. The method of procuring the juice is by boring holes in the trunk of the

Plate 37. *Barroom of the Bump Tavern which beckons the traveller as it did long ago. The pewter tankards, dark green wine bottles, horn tumblers, pewter measures, large earthen mugs, huge carboy used for shipping imported rum, and cider jug all were to be found in the well-equipped tavern bar of 1800. The mantle painting is from the old Van Bergen house built in 1720 at Leeds, New York. The tables are set with pewter plates, trencher, wooden butter dish, and dark green "junk" bottles. (Courtesy of the New York State Historical Association, Cooperstown, New York)*

tree, and fixing faucets of elder; but care should be taken not to tap it in too may places at once, for fear of injuring the tree. If the tree is large, it may be bored in five or six places at once, and bottles are to be placed under the aperture for the sap to flow into. When four or five gallons have been extracted from different trees, cork the bottles very close, and wax them till the wine is to be made, which should be as soon as possible after the sap has been obtained. Boil the sap, and put four pounds of loaf sugar to every gallon, also the peel of a lemon cut thin; then boil it again for nearly an hour, skimming it all the time.

Now pour it into a tub, and as soon as it is almost cold, work it with a toast spread with yeast, and let it stand five or six days, stirring it twice or three times each day. Into a cask that will contain it, put a lighted brimstone match, stop it up till the match is burnt out, and then pour the wine into it, putting the bung lightly in, till it has done working. Bung it very close for about three months, and then bottle it. It will be good in a week after it is put into the bottles.

ANOTHER: Birch wine may be made with raisins, in the following manner: To a hogshead of birch-water, take four hundred of Malaga raisins: pick them clean from the stalks, and cut them small. Then boil the birch liquor for one hour at least, skim it well, and let it stand till it be no warmer than milk. Then put in the raisins, and let it stand close covered, stirring it well four or five times every day. Boil all the stalks in a gallon or two of birch liquor, which, when added to the other, when almost cold, will give it an agreeable roughness. Let it stand ten days, then put it in a cool cellar, and when it has done hissing in the vessel, stop it up close. It must stand at least nine months before it is bottled.

Mackenzie's 5000 Receipts, 1829

BLACKBERRY WINE: Take ripe blackberries; mash them well either with the hands or some broad wooden spoon; then strain the juice through a strong bag. Have your cask measured, and allow one-third of its contents to be pure juice. As soon as the juice is measured, put it into the cask, which must now be placed in a firm position in the cellar, with spigot provided, so that it may be drawn off without having to move the cask. For every gallon that the cask will hold allow three pounds of brown sugar, and dissolve it in a bucket of water, stirring well; then pour this into the cask, and add more water to the sugar remaining in the bucket until all of it is in the cask; then fill up with water to the bung, and leave it open for ten days to ferment. On the tenth day, remove from around the bung-hole all the froth that has collected, using the little finger to reach that inside; then add to a six-gallon cask a half-teacupful of good brandy, and immediately put in the bung pretty tightly. In a day or two, pound it in securely, and let the cask remain undisturbed until the first of January, when it may be quietly racked off, and will be found perfectly clear until the sediment in the bottom is reached. Like all other wine, it improves with age; and although when first drawn it is of a light-red color, it will soon acquire a rich wine tint.

In making all kinds of wine, care must be taken to have the cask perfectly sweet, or the wine will be likely to be sour. If it should smell sour or doubtful, it will be best to have it soaking for a few days beforehand, with a little washing-soda dissolved in the water, rinsing it well before using. Old casks are more desirable than new ones, as, the first time they are used, the wine is likely to taste of the wood.

The Art of Confectionery, 1866

BLACKBERRY WINE: The following is said to be an excellent receipe for the manufacture of a superior wine from blackberries:—Measure your berries and bruise them, to every gallon add one quart of boiling water. Let the mixture stand twenty-four hours, stirring occasionally, then strain off the liquor into a cask; to every gallon add two pounds of sugar; cork tight, and let stand till the following October.

Mrs. Winslow's Receipt Book, 1875

BLACK CURRANT WINE: Take of cold soft water, 10 gallons; black currants, 6 do.; strawberries, 3 do. Ferment. Mix, raw sugar, 25 lbs.; red tartar, in fine powder, 6 oz. orange-thyme, 2 handsful; then add brandy, 2 or 3 quarts. This will make eighteen gallons.

ANOTHER: Take of cold soft water, 12 gallons; black currants, 5 do.; white or red currants, or both, 3 do. Ferment. Mix, raw sugar, 30 lbs. or less; red tartar, in fine powder, 5 oz.; ginger in powder, 5 oz.; then add brandy, 1 gallon, or less. This will make 18 gallons.

ANOTHER, VERY FINE: To every three quarts of juice, add as much of cold water, and to every three quarts of the mixture, add three pounds of good, pure sugar. Put it into a cask, reserving some to fill up. Set the cask in a warm dry room, and it will ferment of itself. When this is over, skim off the refuse, and fill up with what you have reserved for this purpose. When it has done working, add three quarts of brandy to forty quarts of the wine. Bung it up close for ten months, then bottle it. The thick part may be separated by straining, and the percolating liquor be bottled also. Keep it for twelve months.

Mackenzie's 5000 Receipts, 1829

BRITISH CHAMPAGNE: Take gooseberries before they grow ripe, crush them with a mallet in a wooden bowl, and to every gallon of fruit put a gallon of water; let it stand two days, stirring it well; squeeze the mixture well with your hands through a hop-sieve; then measure your liquor, and to every gallon put three pounds and a half of loaf sugar; mix it well in the tub, and let it stand one day: put a bottle of the best brandy in the cask; leave the cask open five or six weeks, taking off the scum as it rises; then make it up, and let it stand one year in the barrel before bottled.

N.B. One pint of brandy is put to seven gallons of liquor.

Family Receipt Book, 1819

CHEAP AND WHOLESOME CLARET: Take a quart of fine draft Devonshire cider, and an equal quantity of good port. Mix them, and shake them. Bottle them and let them stand for a month. The best judge will not be able to distinguish them from good Bordeaux.

Mackenzie's 5,000 Receipts, 1829

CHERRY WINE: Take twenty-four pounds of the finest ripe cherries, (the black English cherry is to be preferred), and after removing defective ones, bruise them in a cloth and press out the juice as dry as possible. Then take the skins and stones, and pound them with a mallet so as to crush the stones and kernels, and put them into the juice again. When it has fermented twelve hours, strain it through a large flannel bag into a pan containing one pound of loaf sugar. Squeeze the bag with the hands, so as to extract as much juice as possible. When the sugar is dissolved, put the liquor into bottles, filling each within an inch of the cork; cork it loosely for a day or two, then cork it tight, and keep it three months before use, in a cool place, or buried in sand in the cellar.

The Young Housekeeper's Friend, 1846

CHERRY WINE: Take of cold soft water, 10 gallons —cherries, 10 gallons—Ferment. Mix raw sugar, 30 lbs.—red tartar, in fine powder, 3 oz. Add brandy, 2 or 3 quarts. This will make 18 gallons.

Two days after the cherries have been in the vat, Mr. Carnell says, we should take out about 3 quarts of the cherry stones, break them and the kernels, and return them into the vat again.

ANOTHER: Take cherries nearly ripe, of any red sort, clear them of the stalks and stones, then put them into a glazed earthen vessel, and squeeze them to a pulp. Let them remain in this state for 12 hours to ferment; then put them into a linen cloth not too fine and press out the juice with a pressing board, or any other convenient instrument. Now let the liquor stand till the scum rises, and with a ladle or skimmer take it clean off; then pour the clear part, by inclination, into a cask, where, to each gallon, put a pound of the best loaf sugar, and let it ferment for seven or eight days. Draw it off, when clear, into lesser casks or bottles; keep it cool, as other wines, and in ten or twelve days it will be ripe.

Mackenzie's 5000 Receipts, 1829

CHERRY WINE: Take the best Cheeries, pick them, stone them, and strain them; into a Gallon of Juice, put two pound of Sugar, put it into a Tub, and let it work, when done, stop it up for two Months, and then draw and bottle it with a little Sugar, and let it be kept six Weeks for use.

Dr. Salmon's Receipes, 1710

CHOCOLET WINE: Take Water 3 quarters of a Pint, choice Red Port, or rather choice Sherry, half a pint; Sugar Chocolet a quarter of a pound, or something better; fine Flower, or white Starch, a quarter of an Ounce, and a little Salt; mix, dissolve and boil, and in about 12 minutes it will be done. But if you make it with chocolet without Sugar, the proportion to the former Water and Wine, will be of Chocolet, two Ounces and a quarter, Double Refined Sugar three Ounces, fine Flower or white Starch, a quarter of an Ounce, & c. as before.

Dr. Salmon's Recipes, 1710

CIDER WINE: Take sweet cider immediately from the press. Strain it through a flannel bag into a tub, and stir into it as much honey as will make it strong enough to bear up an egg. Then boil and skim it, and when the scum ceases to rise, strain it again. When cool, put it into a cask, and set it in a cool cellar till spring. Then bottle it off; and when ripe, it will be found a very pleasant beverage. The cider must be of the very best quality, made entirely from good sound apples.

Miss Leslie's Complete Cookery, 1839

CIDER WINE: Prof. Horsford, a celebrated chemist, communicated the following receipe to the Horticultural Society of Massachusetts, and recommends it for general trial:

"Let the new cider from sour apples, (ripe, sound fruit preferred), ferment from 1 to 3 weeks, as the weather is warm or cool. When it has attained to a lively fermentation, add to each gallon, according to its acidity, from ½ a lb. to 2 lbs. of white crushed sugar, and let the whole ferment until it possesses precisely the taste which it is desired should be permanent. In this condition pour out a quart of the cider and add for each gallon ¼ oz. of *sulphite of lime,* not sulphate. Stir the powder and cider until intimately mixed, and return the emulsion to the fermenting liquid. Agitate briskly and thoroughly for a few moments, and then let the cider settle. Fermentation will cease at once. When after a few days, the cider has become clear, draw off carefully, to avoid the sediment, and bottle. If loosely corked which is better, it will become a sparkling cider wine, and may be kept indefinitely long.

This has been tried with varied success; those who do not think it too much to follow the directions, obtain a good article, but others, supposing it to do just as well without sugar, or drawing off, or bottling, have found but little satisfaction—they have no reason to expect any; and yet they might be well satisfied to obtain a good wine from the orchard, even with all the above requisitions.

Dr. Chase's Recipes, 1869

CIDER WINE: Take of cold soft water, 4 gallons, cider, 15 gallons, honey, 12 pounds, tartar, in fine powder, 2 ounces. Ferment. Mix ginger, in powder, 6 ounces, sage and mint, 2 handsful. Add British spirits, one gallon. This will make eighteen gallons.

Mackenzie's 5000 Receipts, 1829

CIDER RED WINE: Take of cold soft water, 3 gallons, cider, 16 gallons, honey, 10 pounds. Ferment. Add raw sugar, 4 pounds, beet-root, sliced, 4 pounds, red tartar, in fine powder, 6 oz. Mix sweet marjoram and sweetbriar, 3 handsful, rum, 1 gallon. This will make 18 gallons.

Mackenzie's 5000 Receipts, 1829

CIDER WHITE WINE: Take of cold soft water, 2 quarts, cider, 9 gallons, honey, 8 pounds, white tartar, in fine powder, 2 oz. Ferment. Mix cinnamon, cloves, and mace, 2 oz. Add rum, ½ gallon. This will make 9 gallons.

Mackenzie's 5000 Receipts, 1829

CLARET VINE-LEAF WINE: Take of cold soft water, 18 gallons, claret vine-leaves, 3 pecks. Ferment. Mix raw sugar, 50 pounds, barberries, 6 quarts, red tartar, in fine powder, 8 ounces. Add roses, 6 or 8 handsful, sassafras chips, 3 pounds. Brandy, one gallon or more.

Mr. Carnell directs to macerate the vine-leaves in the water 3 days, and then proceed with the general process. This will make 18 gallons.

ANOTHER: Take of cold soft water, 11 gallons, claret vine leaves, 2 pecks. Ferment. Add cider, 9 gallons, raw sugar, 30 pounds, red tartar, in powder, 6 ounces. Mix cinnamon, in powder, 2 oz. 2 nutmegs in powder, brandy, 1 gallon. This will make 18 gallons.

Mackenzie's 5000 Receipts, 1829

CLARY WINE: Boil fifteen gallons of water, with forty-five pounds of sugar, skim it, when cool put a little to a quarter of a pint of yeast, and so by degrees add a little more. In an hour pour the small quantity to the large, pour the liquor on claryflowers, picked in the dry; the quantity for the above is twelve quarts. Those who gather from their own garden may not have sufficient to put in at once, and may add as they can get them, keeping account of each quart. When it ceases to hiss, and the flowers are all in, stop it up for four months. Rack it off, empty the barrel of the dregs, and adding a gallon of the best brandy, stop it up, and let it stand six or eight weeks, then bottle it.

Domestic Cookery, 1807

COMPOUND WINE: An excellent family wine may be made of equal parts of red, white, and black currants, ripe cherries, and raspberries, well bruised, and mixed with soft water, in the proportion of 4 lbs.

of fruit to 1 gallon of water. When strained and pressed, 3 lbs. of moist sugar are to be added to each gallon of liquid. After standing open for 3 days, during which it is to be stirred frequently, it is to be put into a barrel, and left for a fortnight to work, when a ninth part of brandy is to be added, and the whole bunged down. In a few months it will be a most excellent wine.

Mackenzie's 5000 Receipts, 1829

COWSLIP MEAD: Is made in this manner: to 15 gallons of water put 30 pounds of honey, and boil it till 1 gallon be wasted. Skim it, take it off the fire, and have ready 16 lemons cut in halves. Take a gallon of the liquor, and put it to the lemons. Put the rest of the liquor into a tub, with 7 pecks of cowslips, and let them stand all night. Then put in the liquor with the lemons, 8 spoonsful of new yeast, and a handful of sweetbriar. Stir them all well together, and let it work three or four days. Then strain it, put it into the cask, and after it has stood six months, bottle it off.

Mackenzie's 5000 Receipts, 1829

CURRANT WINE: Strain the currants, which should be perfectly ripe. To each quart of juice put a couple of quarts of water, and three pounds of sugar —stir the whole well together, and let it stand twenty-four hours, without stirring—then skim and set it in a cool place, where it will ferment slowly. Let it remain three or four days—if, at the end of that time, it has ceased fermenting, add one quart of French brandy to every fifteen gallons of the liquor, and close up the barrel tight. When it becomes clear, it is fit to bottle. This will be good in the course of six months, but it is much improved by being kept several years.

Kitchen Directory, 1846

CURRANT WINE: Those who have more currants than they have money, will do well to use no wine but of their own manufacture. Break and squeeze the currants, put three pounds and a half of sugar to two quarts of juice and two quarts of water. Put in a keg or barrel. Do not close the bung tight for three or four days, that the air may escape while it is fermenting. After it is done fermenting, close it up tight. Where raspberries are plenty, it is a great improvement to use half raspberry juice, and half currant juice. Brandy is unnecessary when the above-mentioned proportions are observed. It should not be used under a year or two. Age improves it.

American Frugal Housewife, 1833

CURRANT WINE: Gather the currants when dry, extract the juice, either by mashing and pressing the fruit, or putting it in a jar, placed in boiling water; strain the juice, and for every gallon allow one gallon of water and three pounds of sugar. Dissolve the sugar in the water, and take off the scum; let it cool, add it to the currant juice, and put the mixture in a keg, but do not close it tightly till it has ceased fermenting, which will not be under a week. In three or four weeks it may be bottled. The white of an egg beaten, mixed with a tea-spoonful of cream of tartar, and stirred into the liquid, makes the wine look clear and bright.

The Way to Live Well, 1849

CYPRUS WINE (IMITATION): To ten gallons of water put ten quarts of the juice of white elder berries, pressed gently from the berries by the hand, and passed through a sieve, without bruising the seeds: add to every gallon of liquor three pounds of Lisbon sugar, and to the whole quantity two ounces of ginger sliced, and one ounce of cloves. Boil this nearly an hour, taking off the scum as it rises, and pour the whole to cool, in an open tub, and work it with ale yeast, spread upon a toast of bread for three days. Then turn it into a vessel that will just hold it, adding about a pound and a half of bruised raisins, to lie in the liquor till drawn off, which should not be done till the wine is fine.

This wine is so much like the fine rich wine brought from the island of Cyprus, in colour, taste, and flavour, that it has deceived the best judges.

Mackenzie's 5000 Receipts, 1829

DAMSON WINE: Take of cold soft water, 11 gallons, damsons, 8 gallons. Ferment. Mix raw sugar, 30 lbs. red tartar, in fine powder, 6 oz. Add brandy, 1 gallon. This will make 18 gallons.

"When the must," says Mr. Carnell, "has fermented 2 days, (during which time it should be stirred up two or three times), take out of the vat about 2 or 3 quarts of the stones, and break them and the kernels, and then return them into the vat again."

ANOTHER METHOD: Take a considerable quantity of damsons and common plums inclining to ripeness: slit them in halves, so that the stones may be taken out, then mash them gently, and add a little water and honey. Add to every gallon of the pulp a gallon of spring water, with a few bay leaves and cloves; boil the mixture, and add as much sugar as will sweeten it; skim off the froths, and let it cool. Now press the fruit, squeezing out the liquid part; strain all through a fine strainer, and put the water and juice together in a cask. Having allowed the whole to stand and ferment for three or four days, fine it with white sugar, flour and white of eggs; draw it off into bottles, then cork it well. In twelve days it will be ripe, and will taste like weak Port, having the flavour of Canary.

Mackenzie's 5000 Receipts, 1829

DUTCH CURRANT WINE: Take of cold soft water, 9 gallons; red currants, 10 do. Ferment. Mix, raw sugar, 10 lbs.; beet-root, sliced, 2 lbs.; red tartar, in fine powder, 2 oz. Put in bitter almonds, 1 oz.; ginger, in powder, 2 oz. then add brandy, 1 quart. This will make 18 gallons.

Mackenzie's 5000 Receipts, 1829

EGG WINE: Beat up an egg and mix it with a tablespoonful of spring water. Put a wine-glassful of white wine, half a glass of spring water, and sugar and nutmeg to taste, into a small saucepan, place over a slow fire, and when it boils add it gradually to the egg, stirring well; then return the whole to the saucepan, and place over the fire again, stir for a minute, remove and serve with toast. If it boils when placed on the fire a second time, it will curdle.

Practical Housewife, 1860

ELDER WINE, MULLED: Put sufficient wine into a saucepan, warm over the fire, and if requisite add sugar, spice or water. When warmed, serve with thin slips of toast or rusks.

Practical Housewife, 1860

ELDER WINE: Take twelve gallons and a half of the juice of the ripe elderberry, and forty-three pounds of sugar, with thirty-seven and a half of water, in which had been previously boiled six ounces of ginger and nine ounces of pimento, bruised and strained off; and, when it is cooled to blood heat, or a little below, put the whole together, adding a pint of thin brewers' yeast; then let it ferment two weeks in a barrel; then bung it up close for six months; after which it may be bottled.

Farmer's Everyday Book, 1853

ELDER WINE (a very healthful cordial): Put to six gallons and a half of the juice of ripe elderberries, twenty-one pounds and a half of sugar, and eighteen gallons and a half of water, in which have been previously boiled three ounces of ginger, four ounces of pounded allspice. The liquid must be strained through a cloth. When almost cold, add half a pint of brewer's yeast, and let it ferment fourteen days in a cask; then bung it up close. After six months, bottle it. Some persons add a few bitter almonds.

The Young Housekeeper's Friend, 1846

ELDER WINE: Pick the elder-berries when full ripe; put them into a stone jar, and set them in the oven, or a kettle of boiling water, till the jar is hot through; then take them out and strain them through a coarse cloth, wringing the berries, and put the juices into a clean kettle; to every quart of juice put a pound of fine Lisbon sugar; let it boil, and skim it well; when it is clear and fine pour it into a jar; when cold cover it close, and keep it till you make raisin wine; and to every gallon of wine put half a pint of elder syrup.

Family Receipt Book, 1819

ELDERBERRY WINE: Bruise a bushel of picked elderberries; dilute the mass with ten gallons of water, and, having boiled it a few minutes, strain out the juice and squeeze out the husks. Measure the whole, and to every quart put three-quarters of a pound of sugar; then add, while warm, half a pint of yeast, and fill up the cask with some of the reserved liquor: let it ferment for ten days, then cork up. In three months the wine may be drawn off the lees and bottled for use.

The Art of Confectionery, 1866

ELDER-BERRY WINE: Take of cold soft water, 16 gallons, Malaga raisins, 50 lbs. elder-berries, 4 gallons, red tartar, in fine powder, 4 ounces. Mix ginger, in powder, 5 ounces, cinnamon, cloves, and mace, of each 2 ounces, 3 oranges or lemons, peel and juice. Then add 1 gallon of brandy. This will make 18 gallons.

Mackenzie's 5000 Receipts, 1829

ELDER-FLOWER WINE: OR ENGLISH FRONTINIAC: Boil eighteen pounds of white powdered sugar in six gallons of water, and two whites of eggs well beaten; skim it, and put in a quarter of a peck of elder-flowers; do not keep them on the fire. When cool, stir it, and put in six spoonsful of lemon juice, four or five of yeast, and beat well into the liquor; stir it well every day; put six pounds of the best raisins, stoned, into the cask, and tun the wine. Stop it close, and bottle in six months. When well kept, this wine will pass very well for Frontiniac.

ANOTHER: To six gallons of spring water put six pounds of sun raisins cut small, and a dozen pounds of fine sugar; boil the whole together for about an hour and a half. When the liquor is cold, put half a peck of ripe elder-flowers in, with about a gill of lemon juice, and half the quantity of ale yeast. Cover it up, and after standing three days, strain it off. Now pour it into a cask that is quite clean and that will hold it with ease. When this is done, put a quart of Rhenish wine to every gallon; let the bung be slightly put in for twelve or fourteen days; then stop it down fast, and put it in a cool dry place for four or five months, till it be quite settled and fine; then bottle it off.

Mackenzie's 5000 Receipts, 1829

ENGLISH FIG WINE: Take the large blue figs, when pretty ripe, and steep them in white wine, having made some slits in them, that they may swell and gather in the substance of the wine. Then slice some other figs, and let them simmer over a fire in water until they are reduced to a kind of pulp. Then strain out the water, pressing the pulp hard, and pour it as hot as possible on the figs that are imbrewed in the wine. Let the quantities be nearly equal, but the water somewhat more than the wine and figs. Let them stand 24 hours, mash them well together, and draw off what will run without squeezing. Then press the rest, and if not sweet enough, add a sufficient quantity of sugar, to make it so. Let it ferment, and add to it a little honey and sugar-candy; then fine it with whites of eggs and a little isinglass, and draw it off for use.

Mackenzie's 5000 Receipts, 1829

FAMILY WINE: Black currants, red currants, white currants, ripe cherries, raspberries, and gooseberries, each twenty-eight pounds; water, nine gallons. Steep for three or four days, frequently stirring up the mash, then strain with expression, and add to each gallon of the liquor good moist sugar, three pounds; cream of tartar, three drachms. Ferment, cork, and lastly, add good spirit, at the rate of two to five per cent.

Farmer's Everyday Book, 1853

FAMILY WINE: May be made of equal parts of red, white, and black currants, ripe cherries, and raspberries, well bruised, and mixed with soft water, in the proportion of four pounds of fruit to one gallon of water. When strained and pressed, three pounds of moist sugar are to be added to each gallon of liquid. After standing open three days, during which it is to be stirred frequently, and scum it as it may require, it is to be put into a barrel, and left for a fortnight to work, when a ninth part of brandy is to be added, and the whole bunged down; and in two or three years it will be rich and valuable.

Family Receipt Book, 1819

GILLIFLOWER WINE: To three gallons of water

put 6 pounds of the best powder sugar, boil the sugar and water together for the space of half an hour, keep skimming it as the scum rises; let it stand to cool, beat up three ounces of syrup of betony with a large spoonful of ale yeast, put it into the liquor, and brew it well together; then having a peck of gilliflowers cut from the stalks, put them into the liquor, let them infuse and work together three days, covered with a cloth; strain it, and put it into a cask, and let it settle for three or four weeks; then bottle it.

Mackenzie's 5000 Receipts, 1829

GINGER WINE: Alcohol of 98 per cent, 1 quart, best ginger root, bruised, 1 oz.; cayenne 5 grs.; tartaric acid 1 dr.; let stand 1 week and filter, or draw off by faucet above the sediment. Now add 1 gal. of water in which 1 lb. of crushed sugar has been boiled. Mix when cold. To make the color, boil ½ oz. of cochineal, 3/4 oz. of cream of tartar, ½ oz. of saleratus, and ½ oz. of alum in 1 pt. of water until you get a bright red color, and use a proper amount of this to bring the wine to the desired color.

Dr. Chase's Recipes, 1869

GINGER WINE: Put into a very nice boiler ten gallons of water, fifteen pounds of lump sugar, with the whites of six or eight eggs, well beaten and strained; mix all well while cold; when the liquor boils skim it well, put in half a pound of common white ginger, bruised, and boil it twenty minutes. Have ready the rinds (cut very thin) of seven lemons, and pour the hot liquor on them; when cool put it into your cask, with two spoonsful of yeast; put a quart of the warm liquor to two ounces of isinglass shavings, whisk it well three or four times, and put all into the barrel. Next day stop it up, in three weeks bottle it, and in three months it will be a delicious and safe liquor.

Mackenzie's 5000 Receipts, 1829

GOOSEBERRY WINE, RESEMBLING CHAMPAGNE: To each Scotch pint of full ripe gooseberries, mashed, add 1 Scotch pint of water, milk warm, in which has been dissolved 1 lb. of single refined sugar: stir the whole well, and cover up the tub with a blanket, to preserve the heat generated by the fermentation of the ingredients: let them remain in this vessel three days, stirring them twice or thrice a day: strain off the liquor through a sieve, afterwards through a coarse linen cloth; put it into the cask: it will ferment without yeast. Let the cask be kept full with some of the liquor reserved for the purpose. It will ferment for ten days, sometimes for three weeks: when ceased, and only a hissing noise remains, draw off two or three bottles, according to the strength you wish it to have, from every 20 pint cask, and fill up the cask with brandy or whiskey; but brandy is preferable. To make it very good, and that it may keep well, add as much sherry, together with a ¼ oz. of isinglass dissolved in water to make it quite liquid: stir the whole well. Bung the cask up, and surround the bung with clay: the closer it is bunged, the better: a fortnight after, if it be clear at top, taste it: if not sweet enough, add more sugar; 22 lbs. is the just quantity in all for 20 pints of wine; leave the wine six months in the cask; but after being quite fine, the sooner it is bottled, the more it will sparkle and resemble champagne. This process should be carried on in a place where the heat is between 48 deg. and 56 deg. Fahrenheit.—N.B. Currant wine may be made in the same manner.

Mackenzie's 5000 Receipts, 1829

GRAPE WINE: "Ripe, freshly picked, and selected, tame grapes, 20 lbs.; put them into a stone jar and pour over them 6 qts. of boiling soft water; when sufficiently cool to allow it, you will squeeze them thoroughly with the hand; after which allow them to stand 3 days on the pomace with a cloth thrown over the jar, then squeeze out the juice and add 10 lbs. of nice crushed sugar, and let it remain a week longer in the jar; then take off the scum, strain and bottle, leaving a vent, until done fermenting, when strain again and bottle tight, and lay the bottles on the side in a cool place."

Dr. Chase's Recipes, 1869

GRAPE WINE: Bruise the grapes, which should be perfectly ripe. To each gallon of grapes put a gallon of water, and let the whole remain a week, without being stirred. At the end of that time, draw off the liquor carefully, and put to each gallon three pounds of lump sugar. Let it ferment in a temperate situation —when fermented, stop it up tight. In the course of six months it will be fit to bottle.

Kitchen Directory, 1846

GRAPE WHITE WINE: Take of cold soft water, 13 gallons, white grapes, 50 pounds. Ferment. Mix refined sugar, 25 pounds, white tartar, in powder, 3 ounces. Add clary seed bruised, 3 ounces, or clary flowers, 6 handsful, rum, 1 gallon. This will make 18 gallons.

Mackenzie's 5000 Receipts, 1829

GRAPE RED WINE: Take of cold soft water, 5 gallons, black or red grapes, 40 pounds. Ferment. Mix cider, 9 gallons, raw sugar, 20 pounds, barberry leaves, 3 handsful, beet-root sliced, 2 pounds, red tartar, in powder, 4 ounces. Add white elder flowers, 6 handsful, or sassafras chips, 4 pounds, brandy, 1 gallon. This will make 18 gallons.

Mackenzie's 5000 Receipts, 1829

IPOCRAS WINE (HIPPOCRAS): To make Ipocras, take a pottle (bottle) of wine, two ounces of good cinamon, ½ ounce of ginger, nine cloves and six peppercorns, and a nutmeg, and bruise them and put them into the wine with some Rosemary flowers, and so let them steep all night, and then put in Sugar, a pound at least, and when it is well settled, let it run through a wollen bag made for that purpose; thus if your wine be claret, the Ipocras will be red; if white, then of that colour also.

English Housewife, 1615

JUNIPER-BERRY WINE: Take of cold soft water, 18 gallons, Malaga or Smyrna raisins, 35 lbs. juniper berries, 9 quarts, red tartar, 4 ounces, wormwood and sweet marjoram, each 2 handsful, British spirit, two quarts or more. Ferment for ten or twelve days. This will make eighteen gallons.

Mackenzie's 5000 Receipts, 1829

LEMON WINE: Pare off the rinds of 6 large lemons, cut them, and squeeze out the juice. Steep the rinds in the juice, and put to it a quart of brandy. Let it stand three days in an earthen pot close stopped; then squeeze 6 more, and mix with it 2 quarts of spring water, and as much sugar as will sweeten the whole. Boil the water, lemons, and sugar together, and let it stand till it be cool. Then add a quart of white wine, and the other lemons and brandy; mix them together, and run it through a flannel bag into some vessel. Let it stand three months and then bottle it off. Cork the bottles well; keep it cool, and it will be fit to drink in a month or six weeks.

Mackenzie's 5000 Receipts, 1829

MIXED BERRIES FROM A SMALL GARDEN: Take of cold soft water, 11 gallons; fruit, 8 do. Ferment. Mix, treacle, 14 or 16 lbs.; tartar, in powder, 1 oz. Put in ginger, in powder, 4 oz.; sweet herbs, 2 handsful: then add spirits, 1 or 2 quarts. This will make 18 gallons.

Mackenzie's 5000 Receipts, 1829

MIXED WINE: Take equal parts of ripe currants, grapes, raspberries, and English cherries. Bruise them, then mix cold water with them, in the proportion of four pounds of fruit to a gallon of water. Let the whole remain half a day. Stir the whole up well, then strain it—to each gallon of it put three pounds of sugar. Keep it in a temperate situation, where it will ferment slowly, three or four days—stir it up frequently. When fermented, add a ninth part of brandy to it, and stop it up tight—when it becomes clear, bottle it. In the course of a year it will be fit to drink.

Kitchen Directory, 1846

MORELLA WINE: Cleanse from the stalks sixty pounds of Morella cherries, and bruise them so that the stones shall be broken. Now press out the juice and mix it with 6 gallons of sherry wine, and 4 gallons of warm water. Having grossly powdered separate ounces of nutmeg, cinnamon, and mace, hang them separately, in small bags, in the cask containing the mixture. Bung it down and in a few weeks it will become a deliciously flavoured wine.

Mackenzie's 5000 Receipts, 1829

MULBERRY WINE: On a dry day, gather mulberries, when they are just changed from redness to a shinning black; spread them thinly on a fine cloth, or on a floor or table, for twenty-four hours; and then press them. Boil a gallon of water with each gallon of juice; putting to every gallon of water an ounce of cinnamon bark, and six ounces of sugar candy finely powdered. Skim and strain the water, when it is taken off and settled, and put to it the mulberry juice. Now add to every gallon of the mixture a pint of white or Rhenish wine. Let the whole stand in a cask to ferment, for five or six days. When settled, draw it off into bottles, and keep it cool.

Mackenzie's 5000 Receipts, 1829

MULLED WINE: 1. Boil some cloves, mace, cinnamon, and nutmeg, in about a quarter of a pint of water till well flavoured with spice, then add to a pint of port or home-made wine; sweeten to taste, and serve hot with thin toast or rusks. 2. Boil a small stick of cinnamon, a blade of mace, and three cloves, in a breakfastcupful of water for a few minutes; add some grated nutmeg, and a pint of home-made or port wine, sweeten to taste, boil for one minute, and serve hot. 3. Put a bottle of port wine, half a bottle of water, and sugar to taste, into a saucepan, then add allspice, cloves, and a blade of mace; boil all together, serve in a jug with grated nutmeg, and rusks or slips of thin toast. Some persons add lemon-juice to the mull, but it does not generally please.

Practical Housewife, 1860

MULLED WINE: To a pint of water put a teaspoonful of powdered cloves and cinnamon. Set it where it will boil—then separate the whites and yolks of three eggs, and beat the yolks with a large spoonful of powdered white sugar. As soon as the water boils, turn it on to the yolks and sugar—add a pint of wine, and turn the beaten whites of the eggs over the whole.

Kitchen Directory, 1846

ORANGE WINE: Take the expressed juice of eight Seville oranges; and, having one gallon of water wherein three pounds of sugar have been boiled, boil the water and sugar for twenty minutes; skim constantly, and when cooled to a proper heat for fermentation, add the juice, and the outer rind of the fruit, shaved off. Put all into a barrel, stir it frequently for two or three days, and then closely bung it for six months before it is bottled.

Family Receipt Book, 1819

ORANGE WINE: Put 12 lbs. of powdered sugar, with the whites of 8 or 10 eggs well beaten, into 6 gallons of spring water; boil them 3/4 of an hour; when cold, put into it 6 spoonsful of yeast and the juice of 12 lemons, which being pared, must stand with 2 lbs. of white sugar in a tankard, and in the morning skim off the top, and then put it into the water; add the juice and rinds of 50 oranges, but not the white or pithy parts of the rinds; let it work all together 2 days and 2 nights; then add two quarts of Rhenish or white wine, and put it into the vessel.

Mackenzie's 5000 Receipts, 1829

ORANGE AND LEMON WINE: Orange wine of a superior quality may be made with 2 lbs. of clayed sugar, and 1 lb. of Malaga raisins to each gallon of water, to which add the juice and peel of an orange, and to every 100 gallons of fluid 4 lbs. of Rhenish tartar.

Two lbs. of honey, 1 lb. of Malaga raisins, with the juice and peel of a large orange, to every gallon of water, and 4 lbs. of Rhenish tartar to every 100 gallons fluid, will make an orange wine still superior to the former. Steep and press the fruit, and expend the tartar in setting, raising, and cutting the backs: the orange peel and juice are not to be added until the last stage of fermentation, that is on cutting: they will possess infinitely more vinosity than the ordinary orange wines, indeed, nearly as much as the juice of the vine.

Lemon wine, equally delicious, may be made in a similar manner: both these wines, as they advance in age, lose much of the grosser part of the orange and lemon flavour; one approaches the bergamot and the other a fine citron, and become fragrant as they advance in years: they will be more improved if treacle be used, divested of its colour and burnt flavour.

Mackenzie's 5000 Receipts, 1829

PARSNIP WINE: To 12 pounds of parsnips, cut in slices, add 4 gallons of water; boil them till they become quite soft. Squeeze the liquor well out of them, run it through a sieve, and add to every gallon 3 pounds of loaf sugar. Boil the whole three quarters of an hour, and when it is nearly cold, add a little yeast. Let it stand for ten days in a tub, stirring it every day from the bottom, then put it into a cask for twelve months: as it works over, fill it up every day.

Mackenzie's 5000 Receipts, 1829

PEACH WINE: Take of cold soft water, 18 gallons, refined sugar, 25 lbs. honey, 6 lbs. white tartar, in fine powder, 2 ounces, peaches, sixty or eighty in number. Ferment. Then add 2 gallons of brandy. This will make 18 gallons.

The first division is to be put into the vat, and the day after, before the peaches are put in, take the stones from them, break them and the kernels, then put them and the pulp into the vat, and proceed with the general process.

Mackenzie's 500 Receipts, 1829

PEACH AND APRICOT WINE: Take peaches, nectarines, & c. pare them, and take the stones out; then slice them thin, and pour over them from a gallon to two gallons of water, and a quart of white wine. Place the whole on a fire to simmer gently for a considerable time, till the sliced fruit becomes soft; pour off the liquid part into another vessel containing more peaches that have been sliced but not heated; let them stand for twelve hours, then pour out the liquid part, and press what remains through a fine hair bag. Let the whole be now put into a cask to ferment; add of loaf sugar, a pound and a half to each gallon. Boil well, an ounce of beaten cloves in a quart of white wine, and add it to the above.

Apricot wine may be made by only bruising the fruit and pouring the hot liquor over it. This wine does not require so much sweetening. To give it a curious flavour, boil an ounce of mace, and half an ounce of nutmegs, in a quart of white wine; and when the wine is fermenting pour the liquid in hot. In about twenty days, or a month these wines will be fit for bottling.

Mackenzie's 5000 Receipts, 1829

PORT WINE: Fully ripe wild grapes 2 bu.; best alcohol 3 gals.; sugar 25 lbs.; water to fill a barrel.

Mash the grapes without breaking the seed; then put them into a barrel with the sugar and alcohol, and fill up with rain water, and let it lie a few weeks in the sun; or if the weather has become cold, in a warm place; then in the cellar until spring; then rack off and bottle, or place in perfectly clean kegs or barrels, and you have a better article than nine-tenths of what is represented as imported Port.

Dr. Chase's Receipes, 1869

PORT WINE (IMITATION): Take 6 gallons of good cider; 1½ gallons of port wine; 1½ gallons of the juice of elder-berries; 3 quarts of brandy; 1½ ounces of cochineal. This will produce 9½ gallons.

Bruise the chochineal very fine, and put it with the brandy into a stone bottle; let it remain at least a fortnight, shaking it well once or twice every day; at the end of that time procure the cider, and put five gallons into a nine gallon cask, add to it the elder juice and port wine, then the brandy and cochineal. Take the remaining gallon of cider to rinse out the bottle that contained the brandy; and lastly, pour it into the cask, and bung it down very close, and in six weeks it will be ready for bottling.

It is, however, sometimes not quite so fine as could be wished: in that case add two ounces of isinglass, and let it remain a fortnight or three weeks longer, when it will be perfectly bright: it would not be amiss, perhaps, if the quantity of isinglass mentioned was added to the wine before it was bunged down; it will tend very considerably to improve the body of the wine. If it should not appear sufficiently rough flavoured, add an ounce, or an ounce and a half of roche-alum, which will, in most cases, impart a sufficient astringency.

After it is bottled, it must be packed in as cool a place as possible. It will be fit for using in a few months; but if kept longer, it will be greatly improved.

Mackenzie's 5000 Receipts, 1829

POTATO WINE (FROM FROSTED POTATOES): Wine of considerable quality may be made from frosted potatoes, if not so much frosted as to have become soft and waterish. The potatoes must be crushed or bruised; a wooden mallet answers the purpose. If a plank of wood is made hollow, in the manner of a shallow bowl, they may be bruised with a mallet, or put into a cider press. A Winchester bushel must have 10 gallons of water, prepared by boiling it mixed with ½ lb. of hops and ½ lb. of common white ginger. This water, after having boiled for about half an hour, must be poured upon the bruised potatoes, into a tub or vessel suited to the quantity to be made. After standing in this mixed state for three days, yeast must be added, to ferment the liquor. When the fermentation has subsided, the liquor must be drawn off, as pure as possible, into a cask, adding half a pound of raw sugar for every gallon. After it has remained in the cask for three months, it will be ready for use.—*Farmer's Mag.*

Mackenzie's 5000 Receipts, 1829

RAISIN WINE EQUAL TO SHERRY: Let the

raisins be well washed and picked from the stalks; to every pound thus prepared and chopped, add 1 quart of water which has been boiled and has stood till it is cold. Let the whole stand in the vessel for a month, being frequently stirred. Now let the raisins be taken from the cask, and let the liquor be closely stopped in the vessel. In the course of a month, let it be racked into another vessel, leaving all the sediment behind, which must be repeated till it becomes fine, when add to every ten gallons six pounds of fine sugar, and one dozen of Seville oranges, the rinds being pared very thin, and infused in two quarts of brandy, which should be added to the liquor at its last racking. Let the whole stand three months in the cask, when it will be fit for bottling; it should remain in the bottle for a twelve-month.

To give it the flavour of Madeira, when it is in the cask, put in a couple of green citrons, and let them remain till the wine is bottled.

ANOTHER RAISIN WINE: Put two hundred weight of raisins, with the stalks, into a hogshead, and fill it almost with spring water; let them steep for about twelve days, frequently stirring, and after pouring off the juice, dress the raisins and mash them. The whole should then be put together into a very clean vessel that will exactly contain it. It will hiss for some time, during which it should not be stirred; but when the noise ceases, it must be stopped close, and stand for about six or seven months: and then, if it proves fine and clear, rack it off into another vessel of the same size. Stop it up, and let it remain for twelve or fourteen weeks longer, then bottle it off. If it should inot prove clear, fine it down with three ounces of singlass, and a quarter of a pound of sugar-candy, dissolved in some of the wine.

Mackenzie's 5000 Receipts, 1829

RASPBERRY WINE: Take of cold soft water, 6 gallons; cider, 4 do. raspberries, 6 do.; any other fruit, 3 do. Ferment. Mix, raw sugar, 18 or 20 lbs.; red tartar, in fine powder, 3 oz.; orange and lemon peel, 2 oz. dry, or 4 oz. fresh: then add brandy, 3 quarts. This will make 18 gallons.

ANOTHER: Gather the raspberries when ripe, husk them and bruise them; then strain them through a bag into jars or other vessels. Boil the juice, and to every gallon put a pound and a half of lump sugar. Now add whites of eggs, and let the whole boil for fifteen minutes; skimming it as the froth rises. When cool and settled, decant the liquor into a cask, adding yeast to make it ferment. When this has taken place, add a pint of white wine, or half a pint of proof spirit to each gallon contained in the cask, and hang a bag in it containing an ounce of bruised mace. In three months, if kept in a cool place, it will be very excellent and delicious wine.

Mackenzie's 5000 Receipts, 1829

RED CURRANT WINE: Take cold soft water, 11 gallons—red currants, 8 gallons,—raspberries, 1 quart. Ferment. Mix, raw sugar, 20 lbs.—beet-root, sliced, 2 lbs. and red tartar, in fine powder, 3 ounces. Put in 1 nutmeg, in fine powder; add brandy, 1 gallon. This will make 18 gallons.

ANOTHER: Put five quarts of currants and a pint of raspberries to every two gallons of water; let them soak a night; then squeeze and break them well. Next day rub them well through a fine sieve till the juice is expressed, washing the skins with some of the water; then, to every gallon, put four pounds of the best sugar, put it into your barrel, and set the bung lightly in. In two or three days add a bottle of good cogniac brandy to every four gallons; bung it close, but leave out the spiggot for a few days. It is very good in three years, better in four.

Mackenzie's 5000 Receipts, 1829

RED AND WHITE CURRANT WINE: Take of cold soft water, 12 gallons; white currants, 4 do.; red currants, 3 do. Ferment. Mix, raw sugar, 25 lbs.; white tartar, in fine powder, 3 oz. Put in sweet-briar leaves, 1 handful; lavender leaves, 1 do.; then add spirits, 2 quarts or more. This will make 18 gallons.

Mackenzie's 5000 Receipts, 1829

RED AND WHITE GOOSEBERRY WINE: Take cold soft water, 3 gallons, red gooseberries, 1½ gallons, white gooseberries, two gallons. Ferment.

Now mix raw sugar, 5 lbs. honey, 1½ lbs. tartar, in fine powder, 1 oz. Afterwards put in bitter almonds, two ounces, sweet-briar, one small handful, and brandy one gallon, or less. This will make six gallons.

Mackenzie's 5000 Receipts, 1829

RED MEAD OR METHEGLIN WINE: Take of cold soft water, 17 gallons, red currants, 6 quarts, black currants, 2 quarts. Ferment. Mix, honey, 25 pounds, beet root, sliced, 1 pound, red tartar, in fine powder, 4 oz. Add cinnamon, in powder, 2 oz. brandy, 1 gallon. This will make 18 gallons.

Mackenzie's 5000 Receipts, 1829

RHUBARB, OR ENGLISH PATENT WINE: An agreeable and healthful wine is made from the expressed juice of the garden rhubarb.

To each gal. of juice, add 1 gal. of soft water in which 7 lbs. of brown sugar has been dissolved; fill a keg or a barrel with this proportion, leaving the bung out, and keep it filled with sweetened water as it works over until clear; then bung down or bottle as you desire.

These stalks will furnish about three-fourths their weight in juice, or from sixteen hundred to two thousand gallons of wine to each acre of well cultivated plants. Fill the barrels and let them stand until spring, and bottle, as any wine will be better in glass or stone.

Some persons give Mr. Cahoon, of Kenosha, Wis., credit for originating pie-plant wine, but that is a mistake; it has long been made in England, and has even been patented in that country. They first made it by the following directions, which also makes a very nice article, but more applicable for present use than for keeping.

For every 4 lbs. of the stalks cut fine, pour on 1 gal. of boiling water, adding 4 lbs. brown sugar; let stand covered 24 hours, having also added a little cinnamon, allspice, cloves and nutmeg, bruised, as may be desired for flavouring; then strain and let work a few days, and bottle.

Dr. Chase's Recipes, 1869

ROSE WINE: Take a well glazed earthen vessel, and put into it 3 gallons of rose-water drawn with a cold still. Put into that a sufficient quantity of rose leaves, cover it close, and set it for an hour in a kettle or copper of hot water, to take out the whole strength and tincture of the roses; and when it is cold, press the rose leaves hard into the liquor, and steep fresh ones in it, repeating it till the liquor has got the full strength of the roses. To every gallon of liquor put three

Plate 38. *A fine brandy decanter with glasses, pewter, and English earthenware were often seen on cupboards in old New England kitchens. (Courtesy of the New York State Historical Association, Cooperstown, New York)*

pounds of loaf sugar, and stir it well, that it may melt and disperse in every part. Then put it into a cask, or other convenient vessel, to ferment, and put into it a piece of bread toasted hard, and covered with yeast. Let it stand about thirty days, when it will be ripe and have a fine flavour, having the whole strength and scent of the roses in it; and it may be greatly improved by adding to it wine and spiecs. By this method of infusion, wine of carnations, clove gilliflowers, violets, primroses, or any other flower, having a curious scent, may be made.

Mackenzie's 5000 Receipts, 1829

SAGE WINE: Boil 26 quarts of spring water a quarter of an hour, and when it is blood warm, put 25 pounds of Malaga raisins, picked, rubbed, and shred, into it, with almost half a bushel of red sage shred, and a porringer of ale yeast; stir all well together, and let it stand in a tub, covered warm, six or seven days, stirring it once a day; then strain it off, and put it in a runlet. Let it work three or four days, and then stop it up; when it has stood six or seven days, put in a quart or two of Malaga sack; and when it is fine bottle it.

Mackenzie's 5000 Receipts, 1829

SASSAFRAS MEAD: Mix gradually, with two quarts of boiling water, three and a half pounds of best brown sugar, a pint and a half of good molasses, and one fourth of a pound of tartaric acid; stir it well, and when cool strain it into a large jug, or pan, then mix in a quarter of an ounce of essence of sassafras; transfer it to clean bottles, (it will fill about half a dozen), cork it tightly and keep it in a cool place. Have ready a box containing about one fourth of a pound carbonate of soda to use with it. To prepare a glass of it for drinking, pour a little of the mead into a tumbler, fill three-fourths full of cold water, then stir in a small quantity of soda and it will foam to the top.

American Economical Housekeeper, 1850

STRAWBERRY WINE: Take of cold soft water, 7 gallons; cider, 6 do.; strawberries, 6do. Ferment. Mix, raw sugar, 16 lbs.; red tartar, in fine powder, 3 oz.; the peel and juice of 2 lemons: then add brandy, 3 quarts. This will make 18 gallons.

Mackenzie's 5000 Receipts, 1829

SYCAMORE WINE: Boil 2 gallons of the sap half an hour, and then add to it 4 pounds of fine powdered sugar. Beat the whites of 3 eggs to froth, and mix them with the liquor; but take care that it is not too hot, as that will poach the eggs. Skim it well, and boil it half an hour. Then strain it through a hair sieve, and let it stand till next day. Then pour it clean from the sediment, put half a pint of yeast to every twelve gallons, and cover it close up with blankets. Then put it into the barrel, and leave the bung-hole open till it has done working. Then close it up well, and after it has stood 2 months, bottle it. The fifth part of the sugar must be loaf; and if raisins are liked, they will be a great addition to the wine.

Mackenzie's 5000 Receipts, 1829

WHIPT SYLLABUB: Rub a lump of loaf sugar on the outside of a lemon, and put it into a pint of thick cream, and sweeten it to taste. Squeeze in the juice of a lemon, and add a glass of Madeira wine, or French brandy. Mill it to a froth with a chocolate mill, take off the froth as it rises, and lay it in a hair sieve. Fill one half of the glass with red wine, then lay the froth as high as possible, but take care that it is well drained in the sieve, otherwise it will mix with the wine, and the syllabub be spoiled.

Mackenzie's 5000 Receipts, 1829

SOLID SYLLABUB: To a quart of rich cream put a quart of white wine, the juice of two lemons, with the rind of one grated, and sweeten it to the taste. Whip it up well and take off the froth as it rises. Put it upon a hair sieve, and let it stand in a cool place till the next day. Then half fill the glasses with the scum, and heap up the froth as high as possible. The bottom will look clear and it will keep several days.

Mackenzie's 5000 Receipts, 1829

TOMATO WINE: Express the juice from clean, ripe tomatoes, and to each gallon of it, (without any water), put brown sugar 4 lbs.

Put in the sugar immediately, or before fermentation begins—this ought to be done in making any fruit wine. Something of the character of a cheese press, hoop and cloth, is the best plan to squeeze out the juice of tomatoes or other fruits. Let the wine stand in a keg or barrel for two or three months; then draw off into bottles, carefully avoiding the sediment.

It makes a most delightful wine, having all the beauties of flavor belonging to the tomato, and I have no doubt all its medicinal properites also, either as a tonic in disease, or as a beverage for those who are in the habit of using intoxicating beverages, and if such persons would have the good sense to make some wine of this kind, and use it instead of rot-gut whisky, there would not be one-hundredth part of the "snakes in the boot" that now curse our land. It must be tasted to be appreciated. I have it now, which is three years old, worth more than much pretended wine which is sold for three or four shillings a pint.

Dr. Chase' Recipes, 1869

TURNIP WINE: Pare and slice a quantity of turnips, put them in a cyder-press, and press out all the juice. To every gallon of juice put three pounds of lump sugar. Have a vessel ready, just large enough to hold the juice, put your sugar into a vessel, and half a pint of brandy to every gallon of juice. Pour in the juice, and lay something over the bung for a week, to see if it works. If it does, you must not bung it down till it has done working; then stop it close for three months, and draw it off in another vessel. When it is fine, bottle it off.

The London Art of Cookery, 1797

WALNUT MEAD WINE: To every gallon of water put three pounds and a half of honey, and boil them together three quarters of an hour. Then to every gallon of liquor put about two dozen of walnut leaves, pour the boiling liquor upon them, and let them stand all night. Then take out the leaves, put in a spoonful of yeast, and let it work for two or three days. Then make it up, and after it has stood for three months, bottle it.

Mackenzie's 5000 Receipts, 1829

WHITE CURRANT WINE: Ripe, white currants, any quantity; squeeze out the juice, and put on water to get out as much more as there is of the juice, and mix the two, and to each gallon put 2½ lbs. of sugar; let it work without boiling or skimming for 2 or 3 months, then rack off and bottle.

The white currant has less acidity than the red, and does not require as much sugar. I have never tasted currant wine equal to this.

Dr. Chase's Recipes, 1869

WHITE CURRANT WINE: Take of cold soft water, 9 gallons; white currants, 9 do.; white gooseberries, 1 do. Ferment. Mix, refined sugar, 25 lbs.; white tartar, in powder, 1 oz.; clary seed, bruised, 2 oz. or clary flowers, or sorrel flowers, 4 handsful: then add white brandy, 1 gallon. This will make 18 gallons.

ANOTHER: Take of cold soft water, 10 gallons; white currants, 10 do. Ferment. Mix, refined sugar, 25 lbs.; white tartar, in fine powder, 1 oz. then add, bitter almonds, 2 oz. and white brandy, one gallon. This will make eighteen gallons.

Mackenzie's 5000 Receipts, 1829

WHITE GOOSEBERRY OR CHAMPAGNE WINE: Take cold soft water, 4½ gallons, white gooseberries, 5 gallons. Ferment.

Now mix refined sugar, 6 pounds,—honey, 4 pounds,—white tartar, in fine powder, 1 oz. Put in orange and lemon peel, 1 oz. dry, or two ounces fresh; and add white brandy half a gallon. This will make nine gallons.

Mackenzie's 5000 Receipts, 1829

WHITE MEAD WINE: Take of cold soft water, seventeen gallons, white currants, six quarts. Ferment. Mix honey, 30 pounds, white tartar, in fine powder, 3 oz. Add balm and sweetbriar, each 2 handsful, white brandy, 1 gallon. This will make 18 gallons.

Mackenzie's 5000 Receipts, 1829

WINE WHEY: Put half a pint of new milk in a saucepan, set on the fire, and when it boils add as much raisin wine as will turn it; let it boil up, then set the saucepan aside till the curd subsides, but do not stir it. Pour off the whey, then add half a pint of boiling water, and white sugar to taste.

Practical Housewife, 1860

WORTLEBERRY OR BILBERRY WINE: Take of cold soft water, 6 gallons; berries, 8 gallons. Ferment. Mix raw sugar, 20 pounds; tartar, in fine powder, 4 ounces. Add ginger, in powder, 4 ounces; lavender and rosemary leaves, 2 handsful; rum or British spirits, 1 gallon. This will make 18 gallons.

Mackenzie's 5000 Receipts, 1829

Pennellville Hotel,

PENNELLVILLE, N. Y.

Ambrose Gregg, Proprietor.

An Act to Regulate the Liability of Hotel Keepers.

The People of the State of New York, represented in Senate and Assembly, do enact as follows:

SECTION 1. Whenever the proprietor or proprietors of any hotel shall provide a safe in the office of such hotel, or other convenient place for the safe keeping of any moneys, jewels, or ornaments belonging to the guests of such hotel, and shall notify the guests thereof, by posting a notice (stating the fact that such safe is provided, in which such moneys, jewels, or ornaments may be deposited,) in the room or rooms occupied by such guest, in a conspicuous manner, and if such guest shall neglect to deposit such money, jewels or ornaments in such safe, the proprietor or proprietors of such hotel shall not be liable for any loss of such money, jewels or ornaments, sustained by such guest, by theft or otherwise.

AN ACT to prevent fraud and fraudulent practices upon or by Hotel Keepers and Inn Keepers. Passed April 23, 1867.

The People of the State of New York, represented in Senate and Assembly do enact as follows:

SECTION 1. Every person who shall at any hotel or inn order and receive, or cause to be furnished, any food or accommodation, with intent to defraud the owner or proprietor of such hotel or inn out of the value or price of such food or accommodation; and every person who shall obtain credit at any hotel or inn by use of any false pretense or device, or by depositing at such hotel or inn any baggage or property of value less than the amount of such credit or of the bill by such persons incurred; and any person who, after obtaining credit or accommodation at any hotel or inn, shall abscond from such hotel or inn, and shall surreptitiously remove his baggage therefrom, shall upon conviction, be adjudged guilty of a misdemeanor.

§ 1. Every keeper of a hotel, restaurant, boarding house or inn, shall post in a public and conspicuous place in the office or public room, and in every bed room in said house, a printed copy of this act, and a statement of the charge or rate of charges by the day, and for meals or items furnished, and for lodging. No charge or sum shall be collected or received by any such person for any service not actually rendered, or for any item not actually delivered, or for a longer time than the person so charged actually remained at such place. For any violation of this section, or any provision herein contained the offender shall forfeit to the injured party three times the amount so charged, and shall not be entitled to receive any money for the meals, items, services or time charged.

§ 3. This act shall take effect immediately.

A Safe is provided. All money, jewelry and other valuables must be deposited at the office, or the proprietor will not be responsible.

Guests occupying rooms without meals will be charged at the rate of two dollars per day.

Guests are requested to examine their baggage when brought from their rooms. It is also desired that gentlemen receive their baggage from the porters, as any article not claimed will be returned to the hotel.

An extra charge will be made for private parlors, and for meals and lunches served in rooms. Guests having friends to dine will please give notice at the office, so that seats can be provided for them at the table.

Occupants of rooms are requested to bolt their doors on retiring for the night, and also to lock them during the day, and leave the key at the office.

Lights not permitted to be burned after retiring.

Gentlemen will please report to the proprietor any inattention, or misconduct of the servants.

All damage to the furniture or other conveniences, other than ordinary wear and tear will be charged to the parties occupying the apartments.

RATE OF CHARGES.

Board per Week,	$4,50 to 6,00
" Day,	1,50
Breakfast,	.50
Dinner,	.50
Tea,	.50
Lodging,	.50
Fire,	50

Breakfast from 6 to 7 o'clock. Dinner 12 1-2 o'clock. Tea from 6 to 7 o'clock.

Sunday, breakfast at 8. Dinner at 2 1-2

FOR LIVERY, INQUIRE AT THE BAR.

"The Register" Print, Phoenix, N. Y.

CHAPTER EIGHT

Early American Taverns

THE CHURCH AND THE TAVERN

The two basic social institutions of Colonial America were the church and the tavern. Though this may seem shocking to some readers and not at all in harmony with contemporary views of the daily life of the Puritans, investigation into the records of the day will substantiate the close relationship between church and tavern, as inappropriate as it may seem.

Not only were these institutions founded quite simultaneously, but geographically they were usually close neighbors. Often, tavern licenses were issued on the understanding that the tavern must be close to the meeting-house. In 1651, for example, a Boston ordinary-keeper was given permission to operate a house of "common entertainment" provided "hee keepe it neare the new meeting-house."

Frequently the personnel were interchangeable. One such instance was the ordinary-keeper, at Cambridge, Massachusetts' first "house of intertainment," who was also a deacon of the church and later Steward of Harvard College.

Likewise, the edifice itself at times served two purposes. Governor Winthrop's residence at Charlestown, Massachusetts, the Great House, became a meeting-house in 1633, and later a tavern called the Three Cranes, operated by Robert Leary and his family for a long time. When the town was burned in 1775, it was destroyed. It had been here that probably America's first temperance pledge was taken. Governor Winthrop records his own statement against toast drinking in his Diary, as follows:

Plate 39, opposite page. *Rules and regulations of a typical New York State country inn of the mid 19th century. The Pennellville Hotel, which is still standing, was built in 1837 by Rodney Gregg. (Courtesy of Edith M. Gregg)*

The Governor, upon consideration of the inconveniences which had grown in England by drinking one to another, restrained it at his own table, and wished others to do the like; so it grew, little by little, into disuse.

Before the meeting-house edifice could be erected, religious services were often held in the taverns. In Providence, Rhode Island, where Roger Williams served as preacher, and in Fitchburg, Massachusetts, the spacious rooms of the tavern served this purpose.

"Seating the meeting" was often managed at the ordinary. Alice Morse Earle writes that the "Elders, Deacons, and Selectmen" of Cambridge were made a "constant and settled power for regulating the seating of persons in the meeting-house." The following orders and appointments were typical:

Brother Richard Jackson's wife to sit where Sister Kempster was wont to sit. Esther Sparhawke to sit in the place where Mrs. Upham is removed from. Mr. Day to sit the second seat from the table. Ensign Samuel Greene to sit at the Table. Goody Gates to sit at the end of the Deacon's seat. Goody Wines to sit in the Gallery.

Mrs. Earle concludes, "We can imagine the deacons loosening their tongues over the tavern flip and punch, and arguing confidentially over the standing, the wealth, and temper of the various parties to be seated."

Of course, there were always some individuals who, regardless of how close the relationship was between the location of the church and the tavern, were reluctant to attend service. And when the social pressures of the community were removed in the frontier regions during war time, it was sometimes impossible to interest the men in divine service.

The volunteers led by Benjamin Franklin against the French and Indians were no exception. Goodrich in his *Lives of the Signers to the Declaration of Independence* writes, "When, at length, Braddock was defeated, and the whole frontier was exposed to the incursions of the savages and the French, Franklin raised a company of volunteers, at the head of which he marched to the protection of the frontier."

The acting chaplain to this army of five hundred men was Rev. Charles Beatty, one of the first graduates of the Log College. Franklin and his men organized to defend the frontier after the Moravian mission at Gnadenhütten, Pennsylvania was burned.

Franklin tells of the reluctance of the men to attend Rev. Beatty's services:

Dr. Beatty complained to me that the men did not generally attend his prayers and exhortations. When they were enlisted, they were promised, besides hay and provisions, a gill of rum a day, which was punctually served out to them, half in the morning, and the other half in the evening; and I observed they were as punctual in attending to receive it; upon which I said to Mr. Beatty, 'It is perhaps below the dignity of your profession to act as steward of the rum, but if *you* were to deal it out, and only just after prayers, you would have them all about you.'

For obvious reasons, it was important for the townspeople to have the tavern near the place of meeting; the ordinary served as an excellent retreat from an overly long sermon or an unheated church. Earle describes very well problems affecting the physical comforts of the parishioners:

Plate 40. *The village post office was often located in the local tavern. This oil on canvas was painted in 1873 by Thomas Waterman Wood (1823–1903). Note the two characters in the background enjoying a "short snort."* (Courtesy of the New York State Historical Association, Cooperstown, New York)

Through autumn rains, and winter frosts and snows, and fierce northwesters, the poorly-built meeting-house stood unheated, growing more damp, more icy, more deadly, with each succeeding week. Women cowered, shivering, half-frozen, over the feeble heat of a metal footstove as the long sermon dragged on and the few coals became ashes. . . . Gladly and eagerly did all troop from the gloomy meeting-house to the cheerful tavern to thaw out before the afternoon. It was a scandal in many a town that godly church-members partook too freely of tavern cheer at the nooning; the only wonder is that the entire congregation did not succumb in a body to the potent flip and toddy of the tavern-keeper.

Of course there were those who found "going to the tavern" much more attractive than attending church. This practice became so serious in Massachusetts that a law was passed stating that tavern keepers within a mile of church were required to ask all persons "able to go to church" to leave the tavern during the hours of the service. Mr. Fields, a contemporary wit, says, "The townsmen were frozen out of the tavern to be frozen in the meeting-house."

Because of the rigorous limitations set down regarding the running of taverns and because of the generally high-qualitied tavern keeper, both of which will be discussed later, by and large the various "houses of entertainment" were of good standing. Not only was this true in New England, but, as Earle points out, "The history of Pennsylvania shows that its taverns were great in number and good in quality, especially soon after the Revolution." There were a great many public houses in Philadelphia; this met a definite need because of the huge number of visitors to the city and the great wave of immigrants who were entering the country through its port. By 1648, one-fourth of New Amsterdam's buildings had been made into tap-houses to sell beer, brandy and tobacco. And, as elsewhere, restraints were placed on the tavern-keepers, in this instance, by Governor Stuyvesant. It was the Council which was empowered to approve their setting up business. After the English came into power, the same laws prevailed until 1748, and the taverns continued to multiply in number.

Among the strict limitations set down for the operating of taverns, as alluded to previously, were those relating to the harboring of "strangers", for the earliest taverns were not especially run for the convenience of travellers—in fact, as will be noted later, the tavern was of far greater importance to the local citizenry than to those from out of town. For example, a stranger's name would have to be submitted by the tavern-keeper to the selectmen. If the latter wished, they could "warn" them out of town, if they felt they were detrimental to the community or might become a public charge.

Sometimes the restrictions were so severe, few wished to undertake such a venture as running an ordinary. The General Court in 1634 set the price of a meal at six-pence, and not more than a penny could be charged for "an ale-quart of beer out of meal time." Soon, the price of a meal could not exceed twelve-pence, and inn-keepers "were ordered to furnish meals to 'poor people', as simply as called for."

One man discouraged by such strict price-fixing was Richard Cluffe, who is said to have uttered when a poor meal was served him, "What! shall I pay twelve pence for the fragments which the grand jury rogues have left?" But such condemnation of law could not be so attacked in Massachusetts in 1640. Cluffe had to pay three pounds six shillings and eight pence for his derisive remarks.

The first tavern opened in Boston in 1634. It was operated by Samuel Cole. Five years later, on September 4, a law was put into effect by the Massachusetts General Court which reflected Governor Winthrop's sentiments cited earlier: "The common custom of drinking to one another is a mere useless ceremony, and draweth on the abominable practice of drinking healths." But finding that the people could not be controled in this regard and the law not enforced, it was repealed in 1645.

Licenses were issued to William Hudson Jr., Goody Armitage, and Mrs. William Knops, in 1643, to open a "cook's shop" in Boston. They were given the right to operate an "ordinary", but they could not "draw wine."

Among the Dutch, anyone guilty of "unreasonable night-tippling," or "intemperate drinking on the Sabbath" was heavily fined. The 1656 law making it an offense to drink on the Sabbath also made it illegal to take a jaunt in a carriage or a boat, sow, mow, bowl on the green, build, play tick-tack or cards, fish, hunt, dance, or to do any smithing, sawing, or bleaching.

Sports, in general, were forbidden by the Puritan administrators, anyway, whether on the Sabbath or not. Earle writes, "Among the games which were named as forbidden in the ordinaries were 'carding', dicing, tally, bowls, billiards, slidegroat, shuffle-board, quoits, loggets, ninepins." Eventually, shuffle-board and bowling were permitted in private houses, but were not reputable at the ordinary. By the eighteenth century, supervision was beginning to relax and the taverns became centers for drinking, ballad singing, turkey or bear shoot contests, and cock fights. One of the favorite tunes of the day was entitled, "The Parson and the Barrel of Beer."

One of the reasons cited earlier for having a rather high standard upheld in the early taverns was due to the caliber of "tavern landlords". John Dunton, a London bookseller who visited Boston in 1686, paid his tribute to colonial landloards, as follows:

> (George Monk, landlord of the Blue Anchor, is) A person so remarkable that, had I not been acquainted with him, it would be a hard matter to make any New England man believe I had been in Boston; for there was no one house in all the town more noted, or where a man might meet with better accommodation. Besides, he was a brisk and jolly man, whose conversation was coveted by all his guests as the life and spirit of the company.

Very respectable citizens were selected to run the ordinaries and sell their beverages. The first license issued in Cambridge to sell wine and strong water was given to a selectman and Representative to the General Court, Nicholas Danforth. One of the esteemed Deputies, Mr. Constant Southworth, and Mr. William Collier sold wine to their neighbors in the Plymouth Colony. These were not men interested in supplementing their own incomes, which were ample, but rather they assumed the duty of selling wine to aid the colony.

Plate 41. *"I feel provoked to see our . . . taverns made the scenes of frolic and flip on so many occasions. A gingerbread lottery, a vendue, a dance, a singing meeting, a sley ride, everything fills them with young fellows, and our apprentice boys already claim the rights of men against their masters." So wrote Fisher Ames to Thomas Dwight on February 29, 1804. Shown here is a gooseneck sleigh, c. 1830. (Courtesy of the New York State Historical Association, Cooperstown, N.Y.)*

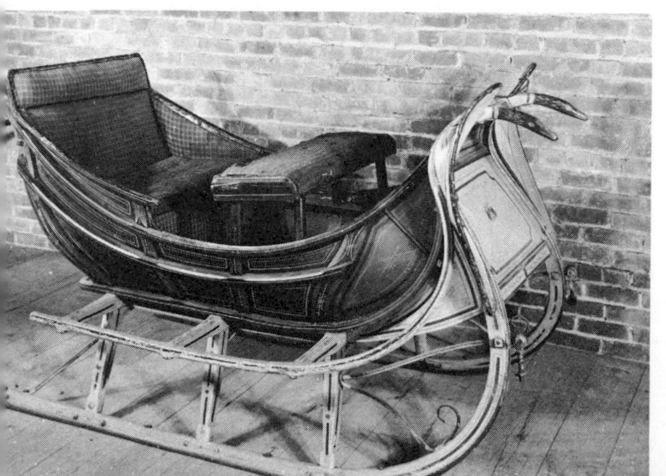

At Duxbury, where the tavern keeper was found to be a little too gay and too much of a reveller himself, one of the tavern inspectors, Mr. Seabury, was appointed in 1678 "to sell liquors unto such sober-minded neighbors as hee shall thinke meet; soe as hee sell not lesse than the quantitie of a gallon att a tyme to one pson, and not in smaller quantities by retaile to the occationing of drunkeness."

Dr. Timothy Dwight in his *Travels* wrote that "To provide for safety and comfort and against danger and mischief they took particular pains in their laws to prevent inns from being kept by unprincipled or worthless men. Every innkeeper in Connecticut must be recommended by the selectmen and civil authorities, constables and grand jurors of the town in which he resides, and then licensed at the discretion of the Court of Common Pleas." He adds, "It was substantially the same in Massachusetts and New Hampshire."

Because all matters of public concern were expressed in the tavern, the innkeeper became a man of great influence. He was the first person to learn about actions of the legislature. Usually, he knew the lawyers well. Those involved in a heated controversy over cards would refer their problem to him, or he would take his own means of settling the argument. He was well informed on everything from the Governor's health to a Sheriff's sale of wood lots. He became a keen judge of human nature and found it his duty to watch for runaway slaves, and to be courteous and attentive to his guests. As to additional civic responsiblities, Earle observes that "He often held public office, was selectman, road commissioner, tax assessor, tax collector, constable, or town moderator; occasionally he performed all these duties." John Adams once observed that men sat at public houses drinking heavily while "plotting with the landlord to get him at the next town-meeting an election either for selectman or representative."

After the Revolution, a favorite vocation for retired officers of the militia or men who had been in the thick of battle and survived was to keep a tavern. They were usually cheery hosts, fond of practical jokes. Sometimes, they would engage in all sorts of April-fool's pranks; one landlord delighted in having the stage coach driver call out, "Stage is ready" before the meal they had just ordered, and paid for, could be eaten.

An Englishman, Henry Wansey, whose journal tells of a visit made to the United States in 1794, wrote of having seen former Revolutionary War officers digging road beds, serving as stablemen, or as tavern keepers. "On our arrival (in Boston), we enquired for the best house of entertainment; and were directed to the Bunch of Grapes, in State street, kept by Colonel Coleman. It is nothing unusual in America for army officers to keep taverns." He seemed to take considerable delight in such an observation.

At times, the tavern keeper in all his gaiety would "par-take too freely of his own 'pure old rye.' " One anecdote relating such an experience is told of an old landlord named Ramsay whose health became a matter of concern to all his family and friends. A doctor, employed to help, de-

Plate 42. *Inn keepers always considered the safety of their guests' horses as a serious responsibility. New York at one time had a notorious gang that engaged in the stealing of draft horses in the North and selling them in the South, where, in turn, they stole driving horses which they disposed of in the North at a very great profit. (Courtesy of the New York State Historical Association, Cooperstown, New York)*

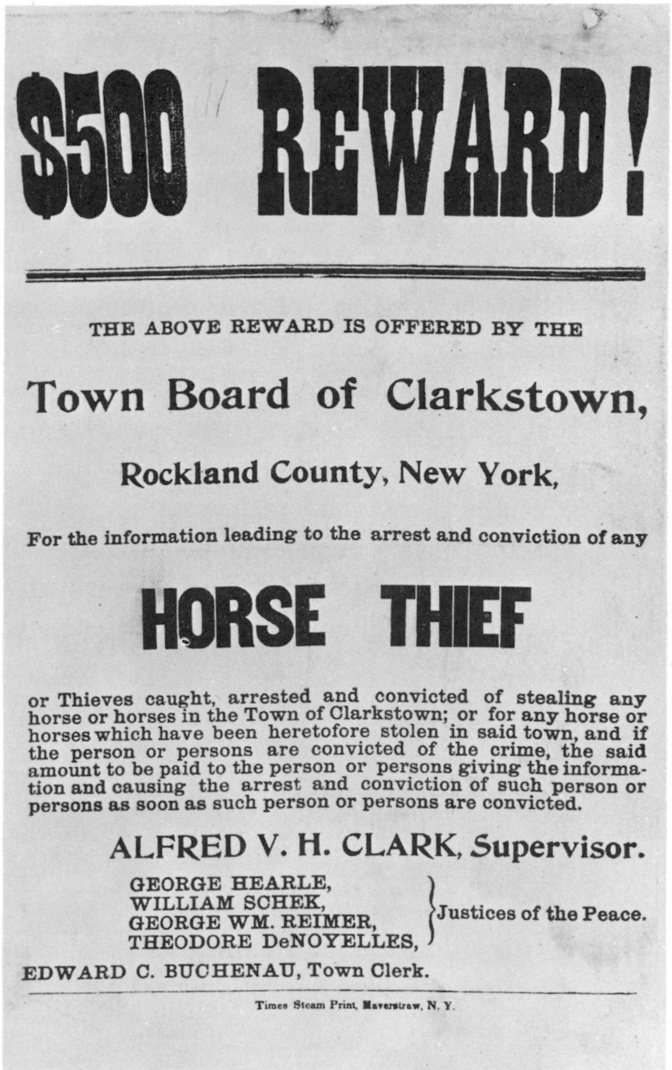

$500 REWARD!

THE ABOVE REWARD IS OFFERED BY THE

Town Board of Clarkstown,

Rockland County, New York,

For the information leading to the arrest and conviction of any

HORSE THIEF

or Thieves caught, arrested and convicted of stealing any horse or horses in the Town of Clarkstown; or for any horse or horses which have been heretofore stolen in said town, and if the person or persons are convicted of the crime, the said amount to be paid to the person or persons giving the information and causing the arrest and conviction of such person or persons as soon as such person or persons are convicted.

ALFRED V. H. CLARK, Supervisor.

GEORGE HEARLE,
WILLIAM SCHEK,
GEORGE WM. REIMER,
THEODORE DeNOYELLES, } Justices of the Peace.

EDWARD C. BUCHENAU, Town Clerk.

Times Steam Print, Haverstraw, N. Y.

vised a scheme of getting his point across through a metaphorical tale about a stagecoach. Entering the taproom and engaging Ramsay in their favorite subject, the doctor finally asked him how long a well-constructed coach would last on the road: "Now, Squire, if you had a fine well-built old coach that had done good service, but showed age by being a little shackling, being sprung a little, having the seams open, would you hitch it up with young horses and put it on a rough road, or would you favor it with steady old stagers and the smoothest road you could find?" The

SPECTATOR-OFFICE—
Middletown, August 21, 1814.
From the Albany Register, Extra. of August 17.

By a Gentleman arrived in the stage from Utica we received a handbill issued from the Utica Gazette Office, this morning, containing the following important information, which we hasten to lay before our readers:

GLORIOUS
VICTORY!!

Extract of a letter, received by express from an Officer of high standing, to M. Hitchcock, Esq. P. M. of this village, dated

[illegible]O, *August* 15—3 *o'clock P. M.*

[illegible]ay gained a most brilliant victory over the enemy this morning. Lieut Gen. Drummond attacked our troops at Fort Erie, about half past two o'clock. The battle was obstinately contested for more than two hours—the British fought hard, but were beaten at every point, with a loss of more than FIVE HUNDRED men killed and wounded, besides near Three Hundred Prisoners. Lt. Gen. Drummond and many other officers are among the slain. Our loss does not exceed fifty, killed and wounded!!"

Plate 43. *Broadsides such as this concerning the sharply contested land action of the War of 1812 always created great excitement at the local tavern. (Courtesy of the New York State Historical Association, Cooperstown, New York)*

squire's reply was, "Well, Doctor, if I had such a coach as that *I would soak it.*"

Each tavern had its characters who adopted the inn as a second home. In 1744, Dr. Alexander Hamilton referred to just such a fellow whom he had met at a tavern in Salem, Massachusetts. Frequently, this old character would stop Dr. Hamilton to visit with him. "When I told him I came from Maryland he said he had frequently read of that place, but never had seen it. This old fellow, by his own account, had read of everything, but had seen nothing. He affected being a scholar, or a man much given to reading or study, and used a great many hard words in discourse, which he generally misapplied."

Not all tavern keepers were men. Many women, especially widows, in early America gained their livelihood from operating inns and taverns. Mrs. Clark was among those who were licensed to open a tavern. Stipulations required of Mrs. Clark were that she "provide a fitt man yt is godlie to manage ye business," in Salem, Massachusetts, in 1645.

Mrs. Nicholas Howard was given a license in 1684 "to entertain Lodgers in the absence of her husband;" other licenses were granted to women to keep victualling-houses, to prepare and sell beer, and to draw wine. Some women, whose husbands were away from home, did not have the same privileges as Mrs. Howard, for they were restricted to the sale of food and drink, and were not allowed to entertain lodgers.

From a study of Vermont law, the writer discovered an act passed November 2, 1798 "directing the mode of obtaining licences, and regulating Inns and houses of publick entertainment." The act concerns the nomination of tavern keepers, the assessment of tavern keepers by the court, "and such clerk shall receive seventeen cents, and the judges of said court thirty-four cents, for each license so granted, and no more."

As a point of interest today when nationally there is such debate over public accommodations, the writer finds of interest Section·4 of this 1798 law. "That *every* person, licensed as aforesaid, shall *at all times* be furnished with suitable refreshments, provisions, and accommodations for travellers, their cattle and horses; on penalty of forfeiting the sum of *three dollars,* to the use of any person who will sue for the same: and may, on complaint to the county court of the same county, (and just cause shown) be deprived of his or her license."

Nor was Vermont without its laws governing intemperance. According to an act passed November 15, 1821, "selectmen (were) to post up notifications, forbidding spirituous liquors to common tiplers." But, according to Section 2 of this act, "Nothing in this act shall prevent any person from administering, as *medicine,* to the person whose name shall be posted up, as aforesaid, such spirituous liquors, and in such quantities, and at such periods as some regular practising physician shall certify to be necessary for the health of such person, so posted up, as aforesaid; nor to prevent any person for whom such person, posted up as aforesaid, shall be labouring, regularly by day's works, or for a longer period, from giving such labourer any spirituous liquors, in the ordinary way of refreshment for labourers, and in such quantities, and at such periods, as cannot be in danger of producing intoxication."

The owner of a tavern who did not keep "a regular and orderly house" was in serious difficulty, for he was to be presented in court, pay a fine, and likely lose his license for the rest of the year.

Unlicensed persons were subject to heavy fines, costs of prosecution, etc., whether he "shall publickly or privately sell any wine, rum, brandy or any other strong liquors; metheglin, strong beer, ale, or cider, by a less quantity than one quart of wine, rum, brandy . . . "

ROLE PLAYED BY TAVERNS

E. L. Bynner writes summarily of the social, political, and military functions of the early tavern:

They were the centres of so much of its life and affairs, the resort at once of judge and jury, of the clergy and the laity, of the politician and the merchant; where the selectmen came to talk over the affairs of the

Plate 44. *Turkey shoots were very popular in the early days and frequently were sponsored by inns. This oil on canvas was painted in 1857 by Tompkins H. Matteson (1813–1884) and depicts a scene described in* The Pioneers *by James Fenimore Cooper. (Courtesy of the New York State Historical Association, Cooperstown, New York)*

> town, and higher officials to discuss the higher interests of the province; where royal governors and distinguished strangers were entertained alike with the humblest wayfarer and the meanest citizen; where were held the carousals of roistering red-coat officers, and the midnight plottings of muttering stern-lipped patriots; where, in fine, the swaggering ensign of the royal army, the frowning Puritan, the obnoxious Quaker, the Huguenot refugee, and the savage Indian chief from the neighboring forest might perchance jostle each other in the common taproom.

For keen insight into the role of taverns in the American Revolution, one finds the following statement by Earle significant: "Many (taverns) served as court-rooms when court-martials were held; others were seized for military prisons; others were fired upon; others served as barracks; some as officers' headquarters; others held secret meetings of partiots; many were used as hospitals."

The Green Dragon Inn was called the headquarters of the Revolution by Daniel Webster. It was used as a hospital during the war. One of its main functions during the conflicts with the British is described by Paul Revere:

> In the fall of 1774 and winter of 1775, I was one of upwards of thirty men, chiefly mechanics, who formed ourselves with a Committee for the purpose of watching the movements of the British soldiers and gaining every intelligence of the movements of the Tories. We held our meetings at the Green Dragon Tavern. This committee were astonished to find all their secrets known to General Gage, although every time they met every member swore not to reveal their transactions even to Hancock, Adams, Otis, Warren or Church.

This was the building, too, in which the first Grand Lodge of Masons, with Warren as its first Grand Master, held its meetings.

As has been said, "The story of our War for Independence could not be dissociated from the old taverns; they are a part of our national history." They served as a rendezvous for the patriotic bands. Here they could listen to the rousing speeches of American rebels. With every bowl of punch consumed, treason to King George magnified.

As John Adams described the tenor of the times:

> Within the course of the year, before the meeting of Congress in 1774, on a journey to some of our circuit courts in Massachusetts, I stopped one night at a tavern in Shrewsbury about forty miles from Boston, and as I was cold and wet, I sat down at a good fire in the bar-room to dry my great-coat and saddle-bags, till a fire could be made in my chamber. There presently came in, one after another, half a dozen, or half a score substantial yeomen of the neighborhood, who, sitting down to the fire after lighting their pipes, began a lively conversation on politics. As I believed I was unknown to all of them, I sat in total silence to hear them. One said, 'The people of Boston are distracted.' Another answered, 'No wonder the people of Boston are distracted. Oppression will make wise men mad.' A third said, 'What would you say if a fellow should come to your house and tell you he was come to take a list of your cattle, that Parliament might tax you for them at so much a head? And how should you feel if he was to go and break open your barn or take down your oxen, cows, horses, and sheep? 'What should I say?' replied the first, 'I would knock him in the head.' 'Well,' said a fourth, 'if Parliament can take away Mr. Hancock's wharf and Mr. Rowe's wharf, they can take away your barn and my house.' After much more reasoning in this style, a fifth, who had as yet been silent, broke out: 'Well, it's high time for us to rebel; we must rebel some time or other, and we had better rebel now than at any time to come. If we put it off for ten or twenty years, and let them go on as they have begun, they will get a strong party among us, and plague us a great deal more than they can now.

After the Sons of Liberty were organized in 1768, they, too, met in taverns. At York, Maine, the sign-board displayed a portrait of Pitt and the words, "Entertainment for the Sons of Liberty." In a Worcester tavern, two girls sang the "New Liberty Song," while John Adams listened, aglow with enthusiasm.

Everywhere, liberty poles and liberty trees were dedicated. One of these was the Liberty Tree which stood in front of the Olney Tavern in Providence. At its dedication in 1768, the orator stood perched among its branches on a platform some twenty feet from the ground. It was he who dedicated this tree to Liberty's cause. One of the most famous of these trees was Boston's Liberty Tree. It was dedicated at a 1765 celebration held in honor of the expected repeal of the Stamp Act. Later, its plaque carried this statement, "This tree was planted in 1646 and pruned by order of the Sons of Liberty February 14, 1766." August 14, 1769 was a day of special celebration in Boston. After the Sons of Liberty met under the Liberty Tree, dinner was served in the tavern. Over three hundred people were served a bountiful meal which included three barbecued pigs. There was much singing, many speeches, and a great many toasts, the last of which follows: "Strong halters, firm blocks, and sharp axes to all such as deserve them." But John Adams, writing of the fourteen toasts offered in Boston, says in his Diary account of the day, "to the honor of the Sons I did not see one person intoxicated or near it."

It was at the Sudbury Wayside Inn and Winchester's Black Horse Tavern where soldiers reassembled after the battle of Lexington. Two years previously, those planning the Boston Tea Party had assembled where Samuel Cole's first ordinary had stood in 1634.

But in peace-time, the taverns were truly "houses of entertainment", including theatrical productions, bear and turkey shoots, bull-baiting, fox chasing, wolf-routs or drives.

The very first attempt at dramatic production in New England was cause for violent opposition. The first "playlets" were entitled drolls. These were performed in the taverns and coffee-houses. Among these were *Pickle Herring, Taylor riding to Brentford,* and *Harlequin and Scaramouch. Otway's Orphans* was produced by two young English actors around 1750, at a Boston coffee-house. Boston magistrates took severe steps to see that such an offense would not be repeated. A clever way to get around the term "play acting" was through the introduction of the "histrionic academies." Sometimes, they were called "Moral Dialogues" as was the case June 10, 1762 at the King's Arms Tavern in Newport, Rhode Island.

The January 11, 1773 issue of the *Boston Evening Post* carried an advertisement for forthcoming "bear and turkey shoots" at the Punch Bowl Tavern in Brookline.

A June, 1806 issue of the *Essex Register* announced a "bull-baiting" and fox chase to be held on Independence Day, at the Half Way House on the Salem Turnpike. The Grand Fox Chase on the Marshes was to start exactly at 6 o'clock.

Not only was fox hunting popular in

New England, but it was especially so in the South. As Alice Morse Earle points out, "The Middle and Southern states saw frequent meets of mounted gentlemen with hounds, usually at the tavern, to which they returned after the day's end with suitable jollity."

The wolf-rout or wolf-drive was an American adaptation, no doubt, of the old English "drift of the forest." At times, this meant that every living forest creature was in danger of being shot. On December 4, 1818 a Bedford County, Pa. newspaper reported that about seven hundred men joined together for such a hunting party. Guns were used only at first; then bayonets, poles, clubs, and pitchforks became instruments of murder. In all, some five bears, fourteen foxes, nine wolves, and three hundred deer were killed. The only cheerful aspect of the expedition is that "it was estimated that more than double the number escaped. The expedition closed with great mirth at the tavern."

But not all the killing was of animals, sometimes it was of people on Execution Day which is said to have been "a grand day for the taverns." Ten thousand people witnessed Burnham's hanging in 1805. In a report of the scene, one learns that "old and young, mothers with babes, lads and lasses, even confirmed invalids thronged to this great occasion."

Perhaps the choice of the tavern as the locale for execution was due in part to the fact that the upper rooms were often used for lockups and temporary jails. One finds among the writings of Mr. S. L. Frey of Palatine Bridge frequent reference to episodes of tavern life connected with this custom.

Perhaps, Mrs Earle's conclusion is the explanation. "Our ancestors found in criminals and all the accompaniments of crime their chief source of diversion. They did not believe in lonely captivity but in public obloquy of criminals. The only exciting and stirring emotions which entered their lives came through the recounting of crimes and offences, and the sight of the punishment of these crimes and offences; rising of course to the highest point of excitement in witnessing the public executions of criminals." This writer wishes that one could now relegate such attitudes to the past. To say they no longer exist, alas, would be a distortion of the truth.

Fortunately, one early custom which can be said to be completely outmoded is the former selling of paupers at the tavern. This was a much more frequent practice than the sale of criminals. It is described by Earle as being—

An exhibition of curious contrasts: the prosperous and thirsty townsmen drinking at the tavern bar, and the forlorn group of homeless, friendless creatures, usually young children and aged folk, waiting to be sold to the lowest bidder for a term of feeble service and meagre keep. . . . The auction at the tavern was frankly brutal, but the end accomplished was so satisfactory that the custom has within a few years been

Plate 45. *An 1852 liquor license issued to Ambrose Gregg to maintain a tavern at what is now Pennellville, Oswego County, in Central New York. Note the stipulation " . . . that a tavern is absolutely necessary for the actual accommodation of travellers." (Courtesy of Edith M. Gregg)*

We the undersigned forming a board of commi-sioners of Excise for the town of Schroeppel in the county of Oswego having been applied to by Ambrose Gregg a resident of the said town who purposes to keep an inn or tavern at his dwelling house in said town of Schroeppel for a license to sell strong & spirituous liquors and wines to be drank in his house and being satisfied that he is of good moral character and of sufficient ability to keep a tavern and that he has the necessary accommodations to entertain trav-elers and that a tavern is absolutely necessary for the actual accommodations of travellers at the place where he purposes to keep the same and for which he has paid a duty of Four Dollars determined by us: we do therefore grant this license and authorize him to sell strong and spirituous liquors and wines to be drank in the ~~town~~ or tavern to be kept at the place mentioned. This license is to be ~~[illegible]~~ force untill the day after the first monday in May next

In witness whereof we have hereunto subscr-ibed our names the 8th day of January 1852

Oliver Breed } Supervisor

A. Diefendorf
J. B. Kin[illegible] } Justices

Ambrose Gregg
License

resumed by the more advanced and thoughtful guardians of paupers in many New England towns.

One is shocked to learn from the above source that "as for the auction sale of aged and infirm paupers, it is not wholly a thing of the past. In Lackwanna township in Pike County, Pennsylvania, paupers are sold to the lowest bidder." In 1899, the following sign was posted at Rowland Station: "A Woman for Sale." As in earlier days, the "vendue" was to be held at a tavern, Rutan's Hotel.

The story of what actually ensued is a tragic one. Mrs. Elmira Quick, the woman to be sold, had three living sons and a daughter. It is said that the bar-room was crowded when seventy-seven year old Mrs. Quick was put up "to be sold to the lowest bidder for keep for a year." There was spirited bidding. It "ran quickly down from four dollars a week. A backwoodsman had just offered to take her for a dollar and a half a week, when Mrs. Quick firmly bid a dollar and a quarter." The Overseer of the Poor was hesitant, but Mrs. Quick assured him that she could maintain herself for such an amount, sixteen cents a day. No one made a lower offer; so he was required to bring the bargain to a close and draw up the sale-papers.

But to return to the statement that taverns served a local community need for a social and political center, and were not primarily intended to provide hospitality for strangers, how did one fare who was a traveller?

Quite frankly, there were few places in the early days where one could stop to dine or spend the night. The few available places were usually of inferior quality. There are numerous accounts of wagon drivers who had to stay over night "upon leaves on the ground with the feet towards a large fire, which they make by the road side wherever night overtakes them, and are covered only with a blanket."

In the South, travellers who were fortunate enough to be invited to spend the night at a planter's house usually fared well in food, drink, and lodging. In fact, southern hospitality had been particularly intended for relatives, neighbors, or an occasional traveller. But when hosts, like Jefferson, gained a reputation for being especially generous, "they were beset by tourists and thought they would like to try it at a great man's house and save a tavern bill." Captain Bacon, Jefferson's overseer, described what happened:

> They were there all times of the year; but about the middle of June the travel would commence from the lower part of the State to the Springs, and then there was a perfect throng of visitors. They travelled in their own carriages and came in gangs, the whole family with carriage and riding horses and servants, sometimes three or four such gangs at a time. We had thirty-six stalls for horses, and only used ten of them for the stock we kept there.

Bacon added that often the rest were full; "I had to send horses off to another place. I have often sent a wagon-load of hay up to the stable, and the next morning there would not be enough left to make a bird's nest. I have killed a fine beef and it would be all eaten in a day or two." Such practices as these explain at least in part why Jefferson died in such economic plight.

Then there were those who found it

necessary to stay overnight at a small farmhouse; often they found "miserable conditions." Those who lodged at an inn, tavern, or ordinary had a real experience, such as that of Madame Knight who journeyed on horseback from Boston to New York in 1704. Her description of her stay at "Haven's Tavern in the Narragansett Country" illustrates how crude life at that time and place was. As she records it in her *Journal,* one also senses her native wit. Having retired to her room which is separated from the kitchen by a single board partition, and to a bed "which tho pretty hard, yet neet and handsome," she is unable to sleep because of an argument in the adjoining room by some topers over the significance of the name of their region, Narragansett:

One said it was named so by ye Indians, because there grew a Brier there, of a prodigious Highth and bigness, the like hardly ever known, called by the Indians Narragansett; And quotes an Indian of so Barberous

Plate 46. *"Horace Tuttle's Livery Stable" is the title of this oil on canvas painted by an anonymous artist c. 1870. A common regulation that inn keepers had to meet was the usual stipulation that provision be made for "a good and sufficient shed or covering for horses, near to his or her house, with a suitable trough or manger, convenient for the accommodation of travellers' horses." (Courtesy of the New York State Historical Association, Cooperstown, New York)*

a name for his Author, that I could not write it. His Antagonist Replyed no—It was from a Spring it had its name, wch hee well knew where it was, which was extreem cold in summer, and as Hott as could be imagined in the winter, which was much resorted too by the natives, and by them called Narragansett, (Hott and Cold,) and that was the originall of their places name—with a thousand Impertinances not worth notice, wch He utter'd with such a Roreing voice and Thundering blows with the fist of wickedness on the Table, that it pierced my very head. I heartily fretted, and wish't 'um tongue tyed; but wth as little succes as a friend of mine once, who was (as shee said) kept a whole night awake, on a Jorny, by a country Left. and a Sergent, Insigne and a Deacon, contriving how to bring a triangle into a Square. They kept calling for tother Gill, wch while they were swallowing, was some Intermission; But presently, like Oyle to fire, encreased the flame.

At this point the philosophical traveller placed her candle upon a chest by her bedside, and "fell to my old way of composing my Resentment, in the following manner:

I ask thy Aid, O Potent Rum!
To Charm these wrangling Topers Dum.
Thou hast their Giddy Brains possest—
The man confounded wth the Beast—
And I, poor I, can get no rest.
Intoxicate them wth thy fumes:
O still their Tongues till morning comes!

Then Madame Knight adds, "And I know not but my wishes took effect; for the dispute soon ended with 'tother Dram; and so Good night!"

It is good to know that this courageous and "fearfull female traiveller" finally reached her destination, New York. After being greeted by Mr. Thomas Burroughs, a prominent merchant, who aided her in attending to the business matters for which she had made the trip and witnessing the sleighing between New York and "the Bowery", she was graciously received by "a handsome Entertainment of five or six dishes and choice Beer and metheglin Cyder," at the home of Madam Dowes.

But some times it was to one's advantage to be kept awake all night by the "topers" in the next room. At least, Phelps of Simsbury, Connecticut, found it so when he was trying to find out the strength of Fort Ticonderoga for Ethan Allen. Phelps had taken a room at a local tavern near the fort. British officers spent the night drinking in the next room. Phelps never dozed a moment. In the morning, he left the tavern as one of the officers did. Inquiring where the nearest barber was, the Britisher explained that he was going there too, and to come along. Passing the Fort, Phelps commented on how it didn't look very strongly fortified. The officer not only agreed but said the fort could be taken with no effort at all; the powder had all gotten wet. Phelps could hardly wait to return to the ferryman and get back across the lake to tell Ethan. But knowing he must not make a wrong move, he sauntered leisurely down the bank after leaving the barber shop, and hailed the ferryman. As soon as he was some distance from the fort, he asked the boatman if he might row. With oars in hand, he made a fast trip across the lake to spread the news.

Ethan Allen, to whom the news was brought, was himself a frequent imbiber of the punch bowl. One such instance was around April 1, 1772, when Ethan hitched his horse in front of Benedict's Tavern in Albany, went in and ordered a bowl of punch. On the wall hung a broadside by the

Governor proclaiming Ethan an outlaw. Ripping down the Governor's poster, Ethan posted his own, strode out of the tavern, jumped on his horse, shouted three cheers for the Green Mountain Boys, and galloped away.

Now, with the siege of Ticonderoga, the rum flowed freely. In the words of Ethan's biographer, John Pell: "Captain Delaplace's liquor was distributed as rapidly as possible. The Green Mountain Boys were having the time of their lives."

But this relatively easy victory at Fort Ticonderoga might not have been possible if Phelps had not been kept awake all night being bombarded with secret bits about the fort by the revellers next door at his tavern.

A traveller from England who stopped at a number of ordinaries in Carolina made the following descriptive observation:

> They were mostly log-huts, or a frame weather-boarded; the better sort consisted of one story and two rooms; the more numerous having no internal divisions. . . . One corner of the room would be occupied by a 'bunk' containing the family bed; another by a pine-wood chest, the family clothes press and larder; a third would be railed off for a bar, containing a rum-keg and tumbler. The rest of the furniture consisted of two chairs and a table, all in the last stage of palsy. . . . If hunger and fatique compelled you to remain, a little Indian corn for your horse, and a blanket on the hearth, with your saddle for a pillow, to represent a bed, were the most you would obtain. . . . As to edibles, whether you called for breakfast, dinner, or supper, the reply was one—eggs and bacon. . . . Ten to one you had to cook the meal yourself. . . . No sooner were you seated than the house dog (of the large wolf breed) would arrange himself beside you and lift his lank, hungry jaws expressively to your face. The young children, never less than a dozen (women seeming to bear them in a litter in those regions), at the smell and sight of the victuals would let up a yell enough to frighten the wolves.

By the beginning of the nineteenth century, however, conditions were better in the taverns. The main room was neater; usually, the floor was sanded and the large fireplace with its numerous benches and chairs was an hospitable sight. Often, in one part of this "lounge", there were tables where customers could eat. The bar was on one side, and was considered an important adjunct to the inn.

There was no such thing as a "private room and bath" in colonial inns. Many times, there were only two bedrooms; one for men, and the other for women. Usually, there was only one bed. This meant that four or more guests would be accommodated together; any late arrivals made themselves as comfortable as possible on the floor.

Another requirement of the inn keeper was "to put and keep up a sign," within thirty days. This may shed some light on the reason why so many artists found sign painting such a lucrative career. Many a tavern sign was painted by Benjamin West in and around Philadelphia. One of these was for the Three Crowns, a tavern which was located on the King's Highway in Salisbury Township in Lancaster County. The tavern was so named because its keeper was an ardent Tory. Often, during the Revolution bullets were fired into the sign by members of the Continental Army. Widow Caldwell's Old Hat Tavern on the old Philadelphia road in Leacock Township also had a West sign-board.

The "Ale Bearers" was another sign painted by West. On one side of this sign there is pictured a man holding a glass of ale and peering through it. Two brewers' porters carrying a cask on a pole with case hooks is on the other side.

West was not the only great artist to have painted signs in the Philadelphia area. According to tradition, several sign-boards were painted by such artists as Gilbert Stuart, Hicks, and the Peales. Matthew Pratt, one of West's pupils, did an elaborate sign for the Federal Convention of 1787 Inn, of Philadelphia. The sign depicted the National Convention which met May 14, 1787 "either in Independence Hall or the State House" to frame the federal Constitution. Washington is seen seated under a panel carrying the state's arms, on one side of the sign. Judge Wilson, with Franklin sitting close by, occupied the chair. And on both sides were these lines:

These thirty-eight men together have agreed
That better times to us shall very soon succeed.

Woodside painted a sign-board which was described in the August, 1820 newspaper announcement in Philadelphia telling of his opening "a house of entertainment." It adds, that Samuel E. Warwick "has copied for his sign Mr. Binn's beautiful copperplate engraving of the Declaration of Independence, by that justly celebrated artist, Mr. Woodside."

Portraits of George Washington and pictures of American eagles were quite in vogue for sign-board motifs during and after the Revolutionary War. James Carson, landlord of the Washington Inn at Holmesburg, Pennsylvania, included the following remarks in an address in 1816: "Here money and merit will secure you respect and honor, and a hearty welcome to choice liquors and to sumptuous fare. Is it cold? You shall find a comfortable fire. Is it warm? Sweet repose under a cool and grassy shade. In short, every exertion shall be made to grace the sign of the hero and

Plate 47, opposite page. *Inn keepers were usually required to put up a sign within thirty days of their opening. This one belonged to the R. Chadwick Inn. (Courtesy of the New York State Historical Association, Cooperstown, New York)*

R CHADWICK
INN

statesman who was first in war, first in peace, and first in the hearts of his countrymen."

Often, there were portraits of William Pitt on sign-boards. A pupil of Gilbert Stuart and Sully, named Jacob Eicholtz, painted the Pitt sign which hung outside Pitt Tavern in Lancaster, Pennsylvania.

Nor were the portraits of Franklin with Lafayette omitted from the subject matter of the sign-board portrait painter. In 1774, the couplet on the Franklin Inn sign in Philadelphia read as follows:

Come view your patriot father! and your friend,
And toast to Freedom and to slavery's end.

Another patriot especially honored by having his portait appear on sign-boards was John Hancock. The sign-board of Hancock Tavern bore his portrait beneath which was painted, "Gov^R^. Hancock." According to tradition, Landlord Duggan, an admirer of Hancock, placed the order to have it painted. Earle describes it as one which "crudely resembles one of Hancock, by Copley." It hung for many years, but in one terrific wind storm, it killed a citizen, as it crashed. Thereafter, it was nailed to the wall. For some time, it was housed at Lexington Memorial Hall but was then moved to Boston.

Birds, animals, and insects also provided sign-board themes. A beehive swarming with active bees was depicted at two taverns; one, in Philadelphia; the other, at Frankford. The former's motto was, "By Industy We Thrive." But an even more appropriate verse was the following:

Here in this hive we're all alive,
Good liquor makes us funny.
If you are dry, step in an try
The flavor of our honey.

In Philadelphia and also in Boston there were similar signs picturing a tree, bird, ship, and a mug of beer. Each sign bore the following tippling-house rhyme:

This is the tree that never grew,
This is the bird that never flew,
This is the ship that never sailed,
This is the mug that never failed.

A good summary of the variety of sign-boards in the Philadelphia area can be gleaned from Palmer, an Englishman, who visited Philadelphia in 1818:

We observed several curious tavern signs in Philadelphia and on the roadside, among others Noah's Ark; a variety of Apostles; Bunyan's Pilgrim; a cock on a lion's back, crowing, with Liberty issuing from his beak; naval engagements in which the British are in a desperate situation; the most common signs are eagles, heads of public characters, Indian Kings, & c.

A similar practice of taverns hanging signs, painted often by recognized artists of the day, prevailed, also, in New England. Such a one hung before Hayden Tavern in Essex, Connecticut. An unusual feature regarding this sign is the fact that on one side there is carved a full-rigged ship flying the Union Jack; and on the other, the British coat of arms. The letters U.A.H. appear at the top on each side together with the date 1766. Uriah and Ann Hayden were the tavern-keepers for whom the sign was made and hence the initials.

The Bissell Tavern sign, dated 1801, hung in front of that ordinary at Bissell's Ferry, East Windsor, Connecticut. Originally this sign carried a portrait of George Washington surrounded by thirteen interlaced links, over which were the words, "The 13 United States", and beneath which was the statement, "Entertainment by David Bissell, A.D. 1777." E. Wolcott's name was painted on in substitution for Bissell in 1787. Joseph Phelps acquired both the house and sign in 1801. At this time a new motif was offered. Earle notes it as being "a copy of the first gold eagle of 1795, and on the other, the reverse side of same coin and the name J. Phelps." When the Ferry Tavern was bought by J. Pelton, in 1816, paint removed all of the design except the initials J. P. which were also his own.

Figures of horses, sporting subjects, and coaches were as popular for sign-board motifs as were people. A 1786 sign at the Perkins Inn, in Hopkinton, New Hampshire depicted a rider with his horse and hounds. On one side of the Williams Tavern sign at Centrebrook, Connecticut were shown a coach and horses. The other side pictured a portly gentleman sitting at a bountiful table drinking a glass of wine.

A favorite subject for portraits was Indian chiefs. Three taverns which had Indians depicted were Stickney Tavern, 1791, in Concord, New Hampshire; the W. Tarlton Inn at Haverhill, New Hampshire; and the E. Wells Tavern in Greenfield Meadows, Massachusetts.

Other designs for taverns and ordinaries might be of Jolly Sailors, a Bunch of Grapes, the King's Head; at times, taverns used slogans on their signs instead of paintings or carvings. Typical of these was the following: "Drink for the thirsty, Food for the hungry, Lodging for the weary, and Good Keeping for Horses." Or, the sign of George A. Chafee of Middletown, Connecticut which read, "As we journey through life, let us live by the way." In Coventry, Connecticut, that of H. Rose said, "A bird in the hand is worth two in the bush."

Plate 48. *Sign used at the Bump Tavern in Ashland near Windham, New York. (Courtesy of the New York State Historical Association, Cooperstown, New York)*

Thompson R. Harlow, Director of the Connecticut Historical Society, discloses the names of some of the recognized artists who engaged in sign painting in Connecticut, in his introduction to *Morgan B. Brainard's Tavern Signs* (1958). Abner Reed of East Windsor, an engraver, also painted signs on various media—glass, wood, canvas, and tin. Newton C. Brainard in his article, "A Jack-of-all Trades," which appeared in the Connecticut Historical Society's *Bulletin,* (July, 1956), mentions Stephanas Knight who painted, repaired, and altered many of the trade signs. At times, according to

Harlow, house painters and paper hangers also painted tavern signs. One of these arts and craftsmen was Chester Andross who was an associate in business with Phipps Deming. John Sutcliff Barrow had many interests including the painting of sleighs and coaches, as well as signs. Also, he was available as instructor for a Drawing School, "upon moderate terms, and at such times as will not interfere with any other school," according to his advertisement. Beatty and Company were a Norwich, Connecticut firm engaged in sign, house and heraldry painting. In Hartford, John C. Bull was both a coach and sign painter. Two men by the name of Janes joined with him in 1805 to form the Janes and Bull firm. Harlow, in discussing portrait painters who also advertised the more practical types of painting, mentions Abraham Delanoy in New Haven, Nathaniel F. Wales of Litchfield, Isaac Sanford and Webster James of Norwich and Hartford.

Thus, the painting of signs provided lucrative opportunities to the artists of the day, and legal identification to the townspeople of proper authorization for such a tavern to operate as a place of entertainment. The term "townspeople" is stressed, for let it be remembered that at first, "strange travellers" were not usually welcome.

PHYSICAL FEATURES

One wonders what the construction of a typical tavern was like. In Wickford, Rhode Island, the old Phillips farm-house was at one time used as a tavern. Its great chimney is over twenty feet square. It takes up so much room that no central staircase was built; rather, there are three separate winding stairs in the same number of corners of the house. Hooks upon which to hang firearms are hung on each chimneypiece. Tobacco and pipe drawers are located at one side. Drawers such as these were often in the taverns. The Dutch located theirs over the front door in the entry, where a narrow three or four steps led to them. Smoking tongs, or pipetongs, would usually hang alongside the drawer or shelf. With these, the smoker could lift a coal from the fire-place with which to light his pipe. A comfortier, a small brazier of metal in which small coals could be handed around with which to also light one's pipe, was often a companion piece to the tongs. Wealthy Dutch settlers also had comfortiers made of silver.

Sometimes the tavern parlor walls were painted with a mural, such as scenes from a forest. In other parlors, wallpaper was used. For example, scenes of a fox-chase might be the paper's motif.

Usually, the parlor was used as a sitting room for women travelling; or a wealthy client might rent it for his personal use. It was a much more sedate room, far less jovial than the taproom. Yet, often in the winter

Plate 49. *Upper hallway of the Bump Tavern at Cooperstown, New York, with wall decorations stenciled in dark green, black, and red on a white background. Doors lead to guest bedrooms and the drover's room. The hallway expands at the front into a ballroom. (Courtesy of the New York State Historical Association, Cooperstown, N.Y.)*

a warm, glowing fire would burn in the open fireplace, resulting in "the old rude-furnished room" bursting "flowerlike into rosy bloom."

The largest room of the tavern was generally the taproom. Here, too, there was an enormous fireplace. It had a sanded floor, seats and chairs. Frequently, a tall, rather crude desk, on which a guest might pen a letter or sign a contract, was situated in the taproom. Here, the landlord could conveniently make out the bills and keep his accounts.

One of the most interesting furnishings in the room was the bar. Often, it was made with a kind of iron grating, which could be closed, if necessary.

Dr. Wayland F. Dunaway in *A History of Pennsylvania* writes:

The taverns were of different types, some more pretentious than others. Those of the humbler class catered to wagoners and drovers, while the others were patronized by the gentry. The better taverns were usually built of stone, and their accommodations and tables were a constant source of pride to the owners. Whatever the class of tavern, however, its one indispensable feature was the bar, which provided liquid refreshments not only for jaded travelers but also for the inhabitants of the countryside.

Dunaway adds a description of the impact on tavern and community life caused by the advent of the turnpike.

Stagecoaches formed an important feature of the life of those early days, and their arrival at towns and hamlets along the way was an eventful occurrence in the day's course, since the coaches brought newspapers and travelers from the outside world to furnish topics for discussion by the worthies gathered of an evening at the tavern. All was animation at the tavern when the stage-coach arrived with horses in full run and with streamers flying and horns tooting. The first through line of stagecoaches from Philadelphia to Pittsburgh was established in 1804, and it took three days to make the trip.

The terms of taverns, inns and ordinaries were not always interchangeable. In New England and New York state, the name tavern was usually used. Inn was a more common term in Pennsylvania, and ordinary was generally the colloquialism of the South. At times, inn and tavern were used to distinguish between a mere drinking place and one where meals were served, also. The word "inn" was despised in some localities, for it seemed too English. The term "hotel", or house was not used widely until after the Revolution.

WILLIAMSBURG ORDINARIES

In Williamsburg, Virginia there was among the early ordinaries one operated by John Burdette. Although meals were served, it was chiefly a drinking and gambling place. An inventory compiled of Burdette's possessions at the time of his death itemizes articles typical of his trade. "1 old Fiddle," "11 pr. dice," "1 billiard table with sticks, balls, etc." and "a Quantity of choice old Madeira Wine, and old Barbados Rum."

Francis Sharp was granted a license in 1718 to offer "good, wholesome and cleanly lodging and diet for travellers." One of the stipulations was to forbid "any unlawful Gaming . . . nor on the sabbath day (to) suffer any person to tipple or drink more than is necessary."

Christiana Campbell's Tavern is described by a French visitor in 1765 as one "where all the best people resorted." He became acquainted with a number of them, including Colonel Byrd. George Washington recorded in his diary when he attended the House of Burgesses in 1772, that he had dined in this ordinary ten times within two months. Washington and some of his friends are said to have had a "club" here, where they could meet for dinner to converse generally and to discuss matters of politics.

Plate 50. *Guest bedroom at Bump Tavern. In such taverns there often were only two bedrooms; one for men and the other for women. Usually there was only one bed and several persons were assigned to it. Late arrivals made themselves as comfortable as possible on the floor. Lice and mosquitoes often made sleep questionable if not impossible. Regulations at the Buckthorn New York Inn stipulated: "No more than five to sleep in one bed—No boots to be worn in bed." (Courtesy of the New York State Historical Association, Cooperstown, New York)*

Chowning's Tavern catered to a less wealthy clientele than others in Williamsburg. It opened in 1766 with Josiah Chowning as host. He announced that his ordinary was one "where all who please to favour me with their Custom may depend upon the best of Entertainment for Themselves, Servants, and Horses, and good Pasturage."

In Virginia, the rates to be charged for the various items were determined each year by the county justices, and it was required that they be "openly set up in the common entertaining room."

Gabriel Maupin served not only as host of Williamsburg's Market Square Tavern when he acquired this property in 1771, but he was also Keeper of the Magazine, situated next door, and proprietor of a saddlery and harnessmaker's business.

King's Arms Tavern served a most dignified clientele including Sir Peyton Skipwith, George Washington and William Byrd III. Here, the Ohio Company of Virginia met in 1778, when they were pressing their land claims to the West.

As ancient is this hostelry
As any in the land may be,
Built in the old Colonial day,
When men lived in a grander way,
With ampler hospitality.
A region of repose it seems,
A place of slumber and of dreams,
Remote among the wooded hills!

LONGFELLOW, *Tales of a Wayside Inn*

AMERICA'S LIVELY HERITAGE

Inns became important as a levelling influence, for as Professors Barck and Lefler have pointed out in their writings concerning colonial America, "class distinctions were not recognized at a bar, and there was no attempt to segregate the customers." Barck and Lefler add, "Thomas Jefferson did most of the drafting of the Declaration of Independence in the Indian Queen Tavern in Philadelphia, while George Washington bade farewell to his officers at Fraunces Tavern in New York City at the end of the Revolution."

The gaiety of tavern life often got out of control. Reverend William Bentley became considerably disturbed over certain observations which he had made and recorded in his diary of 1794: "Not only at our return yesterday, did we observe crowds around the new Tavern at the entrance of the Town, but even at this day, we saw at Perkins' on the neck, persons of all descriptions, dancing to a fiddle, drinking, playing with pennies, & c. It is proper such excesses should be checked."

Fisher Ames wrote to Thomas Dwight, February 29, 1804: "I feel provoked to see our Dedham taverns made the scenes of frolic and flip on so many occasions. A gingerbeer lottery, a vendue, a dance, a singing meeting, a sley ride, everything fills them with young fellows, and our apprentice boys already claim the rights of men against their masters."

In respectful and affectionate retrospect, the writer has re-emphasized and further illustrated the important role of beverages and tavern life in our national fabric.

For the most part, it was only natural for our ancestors to become quite concerned over any excessive gaiety as just described. Few "true New-English men" would care to have the taverns and ordinaries of their peaceful towns change into boisterous abodes of "gay resort", of what they termed "the shewing of vain shews," (display of vanity). To them, these were hostelries of "hospitable convenience," not of riotous or too lively entertainment.

The contemporary view of a 17th c. public house was not too dissimilar to Quarles' poem of that day which likens human life to a stay at an inn, and that view remained in the public mind probably as long as did the ordinary. But by the close of the seventeenth century, as has been indicated, the emphasis was on living and all diversions centered at the tavern. At length, as Earle points out,

Whatever there was of novelty in entertainment or instruction, was delivered at the tavern, and it served as the gathering place for folk on scores of duties or pleasures bent. There was in fact a constant panorama passing within the walls before the doors of an old tavern, not only in the shape of distinguished, picturesque, and unwonted guests, but through the variety of uses to which the tavern was put.

And so it is hoped this insight into early American life through its beverages and its taverns will provide a panorama of America's lively heritage.

Glossary

Definitions taken from *Webster's Collegiate Dictionary*. Springfield, Mass.: G. & C. Merriam Co., 1940.

ARRACK: A spirit distilled in the East from rum.

CAUDLE: A kind of warm drink for sick persons; especially, a mixture of wine or ale with eggs, bread or gruel, sugar, and spices.

COBBLER: A drink made of wine, sugar, orange or lemon; and pounded ice.

CORDIAL: An aromatized and sweetened spirit, used as a beverage; a liqueur.

CREAM: A syrupy liqueur.

DRAM, OR DRACHM: A small drink or draft.

ELIXIR: A compound tincture or medicine; the refined spirit; quintessence.

FLIP: A spiced, sweetened drink of ale, beer, or the like to which beaten egg is sometimes added.

HIPPOCRAS: A highly spiced wine.

LIQUEUR: A spirituous liquor flavored with aromatic substances.

NECTAR: A sweet liquid secreted by the nectaries of a plant; the drink of the Gods.

POP: A beverage which expels the cork with a pop from the bottle.

POSSET: A beverage of hot milk, curdled as by ale, wine, etc., and spiced.

PUNCH: A beverage usually composed of wine or distilled liquor, water, milk or tea, with sugar, lemon juice, and often spice or mint.

RATAFIA: Any liqueur flavored with fruit kernels, especially of a bitter almond flavor.

SPIRITUOUS: Containing, or of the nature of, spirit (alcohol); ardent; as spirituous liquors.

TAMARIND: A tropical tree, the fruit or pod of which has an acid pulp and is sometimes used for preserves and also for a laxative drink.

TANKARD: A tall, one handled drinking vessel; especially one of pewter or silver with a lid.

TODDY: A mixture of spirit and hot water, sweetened, as a rum toddy.

TREACLE: A sovereign remedy; a cure. English molasses, specifically molasses which drains from sugar refining molds.

WHEY: The serum or watery part of milk, separated from the more thick or coagulable part, or curd.

WINE: The fermented, or, loosely, the unfermented, juice of any fruit or plant used as a beverage; as currant wine.

Bibliography

ABBOTT, KATHERINE M. *Old Paths and Legends of the New England Border.* New York: 1909

———. *Old Paths and Legends of New England.* New York: 1909

Acts and Laws of His Majesties Colony of Connecticut in New England. Printed in 1702. Reissued, Hartford: Acorn Club, 1901

ADAMS, JAMES TRUSLOW. *The Founding of New England.* Boston: 1921

———. *Provincial Society: 1690–1763.* Macmillan, 1927

ALLEN, JOSEPH. *History of Northborough, Massachusetts.* Worcester: 1880

The Art of Confectionery. (Collected from the best New York, Philadelphia, and Boston Confectioners, and include a large number from the French and other foreign nations)

AUBURN, THOMAS. *Travels through the Interior Parts of America.* (2 vols.) London: 1789

BACON, EDWIN M. *The Connecticut River.* New York: 1907

———. *Historic Pilgrimages in New England.* Boston: 1898

Badger & Porter's Stage Register. Boston: September 6, 1825

BAGLEY, GEORGE K. *The Family Instructor, or Guide to Health.* Montpelier, Vermont: E. P. Walton and Sons, 1848

BARCK, O. T. and LEFLER, H. T. *Colonial America.* New York: Macmillan Co., 1958

BARRY, Sir EDWARD. *Observations Historical, Critical, and Medical, on the Wines of the Ancients. And the Analogy between them and Modern Wines. With General Observations on the Principles and Qualities of Water, and in particular on those of Bath.* London: Printed for T. Cadell, in the Strand, 1775

BEECHER, (Miss). *Domestic Receipt-Book: Designed as a Supplement to her Traetise on Domestic Economy.* (Third Edition). New York: Harper and Bros., Publishers, 1857

BEERS. *A History of Middlesex County, Connecticut.* New York: 1884

BIGELOW, ELLA A. *Historical Reminiscences of Marlborough, Massachusetts.* Marlborough: 1910

BLAKE, J. L. *The Farmer's Everyday Book. or, Sketches of Social Life in the Country. . . .* Auburn: Derby and Miller, 1853

BLANEY, HENRY R. *Old Boston.* Boston: 1896

BLOOMER, AMELIA, (ed.). *Lily* (a magazine)

Boston News Letter, August 16, 1711

Boston, Antique Views of. Boston: 1882

Boston and Vicinity, The Stranger's New Guide through. Boston: 1869

Boston Street Laying-Out Department, Annual Report of, for the Year 1896. Boston: 1897

BOWEN, CLARENCE W. *An Historical Sketch of Woodstock.*

BRAINARD, M. B. *Morgan B. Brainard's Tavern Signs.* Hartford: Connecticut Historical Society, 1958

Breck, Samuel (1771–1862), Recollections of. Philadelphia: 1877

A Brief and True Report for the Traveller concerning

Williamsburg in Virginia. Richmond: 1935

BRODHEAD, JOHN ROMEYN, E. B. O'Callaghan (ed.). *Documents Relating to the Colonial History of the State of New York*. Albany: 1856

BROWN, FRANK CHOUTEAU. *Dwellings of Old Newbury*. (Monograph Series Recording the Architcecture of the American Colonies)

BROWN, THOMAS ALLSTON. *The History of the New York Stage*. (2 vols.) New York: 1903

BRYANT, WILLIAM ALLEN and GAY, SYDNEY HOWARD. *A Popular History of the United States*. (4 vols.) New York: 1878

Bulletin. Connecticut Historical Society, July, 1956

BUNNER, H. C. "The Bowery and Bohemia." *Scribner's Magazine*, Vol. 15, April, 1894

BURRAGE, WALTER L. (Ed.). *Guide Book of Boston for Physicians*. Boston: 1906

Cambridge, An Historic Guide to, Compiled by D. A. R.: Hannah Winthrop Chapter. Cambridge: 1907

CHAMBERLAIN, ALLEN. *Annals of the Grand Monadnock*.

CHAPIN, CHARLES WELLS. *Sketches of the Old Inhabitants and Other Citizens of Old Springfield*. Springfield, Mass.: 1893

CHASE, A. W. *Dr. Chase's Recipes, or, Information for Everybody: An Invaluable Collection of About Eight Hundred Practical Recipes....* Ann Arbor, Michigan: Published by the Author, 1869

CHILD, (Mrs.). *The American Frugal Housewife. Dedicated to Those Who Are Not Ashamed of Economy*. (Thirteenth Edition). Boston: Carter, Hendre, and Company, 1833

CHILDE, CROMWELL. *Old New York Downtown*. New York: n.d.

CLAPP, WILLIAM W. *A Record of the Boston Stage*. Boston and Cambridge: 1853

COLLES, CHRISTOPHER. *A Survey of the Roads of the United States*. N. Y.: 1789

Connecticut Quarterly, The. Vol. iii, Hartford: 1897

Connecticut Magazine, The. Vols. viii, and ix, Hartford

Connecticut, Laws of, in Regard to Turnpikes. 1806 et seq.

Connecticut, The Laws of: An Exact Reprint of the Original Edition of 1673. Hartford: 1865

"Cooper, Peter, Reminscences of." *Century Magazine*, December, 1883

COPELAND, ALFRED MINOT. *A History of Hampden County, Massachusetts*. (3 vols.) Springfield: 1902

CORNELIUS, (Mrs.). *The Young Housekeeper's Friend: or, A Guide to Domestic Economy and Comfort*. Boston: Charles Tappan and New York: Saxton and Huntington, 1846

CRAWFORD, MARY CAROLINE. *Little Pilgrimages among Old New England Inns*. Boston: 1907

———. *The Romance of Old New England Churches*.

DAGGITT, JOHN A. *A Sketch of the History of Attleborough from its Settlement to its Division*. Boston: 1894

DALGAIRNS, Mrs. *The Practice of Cookery, Adapted to the Business of Every Day Life*. Boston: Munroe and Francis, 1830

DEARBORN, NATHANIEL. *Boston Notions, being an Authentic and Concise Account of "that Village", from 1630 to 1847*. Boston: 1848

Demorest's Monthly Magazine. November, 1869

DEVOE, THOMAS F. *The Market Book*. (2 vols.). New York: 1862

Diary of Samuel Sewall, 1674–1729 in the *Collections of the Massachusetts Historical Society*, 5th Ser., V-VII (1874–82)

"Diary of Daniel Fisher," *Pennsylvania Magazine of History and Biography*, XVII (1893)

DRAKE, FRANCIS S. *The Town of Roxbury*. Roxbury: 1878

DRAKE, SAMUEL ADAMS. *Historic Fields and Mansions of Middlesex*. Boston: 1874

———. *Old Boston Taverns and Tavern Clubs*. Boston: 1886

———. *Old Landmarks and Historic Personages of Boston*. Boston: 1895

DRAKE, SAMUEL G. N. *History and Antiquities of Boston*. Boston: 1856

DWIGHT, TIMOTHY. *Travels in New England and New York, (1821–1822)*. New Haven: S. Converse, Printer, 1822

EARLE, ALICE M. *Customs and Fashions in Old New England*. N.Y.: Charles Scribner's Sons, 1893

———. *Colonial Days in Old New York*. N. Y.: Charles Scribner's Sons, 1896

———. *Colonial Dames and Good Wives*.

———. *Home Life in Colonial Days*. N. Y.: Macmillan, 1910

———. *Stage-Coach and Tavern Days*. New York: Macmillan Company, 1900

———. *The Sabbath in Puritan New England*. N. Y.: Chas. Scnibner's Sons, 1891

Fairfield Historical Society, Annual Reports, 1904–1911

The Family Receipt Book, Containing Eight Hundred Valuable Receipts in Various Branches of Domestic

Economy; Selected from the Works of the Most Approved Writers, Ancient and Modern; and from the Attested Communications of Scientific Friends. (Second American Edition). Pittsburgh: Published by Randolph Barnes, 1819

FARISH, HUNTER D., ed. *Journals and Letters of Philip Vickers Fithian, 1773–1774.* Williamsburg: 1943

Farmer's Magazine, Vol. IX.

FESSENDEN, THOMAS G. *The Husbandman and Housewife.* Bellows Falls: Bill Blake and Co., 1820

FIELD, EDWARD. *The Colonial Tavern.* Providence, R. I.: 1897

FISHER, SYDNEY G. *Men, Women and Manners in Colonial Times.* Philadelphia and London: Lippincott, 1898

FISKE, JOHN. *Old Virginia and Her Neighbours.* Boston and New York: Houghton, Mifflin and Company, 1897

———. *The Dutch and Quaker Colonies in America.* Boston and New York: 1899

———. *The American Revolution*

———. "The Story of a New England Town," *Atlantic Monthly:* December, 1900

FORBES, ESTHER. *Paul Revere and the World He Lived In*

FRANKLIN, BENJAMIN. *Poor Richard's Almanack.* (Collector's ed.) Peter Pauper

FRANKLIN, BENJAMIN. *Poor Richard's Almanac for 1851, as Written by Benjamin Franklin, for the Years 1736–1737–1738.* New York: John Doggett Jr. 1850

———. *Memoirs of The Life of Benjamin Franklin, Written by Himself.* New York: John Doggett Jr., 1850

FRANKLIN, WILLIAM TEMPLE. *The Works of Dr. Benjamin Franklin, in Philosophy, Politics, and Morals: Containing His Diplomatic Correspondence, as Minister of the United States, at the Court of Versailles; His Private Epistolary Correspondence, Miscellaneous, Literary, and Philosophical Subjects, Between the Years 1753 and 1790, Developing the Secret History of His Political Transactions and Negotiations.* Philadelphia: Wm. Duane, 1817

FREESE, JOHN W. *Historic Houses and Spots in Cambridge, Mass. and Near-By Towns.* Boston: 1897

GERARD, JAMES W. "The Old Streets under the Dutch." Address delivered before the New York Historical Society: June 2, 1874

GODDARD, SAMUEL ASPINWALL. *Recollections of Brookline.* Birmingham, (England): 1873

Godey's Lady's Book, Sept., 1858; Oct., 1859; Apr., 1865; Aug., 1866

GOODRICH, CHARLES A. *Lives of the Singers to the Declaration of Independence.* New York: Thomas Mather, 1832

GOOD SAMARITAN. *The American Family Keepsake: or People's Practical Cyclopaedia. A Truthful Book of Facts and Hints upon Useful Subjects: Expressly Adapted to Meet the Wants of Every Man, Woman and Child in the United States.* Boston: 1849

GOSS, ELBRIDGE HENRY. *The Life of Colonel Paul Revere.* (2 vols.) Boston: Howard W. Spurr, 1899

GREEN, BARTHOLOMEW and ALLEN, JOHN. *Acts and Laws of His Majesties Province of the Massachusetts-Bay in New England.* Boston: 1699

GREEN, SAMUEL A. *Groton During the Indian Wars*

GREEN, TIMOTHY. *Acts and Laws of His Majesties Colony of Conn.* New London: 1715

HALE, SARAH J. (Mrs.). *The Way to Live Well, and To Be Well While We Live.* Hartford: Case, Tiffany and Company, 1849

Half-Moon Papers (Historic New York). (2 vols.) New York: 1899

HALL, Captain BASIL, R. N. *Forty Sketches. Travels in North America in the Years 1827 and 1828.* (3 vols.) Edinburgh, 1829

HARLAND, MARION. *Breakfast, Luncheon and Tea.* New York: Charles Scribner's Sons, 1884

HASWELL, CHARLES H. *Reminiscences of an Octegenarian of the City of New York: 1816–1860.* New York: 1897

HEMSTREET, CHARLES. *Literary New York: Its Landmarks and Associations.* New York: 1903

———. *When Old New York was Young.* New York: Scribner's 1902

HIGGINSON, THOMAS WENTWORTH. *Historic Address in Exercise in Celebrating the 250th Anniversary of the Settlement of Cambridge, Held December 28, 1880.* Cambridge: 1881

HILLARD, E. B. *The Last Men of the Revolution.* Hartford: 1864

HOAR, GEORGE FRISBIE. *Historical Address Delivered at Second Centennial of City.* Worcester: 1885

HOUGHTON, ASA. *The Gentlemen's and Ladies' Diary, or an Almanack.* Worcester: 1797

HOUGHTON, GEORGE W. W. *The Coaches of Colonial New York.* Paper delivered before N. Y. Historical Society, March 4, 1890

HOWLAND, Mrs. E. A. (Esther Allen). *The American Economical Housekeeper and Family Receipt Book.*

Worcester: 1850
HUDSON, ALFRED SERENO. *The History of Sudbury, Mass.: 1638–1889*. Published by the town: 1889
Itinerarium of Dr. Alexander Hamilton, 1744. (ed. by Carl Bridenbaugh). Chapel Hill, North Carolina: 1948
JENKINS, STEPHEN. *The Old Boston Post Road*. New York and London: G. P. Putnam's Sons, 1914
JUDD, SYLVESTER. *History of Hadley*
KALM, PETER. *The America of 1750: Peter Kalm's Travels in North America*. (edited by Adolph B. Benson). (2 vols.) N. Y.: 1937
The Kitchen Directory, and American Housewife: Containing the most Valuable and Original Receipts, in All the Various Branches of Cookery; Together with a Collection of Miscellaneous Receipts, and Directions Relative to Housewifery. Also the Whole Art of Carving, Illustrated by Sixteen Engravings. New York: Mark H. Newman and Company, 1844 and 1846
KNIGHT, SARAH (Madam). *The Private Journal of a Journey from Boston to New York, in the Year 1704*. N. Y.: 1825
LATHROP, ELISE. *Early American Inns and Taverns*. N. Y.: 1926
LEE, F. B. *New Jersey as a Colony and As a State*. N.Y.: 1902
LESLIE, (Miss). *Seventy-five Receipts for Pastry, Cakes, and Sweetmeats*. (Tenth edition). Boston: Munroe and Francis, and Joseph H. Francis. New York: Charles S. Francis, 1838
Letters of Robert Carter: 1720–1727: The Commercial Interests of a Virginia Gentleman. (Edited by Louis B. Wright.) San Mario, California: 1940
LINCOLN, WALDO. *Bibliography of American Cookery Books, 1742–1860*. Worcester: American Antiquarian Society, 1929
Litchfield (Conn.) *Monitor*, December 23, 1795
Little Katy; or, The Hot Corn Girl. (a play), 1854
The London Complete Art of Cookery. London: Minerva Press, 1797
LOSSING, BENSON J. *The Diary of George Washington from 1789 to 1791*. New York: 1860
Low's Boston Almanack, 1800
MACKENZIE. *Five Thousand Receipts in All the Useful and Domestic Arts: constituting A Complete Practical Library*. Philadelphia: James Kay, Jun. and Brother, 1829
Maclay, William, Journal of: 1789–1791. New York: 1890
MARKHAM, GERVASE. *English Housewife*. 1615
Mempirs and Letters of Dolly Madison. Boston and New York: Houghton Mifflin and Company, 1886
MERENESS, NEWTON D. (ed.). *Travels in the American Colonies*. New York: 1916
MORTON, LOUIS. *Robert Carter of Nomini Hall: A Virginia Tobacco Planter of the Eighteenth Century*. Williamsburg, Va.: 1941
New England Historical and Genealogical Register. Vol. IV
A New System of Domestic Cookery, Formed Upon Principles of Economy, and Adapted to the Use of Private Families. Boston: Andrews and Cummings, and L. Blake, 1807
New York, The Colonial Laws of. Published by the State. Albany: 1894
Official Letters to the Honorable American Congress, written during the War between the United Colonies and Great Britain, by His Excellency George Washington. New York: 1796
PARKES, H. B. "Morals and Law Enforcement in Colonial New England," *New England Quarterly*, (July, 1932)
PARTON, JAMES. *Life and Times of Benjamin Franklin*. (2 vols.) New York: 1865
PELL, JOHN. *Ethan Allen*. Boston and New York: Houghton Mifflin Company, 1929
PORTER, EDWARD G. *Rambles in Old Boston*. Boston: 1887
POWELL, LYMAN P. (editor). *Historic Towns of New England*. New York: 1902
The Practical Housewife: A Complete Encyclopedia of Domestic Economy and Family Medical Guide. Philadelphia: J. B. Lippincott and Company, c. 1860
Putnam's Monthly Historical Magazine. Published at Salem, Mass.
RANDOLPH, Mrs. MARY. *The Virginia Housewife: or, Methodical Cook*. Philadelphia: E. H. Butler and Co., 1856
RIKEMAN, A. A. *The Evolution of Stuyvesant Village*. Mamaroneck: 1899
The Royal American Magazine, or Universal Repository of Instruction and Amusement. For May, 1774. Boston: I. Thomas, 1774
SALMON, William, M. D. *The Family Dictionary: or Household Companion*. London: 1710
SCHENCK, ELIZABETH HUBBELL. *The History of Fairfield, Fairfield County, Connecticut, from the Settlement of the Town in 1639* to 1818. (2 vols.) New

York: 1889

SEARS, LORENZO. *John Hancock, the Picturesque Patriot.* Boston: 1912

Secret Diary of William Byrd of Westover, 1709–1712. (Edited by Louis B. Wright and Marion Tinling). Richmond, Virginia: 1941

SHEPARD, ODELL. *Connecticut, Past and Present*

SINGLETON, ESTHER. *Dutch New York.* New York: 1909

SLADE, WILLIAM, Jr. (Compiler). *The Laws of Vermont, of a Publick and Permanent Nature: Coming Down to, and Including the Year 1824.* Windsor: Published for the State, by Simeon Ide, 1825

SMITH, CHARLES. *The Gentleman's Political Pocket Almanac.* New York: 1797

SMITH, FRANK. *History of Dover, Massachusetts*

SMITH, THOMAS E. V. *The City of New York in the Year of Washington's Inauguration, 1789.* New York: 1889

STEARNS, SAMUEL. *The American Herbal, or Materia Medica. Wherein the Virtues of the Mineral, Vegetable, and Animal Productions of North and South America are laid open, so far as they are known; and their USES in the Practice of Physic and Surgery exhibited.* Walpole: David Carlisle, 1801

STOWE, HARRIET BEECHER. *Men of Our Times.* Hartford, Conn.: Hartford Publishing Co., 1868

STROHM, GERTRUDE. *The Universal Cookery Book.* N. Y.: Frederick A. Stokes and Bros., 1888

TEMPLE, JOSIAH. *History of Framingham*

THACHER, JAMES, (M. D.). *The American New Dispensatory.* Boston: Thomas B. Wait and Company, 1813

"Travel Diary of William Black," *Pennsylvania Magazine of History and Biography.* I (1877) and II (1878)

TRISTRAM, W. OUTRAM. *Coaching Days and Coaching Ways*

TRUMBULL, JAMES RUSSELL. *History of Northampton, Massachusetts from its Settlement in 1654.* Northampton: 1902

VAN RENSELLAER, Mrs. SCHUYLER. *History of the City of New York in the Seventeenth Century.* (2 vols.) New York: 1909

VAN SCHAICK, JOHN, Rev. (Jr.). *Characters in Tales of a Wayside Inn.* Universalist Publishing House

Virginia Gazette, October, 1737

WARD, ELIZABETH. *Old Times in Shrewsbury, Mass.* 1892

WARNER, CHARLES DUDLEY. *Captain John Smith: 1579–1631. A Study of His Life and Writings.* N. Y.: Henry Holt and Co., 1881

WARREN, EDWARD. *Life of John Collins Warren, M. D.*

WASHBURN, EMORY. *Historical Sketches of the Town of Leicester, Massachusetts.* Boston: 1860

WEBSTER, A. I. (Mrs.). *The Improved Housewife or Book of Receipts.* Boston: Phillips, Sampson, and Co. 1858

WERTENBAKER, T. J. *The Old South: The Founding of American Civilization.* New York: 1949

———. *Patrician and Plebeian in Virginia.* Charlottesville, Va., 1910

———. *Planters of Colonial Virginia.* Princeton: 1922

WHARTON, ANNE HOLLINGSWORTH. *Colonial Days and Dames.* Philadelphia: J. B. Lippincott, 1895

WILCOX, SILAS, (T. P.). *Materia Medica.* Bennington: J.I.C. and A.S.C. Cook, 1843

WINSLOW, (Mrs.). *Domestic Receipt Book,* (1873–1875). Jeremiah Curtis and Sons and John I. Brown and Sons, 1872–1874

WINTHROP, JOHN ESQ. *The History of New England from 1630–1649.* Boston: Thomas B. Wait and Sons, 1826

WOODFIN, MAUDE H. and TINLING, MARION, (eds.). *Another Secret Diary of William Byrd of Westover, 1739–1741.* Richmond, Va.: 1942

Worcester, Old-Time Taverns of. Proceedings of the Worcester Society of Antiquity: 1903

WRIGHT, LOUIS B., (ed.). *The First Gentlemen of Virginia: Intellectual Qualities of the Early Colonial Ruling Class.* San Marino, California: 1940

Writings of George Washington: Being His Correspondence, Addresses, Messages, and Other Papers, Official and Private, Selected and Published from the Original Manuscripts; with A Life of the Author, Notes, and Illustrations. (12 Vols.) Compiled by Jared Sparks. Boston: Russell, Odiorne, and Metcalf, and Hilliard, Gray, and Co., 1835

Indexes

PERSONS

PERSONS—Continued

PERSONS—Continued

PLACES

INNS AND TAVERNS

INNS AND TAVERNS—Continued

RECIPES